PREFACE

1. Scope

This publication provides joint doctrine and principles for planning and executing deployment and redeployment operations. It describes the deployment and redeployment processes and the planning and execution considerations that may impact deployment and redeployment operations to include command relationships and the interactions of combatant commands and Services with the Department of Defense and other US Government departments and agencies, host nations, multinational partners, and intergovernmental and nongovernmental organizations.

2. Purpose

This publication has been prepared under the direction of the Chairman of the Joint Chiefs of Staff (CJCS). It sets forth joint doctrine to govern the activities and performance of the Armed Forces of the United States in operations and provides the doctrinal basis for interagency coordination and for US military involvement in multinational operations. It provides military guidance for the exercise of authority by combatant commanders and other joint force commanders (JFCs) and prescribes joint doctrine for operations and training. It provides military guidance for use by the Armed Forces in preparing their appropriate plans. It is not the intent of this publication to restrict the authority of the JFC from organizing the force and executing the mission in a manner the JFC deems most appropriate to ensure unity of effort in the accomplishment of the overall objective.

3. Application

a. Joint doctrine established in this publication applies to the commanders of combatant commands, subunified commands, joint task forces, subordinate components of these commands, the Services, and combat support agencies.

b. The guidance in this publication is authoritative; as such, this doctrine will be followed except when, in the judgment of the commander, exceptional circumstances dictate otherwise. If conflicts arise between the contents of this publication and the contents of Service publications, this publication will take precedence unless the CJCS, normally in coordination with the other members of the Joint Chiefs of Staff, has provided more current and specific guidance. Commanders of forces operating as part of a multinational (alliance or coalition) military command should follow multinational doctrine and procedures ratified by the United States. For doctrine and procedures not ratified by the United States, commanders should evaluate and follow the multinational command's doctrine and procedures, where applicable and consistent with US law, regulations, and doctrine.

For the Chairman of the Joint Chiefs of Staff:

CURTIS M. SCAPARROTTI
Lieutenant General, U.S. Army
Director, Joint Staff

SUMMARY OF CHANGES
REVISION OF JOINT PUBLICATION 3-35
DATED 07 MAY 2007

- **Deletes training, exercises, and assessments.**
- **Expands on the linkages with the Defense Transportation Regulation.**
- **Incorporates the "joint operation planning process" and adaptive planning and execution in the deployment and redeployment planning process.**
- **Updates the terms and discussions for various operational areas as needed.**
- **Updates responsibilities for deployment and redeployment operations in the conduct of homeland security and civil defense.**
- **Updates predeployment and pre-redeployment activities.**
- **Expands on global force management and force projection.**
- **Expands on force visibility and in-transit visibility programs.**
- **Updates the Joint Operation Planning and Execution System activities, functions, and products.**
- **Incorporates the construct of 'contingency and crisis' action planning.**
- **Modifies the definitions for 'common-user sealift,' 'deployment,' 'force visibility.'**
- **Remove the definition for 'automation network', 'host-nation support agreement', 'information resource', and 'infrastructure.'**
- **Assumes proponency for the term 'cargo increment number.'**

Intentionally Blank

TABLE OF CONTENTS

Intentionally Blank

EXECUTIVE SUMMARY
COMMANDER'S OVERVIEW

- **Discusses Deployment and Redeployment Operations**
- **Outlines Deployment and Redeployment Responsibilities**
- **Details Deployment and Redeployment Planning**
- **Covers Predeployment and Pre-Redeployment Activities**
- **Explains Movement, Movement Control, and Force Visibility**
- **Describes Joint Reception, Staging, Onward Movement, and Integration**

Overview

Deployment and redeployment operations enable the projection of the military instrument of national power.

The deployment and redeployment of US forces in support of combatant commander (CCDR) requirements are a series of operational events enabled by logistics. These activities are planned and executed by both the supported and supporting commanders.

Global Force Management and Force Projection

To effectively support multiple requirements, and apply the right level of priority and resources to each, requires effective global force management (GFM). GFM aligns force assignment, apportionment, and allocation methodologies in support of the National Defense Strategy, joint force availability requirements, and joint force assessments. Force projection is the ability to project the military instrument of national power in response to military operations. Force projection allows a joint force commander (JFC) to position and concentrate forces to set the conditions for mission success.

Joint Deployment and Redeployment Processes

The joint deployment and redeployment processes consist of four phases: planning, predeployment/pre-redeployment activities, movement, and joint reception, staging, onward movement, and integration (JRSOI).

Strategic Mobility

Strategic mobility is the capability to deploy and sustain military forces worldwide in support of national strategy. Beyond the intrinsic capability of US operational forces to self-deploy, the bulk of our nation's strategic mobility requirements are met through common-user sealift, common-user airlift, and pre-positioned stocks, known as the strategic mobility triad [pre-positioning, airlift, and sealift].

Integrated Planning and Execution Process

Adaptive Planning and Execution (APEX), Joint Operation Planning and Execution System (JOPES), and the joint operation planning process (JOPP) provide the processes, formats, and systems which link deployment and redeployment planning for joint force projection to the execution of joint operations. **JOPES** use is directed for planning and executing all deployment and redeployment operations. **JOPP** describes the common activities needed to plan missions across the full range of military operations and defines the required military capabilities and timelines that set the framework for deployment/redeployment planning.

Adaptive Planning and Execution (APEX) System

The joint planning and execution community uses APEX to monitor, plan, and execute mobilization, deployment, employment, sustainment, redeployment, and demobilization activities associated with joint operations.

Joint operation planning is accomplished through the APEX system. APEX incorporates initiatives—such as levels of planning detail, the requirement for more frequent in-progress reviews between CCDRs and Secretary of Defense (SecDef), routine assessments, and the use of collaboration technology to provide more and better options during plan development, increase opportunities for consultation and guidance during the planning process, and promote increased agility throughout deployment and redeployment.

Integrated Employment and Deployment

Force employment plans and schedules drive deployment planning and execution preparation requirements and movement timelines. Deployment operations provide forces ready to execute the supported commander's orders. Deployment plans and schedules align with the operation plans/orders and support the associated force movement requirements, allowing for predeployment preparations required by the Service component. The GFM sourcing processes (preferred forces, contingency sourcing, or execution sourcing) link the requirements to the forces that will ultimately be ordered to deploy.

Force Visibility

Force visibility provides the current and accurate status of forces at the strategic and operational level, their current mission, future missions, location, mission priority, and readiness status. Force visibility provides information on the location, operational tempo, assets, and sustainment requirements of a force as part of an overall capability for a CCDR. Force visibility enhances situational awareness and is required to support force sourcing, allocation, assignment of forces; force position; sustainment forecasting and delivery; and forecasting for future force requirements.

Sustainment Delivery

Sustainment delivery is the process of providing and maintaining levels of personnel and materiel required to sustain combat and mission activity at the level of intensity dictated by the concept of operations (CONOPS). Sustainment is ongoing throughout the entire operation and, like deployment and redeployment, should be aligned with the mission and mission priorities of each phase.

Responsibilities

General

Clearly articulating responsibilities is the first step in fully synchronized and coordinated deployment operations supporting the range of military operations.

Secretary of Defense

SecDef assigns and allocates all forces and resources to the combatant commands (CCMDs) to perform their assigned missions. In addition, SecDef is responsible for transportation planning and operations within the Department of Defense (DOD).

Chairman of the Joint Chiefs of Staff

The Chairman of the Joint Chiefs of Staff's responsibilities most directly related to deployment operations include the following:

- Prepares joint logistic and mobility plans to support strategic plans and recommends the assignment of logistic and mobility responsibilities to the Services in accordance with (IAW) those plans.

- Prepares joint logistic and mobility plans to support joint operation plans (OPLANs), recommends the assignment of logistic and mobility responsibilities to the Armed Forces IAW those logistic and mobility plans, and ascertains the logistic support available to execute the CCDR's general war and joint OPLANs.

- Performs as the global force manager to integrate the force management processes (assignment, apportionment, and allocation of joint forces).

- Assigns movement priorities in support of DOD components based upon capabilities reported by United States Transportation Command (USTRANSCOM).

Supported and Supporting Combatant Commands

Supported CCDRs are responsible for deployment and redeployment operations planned and executed during joint force missions. This responsibility includes identification of the movement, timing, and sequence of deploying and redeploying forces in the time-phased force and deployment data (TPFDD), reception and integration of units and materiel arriving in theater, and assisting these units as required.

Supporting missions during deployment of the joint force could include the deployment or redeployment of forces from or to a supporting CCMD, sponsorship of en route basing or in-transit staging areas (SAs), or provision of sustainment from theater stocks. Regardless of the supporting mission, the primary task for supporting CCMDs is to ensure that the supported CCDR receives the timely and complete support needed to accomplish the mission.

Functional Combatant Commands

Three functional CCMDs could be involved in deployment of the joint force: United States Special Operations Command (USSOCOM), United States Strategic Command (USSTRATCOM), and USTRANSCOM. **USSOCOM** assigned assets may be deployed or redeployed as a result of special operations forces (SOF) mission taskings, or USSOCOM may provide SOF mission support to conventional joint force deployment. **USSTRATCOM** provides advisors upon request by the supported CCDR, who will designate when and where they will report. The advisor coordinates with the mission-planning facilities of USSTRATCOM for the utilization of nuclear weapons; intelligence, surveillance, and reconnaissance; space; and cyberspace forces. **USTRANSCOM** responsibilities include the following:

- As the distribution process owner, USTRANSCOM oversees the overall effectiveness, efficiency, and alignment of DOD-wide distribution activities, including force projection (force movement), sustainment, redeployment, and retrograde operations, and establishes the CONOPS frameworks relating to the planning and execution of the DOD transportation operations. USTRANSCOM also serves as the joint force provider for mobility forces.

- Provide, through its Service component commands, air, land, and sea transportation and common-user port management at air and sea port of embarkation (POE) and/or port of debarkation (POD) for DOD across the range of military operations.

- Exercise responsibility for global air, land, and sea transportation planning (deliberate and crisis action).

- Act as the DOD focal point for items in the transportation pipeline.

Joint Task Forces

Formation of a joint task force (JTF) may complicate deployment planning and execution because of the diverse elements that may come together to form the JTF. A significant challenge in JTF deployment operations is in building the force requirements and TPFDD.

Military Departments and Department of Defense Agencies

The Military Departments and DOD agencies retain the responsibility for organizing, training, equipping, and providing administrative and logistics support (including Service organic transportation) for their respective forces. These forces and other DOD agencies may depend on common-user military transportation services for unit and individual deployment and redeployment operations between POEs and PODs. Each Service is responsible for administrative support and performance of transportation operations assigned by CCDRs at either their local shipping installations or throughout the theater.

Other Government Departments and Agencies

Department of Homeland Security (DHS). DHS responsibilities include customs, aerial and seaport security, and infrastructure hardening and protection.

Department of Transportation. During national defense emergencies, the Secretary of Transportation has a wide range of delegated responsibilities, including executive management of the nation's transportation resources in periods of crisis. Surge sealift-government owned military useful ships maintained in varying states of readiness/reduced operating status by the Military Sealift Command and by the Maritime Administration for activation in time of crisis.

Other Transportation Partners

The Defense Transportation System relies heavily on the commercial transportation industry to perform a multitude of services during deployment operations in peacetime and war. These commercial source capabilities span all modes of transportation and may include the use of contracted US or foreign commercial air and maritime assets as well as host-nation support (HNS) within a joint operations area. Commercial rail, trucking, in-transit visibility (ITV) assets, and other transportation services may also be contracted to support deployment operations.

Deployment and Redeployment Planning

Deployment and Redeployment Planning

Deployment planning is operational planning directed toward the movement of forces and sustainment resources from their original locations to a specific operational area (OA) for conducting the joint operations contemplated in a given plan. Redeployment planning is operational planning directed toward the transfer of forces and materiel from a JFC to support another JFC's operational requirements, or to return personnel, equipment, and materiel to the home and/or demobilization stations from a JFC's OA for reintegration and/or demobilization.

The Joint Operational Planning Process and Deployment and Redeployment Planning

Joint Publication 5-0, *Joint Operation Planning,* describes the seven steps of JOPP and outlines the information that the commander needs from the deployment/redeployment planners to ensure that the courses of action (COAs) presented are feasible from the force and transportation resource standpoint. Specific deployment considerations are first highlighted in step 2 (Mission Analysis), and the deployment concept as a planning product is first mentioned in step 3 (COA Development). Refined TPFDD feasibility estimates are included in step 4 (COA Analysis, under Wargaming), and are among the key inputs to step 5 (COA Comparison), step 6 (COA Approval), and step 7 (Plan or Order Development).

Plan or Order Development

While deployment and redeployment were critical considerations in the previous steps of JOPP, it is in step 7 (Plan or Order Development), that the preponderance of the deployment and redeployment planning takes place. During this step, the supported CCDR and staff, in collaboration with subordinate and supporting components and organizations, expand the approved COA into a detailed joint OPLAN/concept plan or operation order by first developing an executable CONOPS.

Considerations of Operational Requirements

While conducting deployment planning in JOPP, the following operational requirements should be considered: training, protection, communications systems supporting visibility of deployment operations, infrastructure assessment, HNS, and contract support.

Predeployment and Pre-Redeployment Activities

General

Predeployment and redeployment activities is the second phase in the joint deployment and redeployment process. The activities are functions deploying/redeploying planners and unit commanders must accomplish to successfully complete their movement to the POE.

Deployment Prepare the Force Activities

Select forces may deploy within hours or days from receipt of a deployment order while other units may deploy on a timeline of days to several weeks. Deployment timelines will dictate available time to conduct *prepare the force activities,* which include:

- Activate deployment and command and control (C2) support organizations.
- Conduct movement coordination and support meetings.
- Develop deployment equipment list and identify shipping/handling requirements.
- Conduct required training.
- Manage Service members' deployment requirements.

Sustainment

Deployment planners should account for concurrent sustainment activities in their overall plans. Activities in the planning phase may capture the basic requirements for the movement of sustainment, but planners will have to finalize sustainment movement plans as part of their predeployment activities.

Redeployment Prepare the Force Activities

A successful redeployment requires the planning and execution of the *prepare the force activities* used in deployments. The execution of these pre-redeployment activities will not be identical to deployment activities due to the operational environment, available resources, and the force structure of the redeploying units. As such, procedures and unit level activities may vary from those performed during a deployment but these activities require detailed planning for a successful redeployment operation. Redeployment *prepare the force* activities also has a unique sixth activity, *complete equipment disposition actions.*

Schedule Movement for Deployment

Movement scheduling is an iterative process done at every level of supported and supporting commands to transport, move, or deploy the right forces (unit-*related* personnel and equipment) and sustainment (non-unit-related personnel, supplies, and equipment) to the right place at the right time. Supported and supporting CCDRs receive **strategic movement schedules** as they are scheduled and registered in JOPES and the Web Scheduling and Movement application. Movement instructions are published based on JOPES strategic lift schedules and the supported commanders' movement priority.

Schedule Movement for Redeployment

Normally, redeployment TPFDDs are developed with the redeployment plan during force employment planning and updated and refined during redeployment preparations. During redeployment preparation, it is a Service/unit level responsibility to update unit movement data to reflect changes to the deployable equipment list. Subordinate organizations and component commands must verify unit movement data to the supported CCDR for redeployment TPFDD validation. USTRANSCOM develops the redeployment *strategic movement schedule* after receiving the validated TPFDD from the supported CCDR.

Assemble and Marshal Forces for Deployment

Assembly and marshalling involve bringing together personnel, supplies, and equipment in preparation for final movement to the POD. It is comprised of four activities to include: assemble personnel and cargo; conduct unit inspection, load equipment, and prepare; sequence loads; and establish support organization at the POE.

Assemble and Marshal Forces for Redeployment

A successful redeployment also requires the planning and execution for all the *assembling and marshalling forces* activities. These redeployment activities are the same as those performed during a deployment and may require additional time and locations. There is also an additional redeployment activity; *prepare and conduct customs/agricultural inspections.*

Movement

General

During the movement phase, validated TPFDD movement requirements developed during the planning phase and scheduled for movement during the predeployment activities phase must now be physically moved from origin to the designated aerial ports of debarkation (APODs)/seaports of debarkation (SPODs). The movement phase of the joint deployment and redeployment process includes self-deploying forces and forces requiring lift support and is composed of three segments: Movement from origin to aerial ports of embarkation (APOEs)/seaports of embarkation (SPOEs), POE operations, and movement from the POE to POD.

Movement Control

Movement control involves planning, routing, scheduling, and controlling common-user assets and maintaining ITV of forces and materiel moving through the deployment and redeployment processes. Movement control coordinates transportation resources to enhance combat effectiveness and meet the deployment/redeployment and sustainment priorities of the supported CCDR. The supported CCDR has a wide range of options for performing movement control. These options include directing subordinate JFCs and Service components to perform their own movement control or creating a fully integrated joint organization.

Movement

The movement phase of the deployment/redeployment process is divided into three segments; movement from origin to POE, POE operations, and movement from POE to POD. Equipment of deploying forces may either self-deploy or be transported to the POE by commercial rail, truck, or barge. From the APOE/SPOE, deploying forces now move to the APOD/SPOD. While all Services have the organic capability to execute theater opening functions, USTRANSCOM's joint task force-port opening provides the supported geographic combatant commander rapid port opening capability to facilitate crisis response in austere environments.

Force Visibility

The integrated use of C2 systems and innovative information technology makes force tracking through the deployment and redeployment processes possible. Visibility of deploying forces and materiel is established through the logistics management construct of asset visibility and the Global Combat Support System-Joint common operational picture.

Redeployment

Movement in support of redeployment moves forces to support a new mission in another JFC's OA or to return them to their home or demobilization station. Unit integrity should be maintained, to the extent possible, and commanders must have the capability to determine the exact location of unit personnel, equipment, and materiel in the event the redeploying force has to be diverted en route for another mission. **Redeployment movements** are governed by the supported CCDR's redeployment plan and policies and the theater movement control plan.

Joint Reception, Staging, Onward Movement, and Integration

General

JRSOI is the essential process that transitions deploying or redeploying forces, consisting of personnel, equipment, and materiel into forces capable of meeting the CCDR's operational requirements or returns them to their parent organization or Service. The four segments of JRSOI are described below.

- **Reception** operations include all those functions required to receive and clear personnel, equipment, and materiel through the POD.

- **Staging** assembles, temporarily holds, and organizes arriving personnel, equipment, and materiel into forces and capabilities and prepares them for onward movement, tactical operations, or Service reintegration.

- **Onward Movement** is the process of moving forces, capabilities, and accompanying materiel from reception facilities, marshalling areas, and SAs to tactical assembly areas (TAAs) and/or OAs or onward from the POD or other reception areas to the home/demobilization station.

- **Integration** is the synchronized transfer of capabilities into an operational commander's force prior to mission execution or back to the component/Service.

Principles of Joint Reception, Staging, Onward Movement, and Integration

There are three overarching principles of JRSOI [unity of command, synchronization, and balance]. The purpose of **unity of command** is to ensure unity of effort under one responsible commander for every objective. In the context of deployment and redeployment operations, this is the supported CCDR. **Synchronization** links deployed personnel, equipment, and materiel in a timely manner. A well-synchronized flow expedites buildup of mission capability and avoids saturation at nodes and along lines of communications (LOCs), thereby enhancing survivability. **Balance** applies to managing the TPFDD flow. Managing the TPFDD allows the supported CCDR to adjust the movement schedule for units as mission requirements or conditions change.

Elements of Joint Reception, Staging, Onward Movement, and Integration

JRSOI relies on the essential elements [communications systems, force protection, and support organizations and structures] to achieve unity of command, synchronization, and balance. Communications systems are the means by which the CCDR maintains unity of command to balance and synchronize joint force activities and achieve mission success.

Reception

Reception is the process of receiving, off-loading, marshalling, and transporting of personnel, equipment, and materiel from strategic and/or intratheater deployment phase to a sea, air, or surface transportation point of debarkation to the marshalling area. Reception begins with the arrival of deploying forces and equipment into an OA.

Staging

The activities associated with staging will generally include assembling, temporary holding, and organizing of arriving personnel, equipment, and materiel into units and forces, and preparing them for onward movement and employment by the JFC. SAs are specific locations along the LOC. The CCDR usually designates specific locations for staging in order to provide space and focus resources to support staging operations. SAs provide the necessary facilities, sustainment, and other support to enable units to become mission-capable.

Onward Movement

Onward movement is the process of moving forces and sustainment from reception facilities and marshalling or SAs to TAAs or other operating areas. Rail, road, inland or coastal waterway, and/or air can be used to accomplish this movement. Efficient onward movement of personnel, equipment, and materiel requires a balanced, integrated system of node operations, movement control, mode operations, and cargo transfer operations. The onward movement process encompasses support to all Service components of a joint operation, and often includes HNS. Onward movement is complete when force elements are delivered to the designated location at the designated time.

Integration

During deployment or redeployment to a new OA, integration is the synchronized transfer of mission-ready forces and capabilities into the CCDR's force and based on the complexity of the operation, may take hours or days to complete. Integration is complete when the receiving commander establishes C2 over the arriving unit and the unit is capable of performing its assigned mission. In deployment operations, force closure occurs when the supported commander determines that the deploying force has completed movement to the specified OA/destination with sufficient resources and is ready to conduct its assigned mission. In redeployment operations, force closure occurs when the designated commander or Service determines that the redeploying force has returned to home station or other follow-on destination.

CONCLUSION

This publication provides joint doctrine and principles for planning and executing deployment and redeployment operations. It describes the deployment and redeployment processes and the planning and execution considerations that may impact deployment and redeployment operations to include command relationships and the interactions of combatant commands and Services with the DOD and other US Government departments and agencies, host nations, multinational partners, and intergovernmental and nongovernmental organizations.

CHAPTER I
OVERVIEW

> *"I reaffirmed what I already knew, that the US military is far ahead of other militaries in the development of our deployment systems, technologies, and distribution doctrine. Other militaries do not have our force projection capability. Concepts like strategic dominant maneuver are interesting, but are not as relevant to them. For other militaries, end-to-end distribution often means using their commercial transportation assets to deliver supplies to forces that are in a benign area and relatively close. They are generally in awe of our assets and force projection capabilities."*
>
> **Lieutenant General Daniel G. Brown, United States Army**
> **Deputy Commander, US Transportation Command,**
> **September 1999–September 2002**
> ***An Oral History***

1. Introduction

a. The US employs the four instruments of national power (diplomatic, informational, military, and economic) to achieve national strategic objectives. The military instrument's role increases relative to the other instruments as the need to compel a potential adversary through force increases. Military efforts focus on fielding modular, adaptive forces that can be employed across the full range of military operations. Deployment and redeployment operations enable the projection of the military instrument of national power. Joint forces deploy in support of routine, predictable requirements or on short notice, and are increasingly interoperable with multinational forces and other US Government (USG) departments and agencies.

b. The deployment and redeployment of US forces in support of combatant commander (CCDR) requirements are a series of operational events enabled by logistics. These activities are planned and executed by both the supported and supporting commanders. The capability to deploy forces to the operational area (OA) and rapidly integrate them into the joint force as directed by the joint force commander (JFC) is essential. Mission requirements define the scope, duration, and scale of deployment and redeployment operations. These operations involve the efforts of numerous commands, agencies, and processes and as such, unity of effort becomes paramount for the effective and efficient mission accomplishment.

c. **Operational Environment (OE).** Deployment and employment planning decisions are based on the anticipated OE to be encountered in the OA. Understanding the OE helps commanders anticipate the results of various friendly, adversary, and neutral actions and how they impact operational depth and reach, as well as mission accomplishment. The OE is generally described by three conditions: permissive, uncertain, or hostile.

(1) **Permissive Environment.** A permissive environment is an OE in which host nation (HN) military and law enforcement agencies have control, the intent, and the capability to assist operations that a unit intends to conduct. In this situation, entry

operations during deployment are unopposed and the host country is supporting the deployment.

(2) **Uncertain Environment.** An uncertain environment is an OE in which HN forces, whether opposed to or receptive to operations that a unit intends to conduct, do not have totally effective control of the territory and population in the intended OA. In this situation, entry operations during deployment are generally unopposed but could be opposed at any point during the deployment by forces or individuals not under HN control.

(3) **Hostile Environment.** A hostile environment is an OE in which hostile forces have control as well as the intent and capability to effectively oppose or react to the operations that a unit intends to conduct. In this situation, the deploying force must conduct forcible entry operations to secure a lodgment for reception of the joint force to provide for the continuous landing of forces and materiel and provide space for subsequent operations, such as onward movement and integration. Should US forces be denied temporary physical access to a specific geographic location, the JFC should plan forcible entry operations from an existing forward operating site or consider the use/formation of an intermediate staging base (ISB) near the objective area or forward deployed maritime forces.

2. Global Force Management and Force Projection

a. **Global Force Management (GFM).** At any given time there could be multiple requirements to employ military forces. Each operation could have a different strategic priority and could be of a different size and scope. To effectively support multiple requirements, and apply the right level of priority and resources to each, requires effective GFM. The GFM and the Adaptive Planning and Execution (APEX) processes have separate and distinct purposes but are interdependent by design, with APEX focusing on designing, organizing, and executing operations to create desired effects and GFM focusing on identifying, providing, and managing the forces and capabilities needed to support those operations. GFM aligns force assignment, apportionment, and allocation methodologies in support of the National Defense Strategy, joint force availability requirements, and joint force assessments. It provides comprehensive oversights into the global availability of US military forces/capabilities and provides decision makers a process to quickly and accurately assess the impact and risk of proposed changes in forces/capability assignment, apportionment, and allocation.

(1) The GFM process cycle starts and ends with the Secretary of Defense (SecDef). In accordance with (IAW) Title 10, United States Code, SecDef assigns and allocates forces/capabilities, provides planning guidance to combatant commands (CCMDs), and provides overarching strategic guidance to the Chairman of the Joint Chiefs of Staff (CJCS). The CJCS apportions forces/capabilities to CCMDs for adaptive planning and develops strategic-level guidance. CCMDs, in turn, coordinate force/capability requirements with the CJCS or delegated CCDR based on SecDef's guidance across the three processes; develop Guidance for Employment of the Force (GEF)-directed plans with forces apportioned by the CJCS, and forward designated plans to SecDef for approval.

(2) The Unified Command Plan (UCP) establishes CCMD missions, responsibilities, and force structure. CCDRs are directed by the UCP, strategic guidance, and various orders to plan for and execute operations and missions. CCDRs are assigned forces to accomplish those missions; however, in the dynamic world environment, a mission may require adjusting the distribution of assigned forces among the CCDRs and Services through a process called allocation. Assignment, apportionment, and allocation of forces to support UCP missions are accomplished through GFM.

For more information on GFM, see Joint Publication (JP) 5-0, Joint Operation Planning.

(3) **During the initial and subsequent deployments, the Department of Defense (DOD) leadership will use requests for forces (RFFs) and deployment orders (DEPORDs).** Commanders and their staffs must understand the dynamic nature of force flow.

For additional information on GFM processes, see the Global Force Management Implementation Guidance; *Chairman of the Joint Chiefs of Staff Manual (CJCSM) 3122.01,* Joint Operation Planning and Execution System (JOPES) Volume I, Planning Policies and Procedures; *CJCSM 3122.02,* Joint Operation Planning and Execution System (JOPES) Volume III, Crisis Action Time-Phased Force and Deployment Data Development and Deployment Execution; *and JP 5-0,* Joint Operation Planning.

(4) Timely response to crisis situations is critical to US deterrent and warfighting capabilities. The timeliness of US response is a function of US forward deployed forces and pre-positioned assets, forces with organic movement capability, and adequate strategic and intratheater mobility capability assets. The combination of organic force movement and rapid mobility, bolstered by pre-positioned assets, provides the supported JFC with flexible mobility options that can be tailored to meet any crisis situation. Deployment operations normally involve a combination of organic and common-user lift supported movements using land (road and rail), sea, and air movement resources, as necessary. **Successful movement depends on the availability of sufficient transportation capabilities to rapidly deploy combat forces, sustain them during an operation, and redeploy them to meet changing mission requirements or to return them to home and/or demobilization stations upon completion of their mission.**

b. **Joint Force Projection.** Force projection is the ability to project the military instrument of national power in response to military operations. Force projection allows a JFC to position and concentrate forces to set the conditions for mission success. Force projection, enabled by GFM, forward presence, and agile force mobility, is critical to US deterrence and warfighting capabilities. The President or SecDef could direct CCDRs to resolve a crisis by employing immediately available forward-presence forces. However, when this response is not sufficient or possible, the rapid deployment of forces from other locations may be necessary.

3. Joint Deployment and Redeployment Processes

a. **The joint deployment and redeployment processes consist of four phases: planning, predeployment/pre-redeployment activities, movement, and joint reception, staging, onward movement, and integration (JRSOI).** Both processes are similar; however, each has unique characteristics. See Figure I-1 for a depiction of the phases. These phases are iterative and may occur simultaneously throughout an operation.

(1) **Deployment and redeployment planning** is the first phase of the process and occurs during deliberate planning and crisis action planning (CAP) currently as part of the JOPES and APEX process. It is conducted at all command levels and by both the supported and supporting commanders.

(2) **Predeployment and pre-redeployment activities** are actions taken by the joint planning and execution community (JPEC), before actual movement, to prepare to execute a deployment or redeployment operation. This includes training, organizing and equipping the force to be able to perform the mission specified in the force requirement.

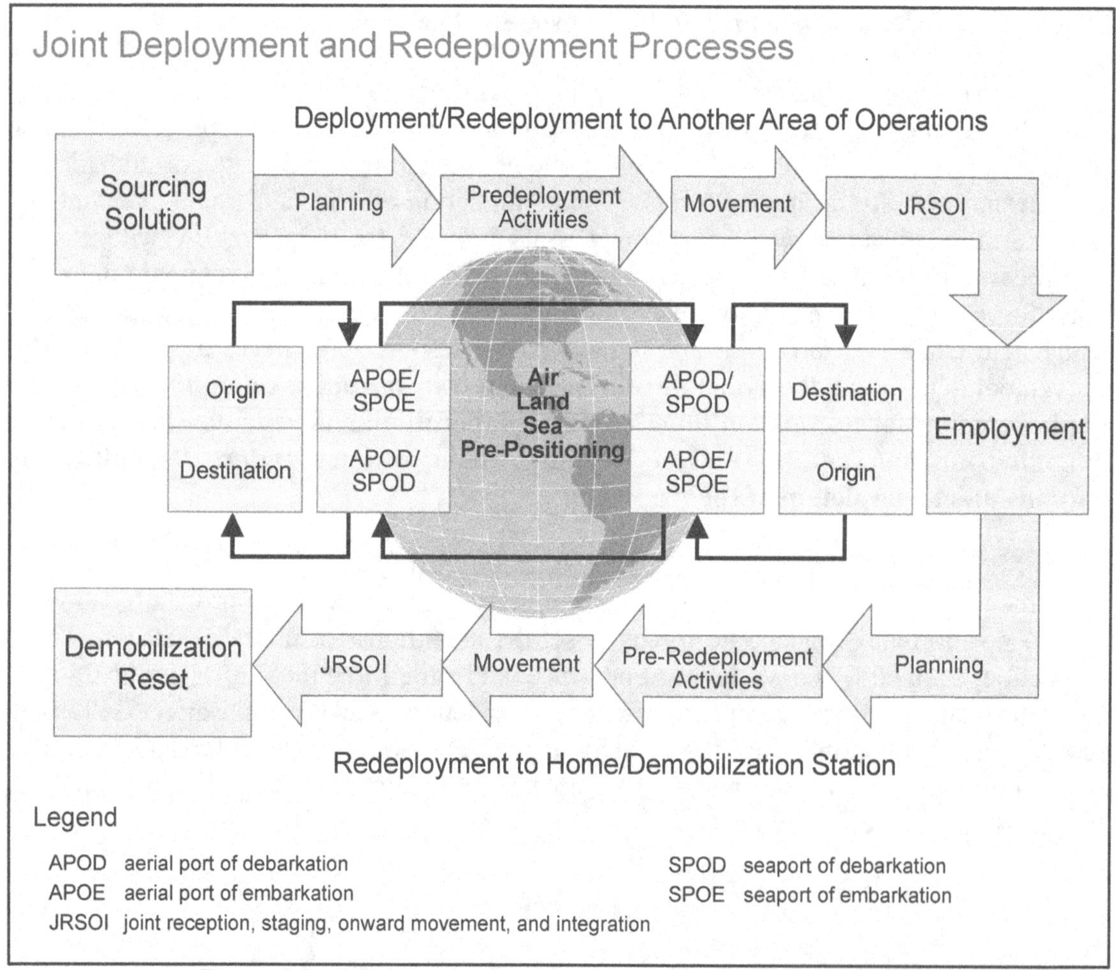

Figure I-1. Joint Deployment and Redeployment Processes

(3) **Movement** includes the activities to physically move joint forces from origin to destination. It includes three segments: origin to port of embarkation (POE), activities at the POE, and POE to port of debarkation (POD) including movement and transit through intermediate locations as required. However, in order for joint deployment to produce a seamless, end-to-end deployment movement process, consideration should be given to JRSOI.

(4) **JRSOI,** the final phase, is the essential process that transitions deploying or redeploying forces, consisting of personnel, equipment, and materiel arriving in theater, into forces capable of meeting the CCDR's operational requirements, or completes the redeployment of forces to home or demobilization station as a result of end-of-mission or rotation.

b. **Deployment**

(1) **Deployment** encompasses all activities from origin or home station through destination, specifically including in the continental United States (CONUS), intertheater, and intratheater movement legs, staging, and holding areas.

(2) **Deployment planning and execution.** The joint deployment process has numerous process stakeholders and process seams, resulting from the multitude of organizations and functional processes involved in deployment planning and execution. Deployment stakeholders include the supported and supporting CCDRs, their Service components, and the entire JPEC. Process seams may occur at functional or organizational interfaces when physical resources or information is transferred. Friction between operational and supporting stakeholders or process seams reduces the operational effectiveness and efficiency of the deployment process. Supported commanders can enhance mission accomplishment during deployment execution by:

(a) Linking deployment to employment mission and force requirements;

(b) Determining RFF timing and duration and specifying level of operational control (OPCON) required;

(c) Providing rapid notification of changes to the concept of operations (CONOPS) when they occur;

(d) Conducting effective coordination and collaboration with other process stakeholders;

(e) Requiring accurate and early reporting of movement support requirements;

(f) Following JOPES deployment procedures.

c. **Deployment operations** are the sum of activities required to plan, prepare, and move forces and materiel from home station to a destination within an OA, to achieve the employment of an operational capability required to execute a mission. The focus of these operations is to globally position forces in time to conduct campaigns and major operations and to respond to other contingencies.

For additional information on movement and maneuver, see JP 3-0, Joint Operations.

d. **Redeployment**

(1) **Redeployment** is the transfer of deployed forces and accompanying materiel from one OA to support another JFC's operational requirements within a new OA or home/demobilization station as a result of end-of-mission or rotation.

(2) Redeployment planning and execution. Similar to deployment operations, redeployment planning decisions are based on the OE in the OA at the time of redeployment. As already described, the redeployment process consists of four phases; **redeployment planning, pre-redeployment activities, movement, and JRSOI.** The supported geographic combatant commander (GCC) is responsible for redeployment planning in the area of responsibility (AOR). This planning should be considered at the outset of an operation and continually be refined as the operation matures. The individual activities within each phase of redeployment are similar to those described in the deployment process; however, significant differences exist during the JRSOI phase. These differences are apparent when the force is redeploying to a new OA or to home or demobilization station. These distinctions and the command relationships during redeployment are addressed later in this publication.

e. **Redeployment operations** are the sum of activities required to plan, prepare, and move forces and accompanying materiel from origin to destinations within a new OA or to home station to achieve the operational status required to execute a mission or demobilize.

4. Strategic Mobility

a. **Strategic mobility** is the capability to deploy and sustain military forces worldwide in support of national strategy. Beyond the intrinsic capability of US operational forces to self-deploy, the bulk of our nation's strategic mobility requirements are met through common-user sealift, common-user airlift, and pre-positioned stocks, known as the strategic mobility triad, shown in Figure I-2.

b. **The Strategic Mobility Triad.** Successful deployment and redeployment of forces and capabilities in military operations depends on sufficient port throughput capacity coupled with the availability of sufficient mobility assets to rapidly deploy operational forces, sustain them as long as necessary to meet US military objectives, and reconstitute and redeploy them to meet changing mission requirements or return to home and/or demobilization stations upon completion of their mission. To meet this challenge, the United States Transportation Command's (USTRANSCOM's) transportation component commands (TCCs), Air Mobility Command (AMC), Military Sealift Command (MSC), and Military Surface Deployment and Distribution Command (SDDC) exercise command and control (C2) of assigned, allocated, apportioned, or chartered transportation assets for use by all DOD elements and, as authorized, other USG departments and agencies or other approved users. Deployment operations normally involve a combination of land (road and rail), sea commercial shipping; US privately owned, foreign flag commercial shipping; and foreign owned and operated commercial shipping. With respect to sealift, Commander, United States Transportation Command (CDRUSTRANSCOM), is delegated authority to procure commercial transportation services and, with the approval of SecDef, to activate the Maritime Administration Ready Reserve Force and the VISA.

For more information on common-user sealift, see JP 4-01.2, Sealift Support to Joint Operations.

(3) **Pre-positioned force, equipment, or supplies programs are both land and sea-based.** They are critical programs for reducing closure times of combat and support forces needed in the early stages of a contingency. They also contribute significantly to reducing demands on the DTS.

For more information on pre-positioned stocks, see JP 4-01, The Defense Transportation System.

c. **Other mobility considerations.** Other transportation resources may be available to a CCDR to support deployment operations that do not fit within the context of the strategic mobility triad. As proven in operations in Afghanistan, land transportation may augment traditional strategic mobility capabilities. Land transportation may include road and/or rail modes in areas where there is limited air or sea port infrastructure to meet the CCDR's requirements. This intratheater mode may be effective in delivering forces and sustainment to support the CCDR's mission.

5. Integrated Planning and Execution Process

APEX, JOPES, and the joint operation planning process (JOPP) provide the processes, formats, and systems which link deployment and redeployment planning for joint force projection to the execution of joint operations. The incorporation of collaboration capabilities, relational databases, and decision-support tools promotes deployment and redeployment planning with real-time access to relevant information and the ability to link planners and selected subject matter experts regardless of their location.

a. **JOPES** use is directed for planning and executing all deployment and redeployment operations. JOPES has three operational activities: situation awareness, planning, and execution. JOPES provides the process, structure, reports, plans, and orders that orchestrate the JPEC's delivery of the military instrument of national power.

b. **JOPP** describes the common activities needed to plan missions across the full range of military operations and defines the required military capabilities and timelines that set the framework for deployment/redeployment planning. It applies to both supported and supporting JFCs and to joint force component commands when the components participate in joint planning. This process is designed to facilitate interaction between the commander, staff, and subordinate headquarters (HQ) throughout planning. JOPP helps commanders and their staffs organize their planning activities, share a common understanding of the mission and commander's intent, and develop effective plans and orders. This planning process applies to deliberate planning and CAP within the context of the responsibilities specified by the CJCSM 3122 Series and the CJCSM 3130 Series. JOPP also is used by joint organizations that have no specific JOPES responsibilities. Furthermore, JOPP supports deployment and redeployment planning after the CJCS, at the direction of the President or SecDef, issues the execute order. In common application, JOPP proceeds according to planning milestones and other requirements established by the commanders at various levels. However, the CJCSM 3122 Series and the CJCSM 3130 Series specifies JPEC milestones, deliverables, and interaction points for contingency and crisis action plans developed per the formal JOPES process. Figure I-3 shows the primary steps of JOPP.

For more discussion on APEX and JOPES, see CJCSM 3122 Series, and the CJCSM 3130 Series. For information on JOPES and JOPP, as adaptive processes, see JP 5-0, Joint Operation Planning.

6. Adaptive Planning and Execution System

a. Joint operation planning is accomplished through the APEX system. The JPEC uses APEX to monitor, plan, and execute mobilization, deployment, employment, sustainment, redeployment, and demobilization activities associated with joint operations. APEX occurs in a networked, collaborative environment, which facilitates dialogue among senior leaders, concurrent and parallel plan development, and collaboration across multiple planning levels. This facilitates responsive deployment and redeployment planning and execution throughout the JPEC. Figure I-4 outlines joint operation planning activities, functions, and products.

b. APEX incorporates initiatives—such as levels of planning detail, the requirement for more frequent in-progress reviews between CCDRs and SecDef, routine assessments, and

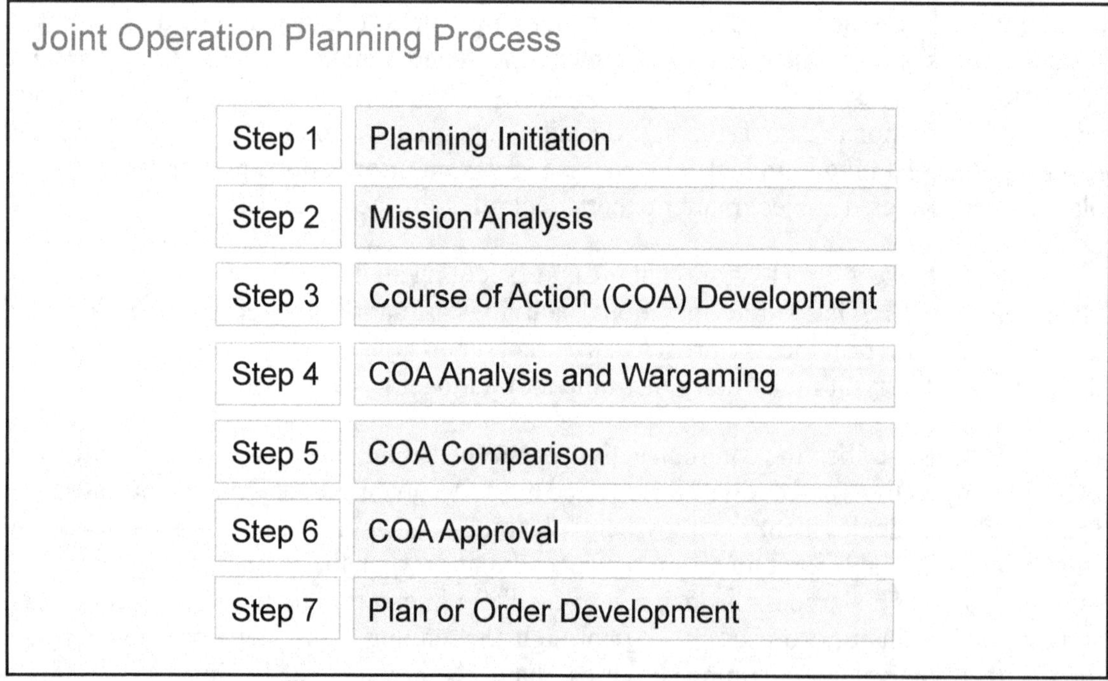

Figure I-3. Joint Operation Planning Process

the use of collaboration technology to provide more and better options during plan development, increase opportunities for consultation and guidance during the planning process, and promote increased agility throughout deployment and redeployment.

c. Joint operation planning encompasses a number of elements, including three broad operational activities, four planning functions, and a number of related products.

(1) Operational Planning. The GEF guides the development of **contingency plans**, which address potential threats that put one or more end states at risk in ways that warrant

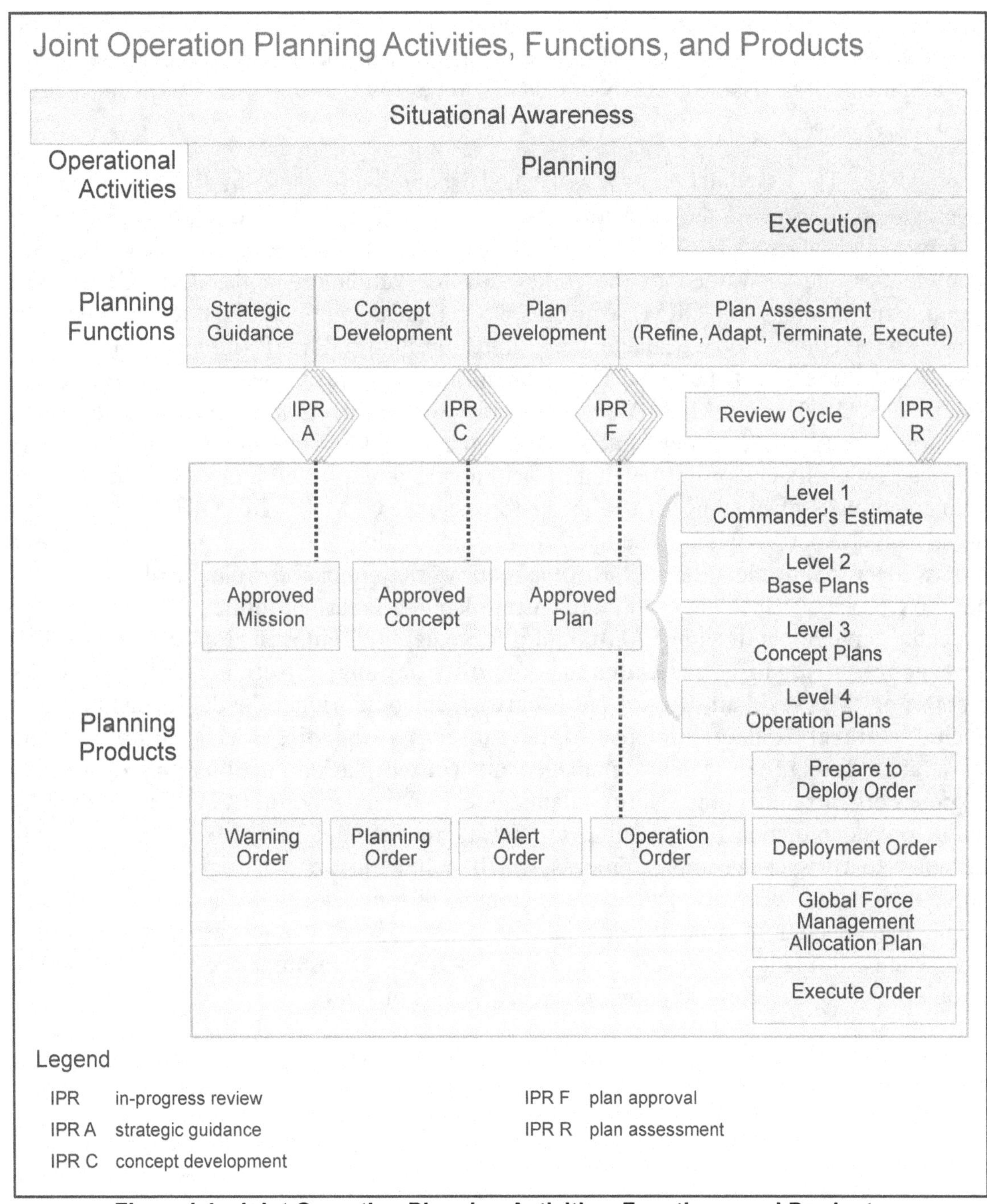

Figure I-4. Joint Operation Planning Activities, Functions, and Products

military operations. Both deliberate planning and CAP are employed to further refine a contingency plan to best meet the CCDR's operational requirements.

(a) Deliberate planning enables supported CCDRs to create and define valid courses of action (COAs) in anticipation of the need for a military response to predictable scenarios. The selected COA becomes the basis for the operation plan (OPLAN), which contains a deployment concept and will contain a time-phased force and deployment list (TPFDL) or a time-phased force and deployment data (TPFDD) as required by the CONOPS.

(b) CAP is triggered in response to an event. If an applicable and usable OPLAN or concept plan (CONPLAN) exists, it will be used to accelerate orders development. If no usable OPLAN or CONPLAN exists, the supported CCDR must begin the CAP process.

(2) The CONOPS with the associated list of required capabilities and/or forces and deployment concept are the basis for deployment planning. For forces not included in an approved and validated TPFDD, RFFs are drafted, submitted, and endorsed by the supported commander and forwarded to the Joint Staff for validation in the Joint Capabilities Requirements Manager (JCRM) software. Upon SecDef approval, the CJCS publishes an annex to the Global Force Management Allocation Plan (GFMAP) directing forces to be allocated to the supported CCDR. It also directs the joint force provider (JFP) to release the global DEPORD, or GFMAP Annex Schedule, which directs force providers to deploy specific forces at the time and duration specified by SecDef. Subsequently, DEPORDs are released by each echelon in the chain of command down to the unit or individual level implementing SecDef authority to allocate forces in the GFMAP. DEPORDs generally get progressively more detailed. The SecDef decision to allocate forces, or not, and the actual forces identified to meet the CCDR force requests may impact the plan, making CAP an iterative process. Once allocated, movement planning is further refined in the TPFDD to meet the deployment timeline. **Actual joint force deployment is in response to an action or event requiring force projection to accomplish national objectives and is directed by SecDef or the President.** Actions or events which could trigger the deployment process include **natural disasters**, **defense support of civil authorities**, **foreign humanitarian assistance**, foreign consequence management, **United Nations actions and support** to regional organizations (e.g., North Atlantic Treaty Organization [NATO] operations), or joint force deployments in response to **threats to national interests.** Deployment in response to a crisis is a complex process, which includes all actions from planning through force integration. It involves all levels of command from strategic to tactical. Planning of deployment operations is inextricably linked with and dependent upon the operational design and scheme of maneuver described in the CONOPS. To ensure successful execution, it should be given due consideration in the early stages of JOPP.

For more information on APEX, see JP 5-0, Joint Operation Planning, and CJCS Guide 3130, *Adaptive Planning and Execution (APEX) Overview and Policy Framework.*

7. Integrated Employment and Deployment

Force employment plans and schedules drive deployment planning and execution preparation requirements and movement timelines. Deployment operations provide forces ready to execute the supported commander's orders. Plan force requirements identify when and where forces are required and list the missions they are expected to perform. Deployment plans and schedules align with the OPLANs/operation order (OPORDs) and support the associated force movement requirements, allowing for predeployment preparations required by the Service component. The GFM sourcing processes (preferred forces, contingency sourcing, or execution sourcing) link the requirements to the forces that will ultimately be ordered to deploy. Employment is normally divided into a series of phases. Within those phases, missions are identified and prioritized. Forces are selected based on their ability to execute specific required missions. Any mission may require integrated or synchronized support from one or more Service forces. Deployment processes, systems, and plans must provide the supported commander with a joint force and the flexibility to redeploy forces as required to achieve the transition criteria for each phase of the operation and ultimately, mission success.

a. **Operation Phase Model. The operation phase model is an element of operational design and is used to arrange operations.** It assists the JFC to visualize and think through the entire operation to define requirements in terms of forces, resources, time, space, and purpose. The model consists of six phases: ***shape, deter, seize initiative, dominate, stabilize, and enable civil authority*** **(see Figure I-5).** Predeployment activities and the initial deployment into a theater normally occur during the ***deter phase***; however, deployment and redeployment can occur during any of the phases. Redeployment operations will often begin during the ***stabilize phase***; however, planning for rotational deployments and redeployment operations should begin as early as possible and continue through all phases of the operation. The operation or campaign concludes when the national strategy end state is achieved and redeployment operations are complete.

For more discussion on phasing, see JP 3-0, Joint Operations, *or JP 5-0,* Joint Operation Planning.

b. **Force Planning.** Force planning consists of determining the force requirements by operation phase, mission, mission priority, mission sequence, and OA. It includes major force phasing, and integration planning and force list structure development followed by force list development. The supported CCDR determines force requirements, develops a TPFDD and letter of instruction (LOI), and designs force modules to align and time-phase the forces IAW the CONOPS. If the plan is directed for execution, the force requirements are forwarded to the Joint Staff for validation and tasked to the JFPs to provide sourcing recommendations to SecDef. When SecDef accepts the sourcing recommendation, the JFPs are ordered to deploy the force to meet the requested force requirement. After the actual forces are sourced, the CCDR refines the force plan to ensure it supports the CONOPS, provides force visibility, and enables flexibility. Deployment and redeployment movement planning is paramount throughout force planning.

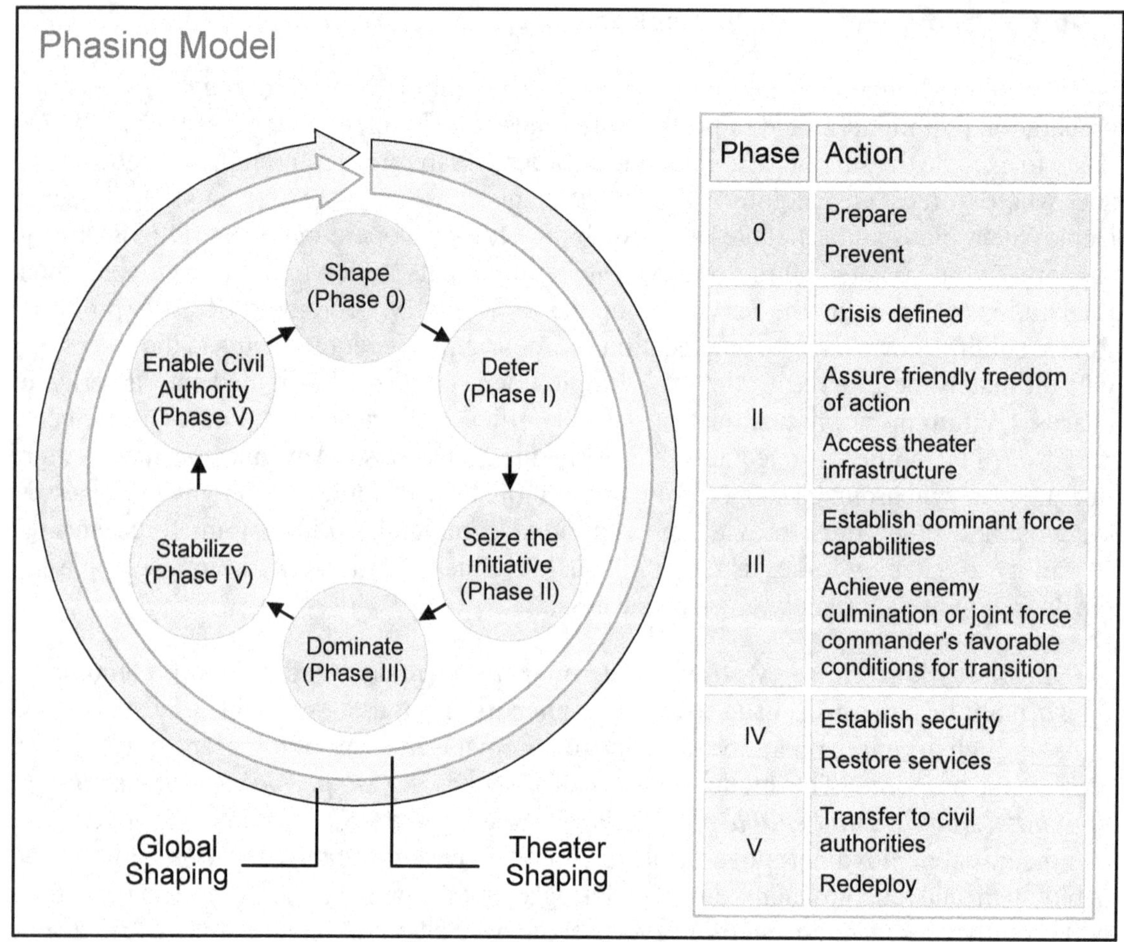

Phase	Action
0	Prepare Prevent
I	Crisis defined
II	Assure friendly freedom of action Access theater infrastructure
III	Establish dominant force capabilities Achieve enemy culmination or joint force commander's favorable conditions for transition
IV	Establish security Restore services
V	Transfer to civil authorities Redeploy

Figure I-5. Phasing Model

8. Force Visibility

Force visibility provides the current and accurate status of forces at the strategic and operational level, their current mission, future missions, location, mission priority, and readiness status. Force visibility provides information on the location, operational tempo, assets, and sustainment requirements of a force as part of an overall capability for a CCDR. Force visibility integrates operations and logistics information, facilitates GFM, and enhances the capability of the entire JPEC to adapt rapidly to unforeseen events, to respond and ensure capability delivery. **Force visibility enhances situational awareness and is required to support force sourcing, allocation, assignment of forces; force position; sustainment forecasting and delivery; and forecasting for future force requirements.** Force visibility is achieved through effective force and phase planning for contingencies and crises, detailed deployment planning, and sound reporting procedures. Within force visibility are the following:

a. **Asset visibility (AV) is a subcomponent of force visibility.** Having it provides commanders and planners with timely and accurate information on the location, movement, status, and identity of units, personnel, equipment (maintenance and retrograde actions), and supplies by class of supply, nomenclature, and unit during deployment operations. AV is in the Global Combat Support System-Joint (GCSS-J) family of systems and includes in-transit visibility (ITV) over equipment, supplies, or personnel.

b. **ITV is a component of AV.** When applied to an operation, it provides visibility of deploying and redeploying forces as well as sustainment en route to an operation or a unit. ITV preserves the link between the in-transit force and that force's mission within an operation phase through the force requirement number (FRN). ITV can be divided into levels of visibility: force movements associated with a specific operation; force movements for a specific phase, mission, and OA/destination; the movements of a force or unit as a capability with a specific mission; visibility of a lift mission; and in the box or item visibility. Movement of all non-unit personnel, equipment, and supplies to include contractors and other non-DOD lift requestors, and retrograde actions will generally not have transportation and item level visibility unless they are included in a TPFDD. Patient movement ITV is documented utilizing the USTRANSCOM Regulating and Command and Control Evacuation System (TRAC2ES).

For more information on force visibility, see Chapter V, "Movement," and JP 4-01, The Defense Transportation System.

9. Sustainment Delivery

Sustainment delivery is the process of providing and maintaining levels of personnel and materiel required to sustain combat and mission activity at the level of intensity dictated by the CONOPS. Sustainment is ongoing throughout the entire operation and, like deployment and redeployment, should be aligned with the mission and mission priorities of each phase. Sustainment delivery must frequently be balanced against force deployment or redeployment requirements because these operations share the same deployment and distribution infrastructure and other resources. However, deployment and force integration can be adversely affected by excess or insufficient sustainment support; hence operation planning must integrate deployment and sustainment operations.

CHAPTER II
RESPONSIBILITIES

"All over the ship the tension that had been slowly building up since our departure was now approaching its climax. Even the Yellow Sea rushing past the ship's sides seemed to bespeak the urgency of our mission. That night, about half past two, I took a turn around the deck. The ship was blacked out from stem to stern. At their posts and battle stations the crew members were alert and silent, no longer exchanging the customary banter. At the bow I stood listening to the rush of the sea and watched the fiery sparklets of phosphorescence as the dark ship plowed toward the target, the armada of other craft converging on the same area, all now past the point of no return. Within five hours, 40,000 men would act boldly, in hope that 100,000 others manning the thin defense lines in South Korea would not die. I alone was responsible for tomorrow, and if I failed, the dreadful results would rest on judgment day against my soul."

Thoughts of General Douglas MacArthur in the predawn hours prior to the Inchon landings,
Reminiscences, General of the Army, Douglas MacArthur

1. General

a. This chapter identifies the responsibilities, roles, and relationships of the commands and agencies involved in deployment operations.

b. Basic responsibilities for commands and entities involved in joint deployment operations are outlined in JP 1, *Doctrine for the Armed Forces of the United States,* JP 3-0, *Joint Operations*, and JP 4-01, *The Defense Transportation System.* Clearly articulating responsibilities is the first step in fully synchronized and coordinated deployment operations supporting the range of military operations.

2. Secretary of Defense

SecDef assigns and allocates all forces and resources to the CCMDs to perform their assigned missions. In addition, SecDef is responsible for transportation planning and operations within the DOD.

a. Under Secretary of Defense for Acquisition, Technology, and Logistics establishes policies and provides guidance to DOD components concerning the effective and efficient use of the DTS.

b. SecDef has designated the Joint Staff Operations Directorate the primary joint force coordinator for conventional forces (except designated forces sourced by United States Special Operations Command [USSOCOM], United States Strategic Command [USSTRATCOM], and USTRANSCOM).

c. The CDRUSTRANSCOM is designated DOD's single manager for transportation and the distribution process owner (DPO) and the JFP for mobility forces. Commander,

United States Special Operations Command (CDRUSSOCOM), is the JFP for special operations forces (SOF). The Commander, USSTRATCOM, is designated as the joint functional manager for intelligence, surveillance, and reconnaissance (ISR) and associated processing, exploitation, and dissemination forces and missile defense forces.

3. Chairman of the Joint Chiefs of Staff

As the principal military advisor to the President, National Security Council, and SecDef, the CJCS is assigned specific supervisory and joint operation planning responsibilities in the areas of strategic direction, strategic planning, and joint operation planning. The CJCS's responsibilities most directly related to deployment operations include the following:

a. Prepares joint logistic and mobility plans to support strategic plans and recommends the assignment of logistic and mobility responsibilities to the Services IAW those plans.

b. Reviews joint OPLANs, ensuring conformance with policy guidance from the President and SecDef.

c. Prepares joint logistic and mobility plans to support joint OPLANs, recommends the assignment of logistic and mobility responsibilities to the Armed Forces IAW those logistic and mobility plans, and ascertains the logistic support available to execute the CCDR's general war and joint OPLANs. The CJCS will also review and recommend to SecDef appropriate logistic guidance for the Services that, if implemented, will result in logistic readiness consistent with approved plans.

d. Advises SecDef on critical deficiencies and strengths in force capabilities identified during the preparation and review of OPLANs and assesses the effect of noted deficiencies and strengths on meeting national security objectives, policies, and strategic plans.

e. Prepares integrated plans for military mobilization.

f. Participates, as directed, in the preparation of multinational plans for military action in conjunction with the other nations' armed forces.

g. Oversees the activities of the CCMDs upon assignment by SecDef. Such assignment does not confer any command authority on the CJCS and does not alter the responsibilities of the CCDRs.

h. Reviews the plans and programs of CCDRs to determine their adequacy, consistency, acceptability, and feasibility for the performance of assigned missions.

i. Provides guidance and direction to the CCDRs on aspects of C2 that relate to the conduct of operations.

j. Performs as the global force manager to integrate the force management processes (assignment, apportionment, and allocation of joint forces).

k. Develops a standardized joint planning and execution process, with common data elements and terms, supported by clearly delineated procedures for implementation throughout the JPEC.

l. Establishes procedures (in coordination with the Deputy Assistant Secretary of Defense [Transportation Policy], the Secretaries of the Military Departments, and the Defense Logistics Agency [DLA]) for the submission of movement requirements by DOD user components to USTRANSCOM and for the submission of evaluated requirements and capabilities by USTRANSCOM and the TCCs to the CJCS.

m. Prescribes a movement priority system in agreement with Uniform Material Movement and Issue Priority System that will ensure responsiveness to meet the needs of the CCDR.

n. Advises SecDef of mobility support force capabilities and assesses their impact on CCDR and DOD component requirements.

o. Assigns movement priorities in support of DOD components based upon capabilities reported by USTRANSCOM.

p. Apportions strategic lift assets.

q. Allocates strategic lift assets through the CJCS execute order to the supported CCDR.

r. Acts on the recommendations of the CJCS Joint Transportation Board (JTB) with respect to the establishment of priorities and apportionment for the use of airlift, sealift, and surface transportation capability. The JTB monitors the balance between DOD transportation requirements and capabilities through close liaison with the CCDRs and USTRANSCOM. Once armed with CJCS priorities, USTRANSCOM closely collaborates with the CCDR(s) and other CJCS-designated agencies to meet President or SecDef objectives while keeping the Joint Staff directorates informed. A joint deployment and distribution operations center (JDDOC), established in each GCC's AOR and acting in consonance with the GCC's priorities, uses reachback linkages to USTRANSCOM, DLA, the Services, and other partners to synchronize and optimize the flow of forces and sustainment in, through, and out of a theater. Service participation and considerations in transportation decision making are appropriately raised through supported Service components to the CCDR. CDRUSTRANSCOM refers problems with recommended COAs to the JTB for resolution or adjudication if a balance of transportation requirements and capabilities cannot be maintained.

s. Serves as the joint development trainer through the Joint Deployment Training Center. Develops, implements, monitors, and assesses joint education and training programs to improve deployment and redeployment planning and execution.

t. Ensures that deployment and redeployment planning and execution are assessed during all joint force operations as well as CJCS and CCMD-sponsored joint exercises.

u. Recommends allocation recommendations from the JFPs to SecDef.

v. Issues prepare to deploy orders, DEPORDs, and orders for execution of deployment operations upon authorization by SecDef.

w. Serves as the joint force coordinator for conventional forces while coordinating with USSTRATCOM for ISR forces and associated processing, exploitation, and dissemination. Identifies and recommends force sourcing solutions to SecDef for Joint Staff validated conventional force requests.

4. Supported and Supporting Combatant Commands

a. A CCDR's joint operation planning responsibilities are described in the *Unified Command Plan (UCP),* JP 1, *Doctrine for the Armed Forces of the United States,* and JP 5-0, *Joint Operation Planning.* Supported CCDRs are responsible for coordinating with USTRANSCOM and other supporting CCDRs to provide an integrated transportation system from origin to destination during deployment and redeployment operations.

b. **Responsibilities of Supported Combatant Commanders.** Supported CCDRs are responsible for deployment and redeployment operations planned and executed during joint force missions. This responsibility includes identification of the movement, timing, and sequence of deploying and redeploying forces in the TPFDD, reception and integration of units and materiel arriving in theater, and assisting these units as required. Throughout this process, GCCs must maintain personnel accountability and strength reporting by location. Working through the Department of State (DOS), supported CCDRs negotiate HN diplomatic clearances and reception POD access when required, for deploying forces. For air movements, supported CCDRs must ensure that overflight and landing clearances are secured prior to the departure of forces from aerial ports of embarkation (APOEs). Additionally, the CCDR will establish and publish policies, procedures, and standards to accomplish the personnel visibility mission in their AOR. Supported CCDRs have three major responsibilities relative to deployment operations: build and validate movement requirements based on the CONOPS; determine predeployment standards (i.e., preparation for movement and predeployment training; plan to use DOD/Service-owned/leased containers in preparation for intertheater distribution operations during initial deployment stage); and balance and regulate the transportation flow.

(1) **Build and Validate Movement Requirements.** Based on an approved CONOPS, the supported CCDR determines the forces or capabilities required for the mission and builds TPFDD movement requirements.

(a) Designate latest arrival date (LAD) and required delivery date (RDD). The supported CCDR specifies key employment information regarding when, where, and how forces will be employed by phase.

(b) Publishes a TPFDD LOI or supplement to the standing joint TPFDD LOI which provides specific guidance for supporting CCDRs, Services, and agencies.

(2) **Determine Predeployment Standards.** Supported CCDRs establish predeployment standards for forces, capabilities, and personnel supporting their operations. Predeployment standards outline the basic command policies, training, and equipment requirements necessary to prepare supporting personnel and forces for the tactical, environmental, and/or medical conditions in theater. The Services and CDRUSSOCOM's role is to ensure that designated forces for CCMDs are organized, trained, equipped, maintained, and ready IAW these predeployment standards. Predeployment standards help ensure that all supporting personnel and forces arrive in theater fully prepared to perform their mission.

(a) **Preparation for Deployment.** Preparation for deployment is primarily a Service responsibility. Specific responsibility for preparation for deployment rests with the deploying unit or Service in the case of individual augmentees, replacements, and contractors. For in lieu of and joint sourcing solutions, the resourcing of preparation and training will be IAW Service to Service memorandums of agreement. Usually, the deploying unit commander must acknowledge completion of specified preparation for deployment requirements to the supported command during predeployment activities. In some instances, constraints may affect personnel readiness if specific training requirements have not been completed.

(b) **Predeployment Training.** In addition to preparation for movement, supported CCDRs may identify mission-specific training requirements that supporting individuals or units must complete before operational employment. These requirements are included in the force requests submitted in either the annual submission or in an emergent RFF. This training may be conducted at home station prior to deployment, en route to the OA, or at the ISB. The supported CCDR should, at a minimum, specify theater-unique

PREDEPLOYMENT PREPARATION: TWO PERSPECTIVES

"Prior to a unit's initial deployment, there was usually time for some final training and organization, but not always. Haste often undermined a unit's readiness...Although the 1st Cavalry [Division] had been training for two years as the 11th Air Assault Division at Fort Benning, its members had received no jungle training and the division was issued M16 rifles only ten days prior to its departure, resulting in a hurried familiarization program."

"Marines, prior to shipping out to 'WestPac,' returned from leave to a staging battalion. Staging battalions provided a final bit of pre-Vietnam refresher training and was a catchall for shots and paperwork before departure. Even Marines who had previously been to Vietnam went through a staging battalion before returning for another tour...Marine replacements went through a staging regimen that included three weeks of refresher infantry training, instruction in topics relating to Vietnam—such as booby traps—and the bureaucratic paper-pushing that accompanies all military moves."

SOURCE: ***A Life in a Year: The American Infantryman in Vietnam 1965–1972,*** **by James R. Ebert**

clothing and equipment requirements and mission-essential tasks to be trained prior to arrival in theater.

(3) **Balance and Regulate the Force Flow.** The requested start dates on the request for each individual force or capability must support the overall CONOPS. SecDef approved ordered start dates also support the CONOPS while balancing operational capabilities. To the maximum extent possible, the supported CCDRs should balance and regulate the flow of forces with the flow of sustainment. OE, available infrastructure, protection risk assessment, and the CONOPS are major factors in determining how to balance the flow of forces and capabilities. The supported CCDR manages the flow of forces via the TPFDD supported by strategic, operational, and tactical movement control organizations, to ensure effective interfaces between intertheater and intratheater movements. Balance is primarily a function of effective mission prioritization, alignment of forces, force composition, and force flow. Consideration must also be given to planned theater distribution (TD) and JRSOI requirements and capabilities. Force composition and transportation flow must accommodate mission requirements, providing the supported CCDR with the operational flexibility and freedom of action required for successful mission execution.

c. **Responsibilities of Supporting Combatant Commanders.** Supporting missions during deployment of the joint force could include the deployment or redeployment of forces from or to a supporting CCMD, sponsorship of en route basing or in-transit staging areas (SAs), or provision of sustainment from theater stocks. Regardless of the supporting mission, the primary task for supporting CCMDs is to ensure that the supported CCDR receives the timely and complete support needed to accomplish the mission. Supporting CCDRs have five major deployment responsibilities: source, prepare, and verify forces; ensure units retain their visibility and mobility; ensure units report movement requirements rapidly and accurately; regulate the support flow; and coordinate.

(1) **Source, Prepare, and Verify Forces.** The GFMAP is a SecDef approved consolidated allocation order, by fiscal year (FY) that authorizes the transfer and attachment of forces from designated CCDRs, Services, and combat support agencies (CSAs) to supported CCDRs or back following completion of mission requirements by the supported CCDR. Annexes within the GFMAP contain all the information inherent within a written order.

(2) **GFMAP Annex Schedules.** The GFMAP annexes published by the Joint Staff also delegate authority and responsibility for designated JFPs to manage deployments per the JFP authorities and to publish the JFP GFMAP annex schedule. The content of SecDef approved annexes is the basis of the JFP GFMAP annex schedule.

(a) The JFP GFMAP annexes schedule units and individuals in support of the approved force requirements and serve as the DEPORDs.

1. The GFMAP provides SecDef direction to the JFPs, working with all force providers through their assigned Service component and CSA to identify specific forces, units, and individuals for deployment in support of the GFMAP.

2. The actual units sourced by the force provider are not included in the GFMAP annexes. Unit sourcing is available in the JOPES/APEX and GFM information technology systems. Each unit line number (ULN) should reference the force tracking number (FTN) in order to trace back the force requirement to the originator as well as SecDef authority to allocate back through the JFP GFMAP annex schedule to the GFMAP annex.

(b) All CCDRs, Services, and CSAs support JFP planning and deploy forces specified in the JFP GFMAP annex schedules.

(c) Any additional FY annual forces, as well as emergent requirements, are allocated in subsequent annex modifications to the base GFMAP annex upon SecDef approval.

(d) JFPs publish modifications as required to their respective GFMAP annex schedules in their entirety and supersede previous versions. This allows the JPEC to reference one final order rather than having to put together the dozens of modifications to the GFMAP annexes.

(3) Supporting and supported CCDRs will publish DEPORDs implementing the orders in the JFP GFMAP annex schedules. All orders, down to the individual level, that implement the GFMAP annexes will reference the FTN and FTN line number. Individual Marines, Soldiers, Sailors, Coast Guardsmen, and Airmen deploying should be able to trace their DEPORDs back to the CCDR requirements via the FTN. Supporting and supported CCDRs, Services, and DOD agencies utilize JOPES as the system of record for execution, to implement the deployment guidance in the JFP GFMAP annex schedules.

(4) **Command Relationships.** Unless otherwise specified in the GFMAP or in a separate SecDef approved order, supported commanders accept deploying forces and exercise OPCON upon arrival in their AOR, and relinquish OPCON of redeploying forces upon departure from their AOR. Supporting commanders who provide forces transfer forces and relinquish OPCON to the supported commander upon arrival in the supported commander's AOR. CCDRs who provided forces exercise OPCON of their redeploying forces upon departure from the supported commander's AOR.

5. Functional Combatant Commands

Supported CCDRs capitalize on the power inherent in joint operations by synchronizing the complementary capabilities of all the Services and supporting commands into a unified effort. Moreover, CCDRs are responsible for unified actions that are synchronized in time, space, and purpose with actions of other military forces and nonmilitary organizations. Because of the numerous process stakeholders, successful deployment operations require unity of effort. Normally, several functional CCMDs are involved in every phase of a joint operation. Three functional CCMDs could be involved in deployment of the joint force: USSOCOM, USSTRATCOM, and USTRANSCOM.

a. **United States Special Operations Command.** USSOCOM assigned assets may be deployed or redeployed as a result of SOF mission taskings, or USSOCOM may provide

SOF mission support to conventional joint force deployment. USSOCOM also serves as the JFP for SOF. USSOCOM identifies and recommends force sourcing solutions for SecDef validated SOF requests.

(1) On occasion, USSOCOM may require common-user transportation assets to deploy or redeploy SOF. Compared to conventional force operations, SOF deployment operations are relatively small in scale; however, deployment planners may need to consider conventional support requirements which may also accompany SOF. Given the nature of most SOF missions, time constraints, planning considerations, or special mission requirements may place unique demands on common-user transportation assets utilized for deployment of SOF.

(2) **Special Operations Forces Mission Support.** SOF core operations and activities could directly impact support to joint force deployment operations. Based on mission requirements and the OE, SOF could provide the JFC with the capability to facilitate the JFC's operational goals. USSOCOM, through the theater special operations command, provides combat-ready SOF to the GCC to conduct selected special operations (SO).

For additional information, see JP 3-05, Special Operations, *JP 3-13.2,* Military Information Support Operations, or *JP 3-57,* Civil-Military Operations.

b. **United States Strategic Command.** USSTRATCOM provides advisors upon request by the supported CCDR, who will designate when and where they will report. The advisor coordinates with the mission-planning facilities of USSTRATCOM for the utilization of nuclear weapons, ISR, space, and cyberspace forces.

c. **United States Transportation Command.** USTRANSCOM responsibilities include the following:

(1) **Department of Defense Distribution Process Owner.** As the DPO, USTRANSCOM oversees the overall effectiveness, efficiency, and alignment of DOD-wide distribution activities, including force projection (force movement), sustainment, redeployment, and retrograde operations, and establishes the CONOPS frameworks relating to the planning and execution of the DOD transportation operations. USTRANSCOM also serves as the JFP for mobility forces. USTRANSCOM identifies and recommends force sourcing solutions to SecDef for Joint Staff validated mobility force requests.

(2) Provide, through its Service component commands, air, land, and sea transportation and common-user port management at air and sea POE and/or POD for DOD across the range of military operations. Also provide air transportation to numerous non-DOD agencies at the direction of the President or SecDef through the CJCS.

(3) Exercise authority over RC forces when mobilized or ordered to active duty for other than training. This includes CRAF and National Defense Reserve Fleet lift assets.

(4) Exercise responsibility for global air, land, and sea transportation planning (deliberate and crisis action).

(5) Act as the DOD focal point for items in the transportation pipeline. Ensure effective interfaces between the Integrated Data Environment/Global Transportation Network Convergence (IGC) and JOPES leading to force ITV.

(6) Provide ITV for all force movements supported by transportation activities and all sustainment movements. Report all Service and transportation system interface failures during CAP operations. Report incorrectly prepared, delayed, or frustrated cargo and personnel to the Service and the CCDR to support operation decision making and ensure accurate corrections without loss of visibility.

(7) Provide DOD global patient movement in coordination with GCCs through DTS.

(8) Provide GCCs with coordinated transportation planning expertise required during the deliberate planning process. This includes reviewing the Joint Strategic Capabilities Plan tasking, analyzing supported CCDR requirements registered in the JOPES for transportation feasibility, and advising the CCDR of changes required to produce a sustainable force deployment concept. In addition, provide plan maintenance support to the supported CCDR as required or directed by the CJCS.

(9) Provide deployment lift estimates and total lift asset availability to the President or SecDef and supported CCDRs for development of alternative COAs and optimal flow of forces during CAP. USTRANSCOM will also advise supported CCDRs and the CJCS concerning use of or changes to lift allocations.

(10) Assist the supported CCDR and ensure that validated movement requirements are routed and scheduled IAW the CONOPS. Recommend reallocation of strategic lift assets to optimize their use and support plan execution during deployment, employment, sustainment, reconstitution, and redeployment.

(11) **Provide Single Port Management.** In addition to its other responsibilities, USTRANSCOM is designated by SecDef as the single worldwide manager for common-user POEs and PODs. Operational experience shows the single port manager (SPM) is necessary to improve the planning and execution of port management operations and ensure the seamless transfer of cargo and equipment in any given theater. Under SPM, USTRANSCOM, through AMC, operates strategic aerial ports in theaters. Additionally, USTRANSCOM, through SDDC, manages seaports of embarkation and debarkation in any given theater. Key aspects of the SPM construct are that SDDC will provide planners to supported CCMDs to develop seaport management and operations requirements; at the request of the supported CCDR, conduct seaport assessments, establish contact with local seaport authorities, and determine availability of host-nation support (HNS); and when required, act as seaport manager throughout the operation.

(12) **Provide Liaison.** USTRANSCOM provides liaison officers (LNOs) to all GCCs to assist in coordination of strategic mobility issues. USTRANSCOM and its components may provide additional technical experts to facilitate planning and execution on an as needed basis as requested by the supported CCDR.

6. Joint Task Forces

Joint Task Force (JTF) Deployment and/or Redeployment Planning Responsibilities. Formation of a JTF may complicate deployment planning and execution because of the diverse elements that may come together to form the JTF. A significant challenge in JTF deployment operations is in building the force requirements and TPFDD. This is particularly true during crisis action situations when limited planning time prompts the development of a fully coordinated OPLAN/CONPLAN with TPFDD or TPFDL.

See JP 3-33, Joint Task Force Headquarters, *for additional information.*

7. Military Departments and Department of Defense Agencies

The Military Departments and DOD agencies retain the responsibility for organizing, training, equipping, and providing administrative and logistics support (including Service-organic transportation) for their respective forces. They are also responsible for maintaining personnel trained in joint operation planning who can participate in joint planning and add data into JOPES. These forces and other DOD agencies may depend on common-user military transportation services for unit and individual deployment and redeployment operations between POEs and PODs. In the role of common-user military transportation services, the Army, Navy, Air Force, Marine Corps, DLA, and other DOD agencies are all generically called shipper services. Each Service is responsible for administrative support and performance of transportation operations assigned by CCDRs at either their local shipping installations or throughout the theater. USTRANSCOM, as the DPO, is responsible for coordinating with its components, the Services, and DLA to ensure integration and synchronization of distribution-related requirements. In addition to these responsibilities, logistic elements of the Services that provide key support and enable the operations staff to execute the commander's requirements for deployment operations are noted below.

a. **US Army**

(1) The Department of the Army (DA) is responsible for the assignment, preparation, and support of Army forces necessary for employment across the range of military operations. For deployment operations, DA is responsible for training, mobilizing, modernizing, administering, organizing, and demobilizing Army forces. The Army's ability to project the military instrument of national power, specifically land power capabilities from the US or another theater, in response to requirements for military operations or force projection encompasses the process of mobilization, deployment, employment, sustainment, and redeployment. DA also establishes policy and procedures for reconstitution of the Army and is the DOD executive agent for repatriation operations. The majority of Army combat assets cannot self-deploy and must be transported by other DOD assets in support of joint force operations. Army units and their sustainment requirements will be submitted by the Army Service component command (ASCC) for inclusion on the joint force TPFDD by supported CCMD planners for scheduling of common-user transportation assets. However, certain quantities of Army pre-positioned stocks in unit equipment sets, sustainment stocks, operational projects, or war reserve stocks for allies may be available either shore-based or afloat to support Army component operations.

(2) DA is responsible for making land transportation available in overseas areas (normally under the GCC's Army Service component commander) for the other Services and for coordinating all planning and requirements for the use of DOD-controlled land transportation equipment and facilities. In some overseas areas, the ASCC has been assigned common-user land transportation (CULT) responsibility for peacetime land transportation; the ASCC will normally designate the theater sustainment command to supervise and execute any common-user transportation requirements delegated to it. Wartime CULT requirements are the responsibility of the CCDR, and normally the JDDOC or the component assigned the mission will consolidate planned wartime movement requirements of all component commands. While DA is responsible for overseas land transportation, USTRANSCOM manages the CONUS land movements.

For more information on TD responsibilities, see JP 4-09, Distribution Operations.

b. **US Marine Corps.** For deployment operations, both the Marine Corps component and Marine air-ground task force (MAGTF) have force deployment officers, MAGTF planners, and strategic mobility/embarkation officers who work as a team during the planning and execution of force deployment operations in support of the MAGTF commander or JFC. Force deployment officers and MAGTF planners build the MAGTF's force deployment TPFDD plan within the guidelines set forth by the CCDR and to support the MAGTF commander's OPLAN. During force deployment execution, force deployment officers ensure proper execution of intertheater and intratheater lift and the strategic mobility officers coordinate Marine Corps movement requirements with the supported GCC, JDDOC, and USTRANSCOM. The Marine Corps activates a MAGTF deployment and distribution operations center (MDDOC) within theater to coordinate and provide transportation services to all land-based elements of the MAGTF. As the Marine Corps primary movement control agency within the theater, the MDDOC is responsible for establishing liaison and communications with and forwarding all transportation shortfalls to the theater JDDOC, or to the component commander.

c. **US Navy**

(1) The Navy component commanders for the GCCs (Commander, US Pacific Fleet; Commander, US Fleet Forces Command; Commander, US Naval Forces Europe; Commander, US Naval Forces Africa; Commander, US Naval Forces Southern Command; and Commander, US Naval Forces Central Command) are responsible for Navy theater deployment and logistics support.

(2) The majority of Navy combat assets self-deploys in support of joint force operations and will be documented in the TPFDD. Forces will be validated for movement by the supported CCDR and will move to meet the LAD, RDD, and CCDR's required date timelines. Navy expeditionary forces which do not self-deploy, including the engineering force, security forces, expeditionary logistics, fleet hospital personnel, and equipment, must be time phased to support the JFCs. The supported CCDR will validate forces for movement, which will then move to meet ready-to-load date (RLD), available-to-load date (ALD), earliest arrival date (EAD), LAD, and CCDR's required date timelines.

(3) In large mobilization scenarios, the Navy may establish naval advanced logistic support sites (NALSSs) to serve as the primary shore-based reception and transshipment points for personnel, equipment, and materiel. Based on the number of carrier strike groups, amphibious ready groups, other Navy units ashore in the Naval component commander AOR, and level of joint tasking, the NALSS may be staffed and equipped to perform both Navy reception, staging, onward movement, and integration and limited JRSOI duties.

(4) A naval forward logistic site (NFLS) is the forward-most land-based transshipment point that provides the bridge between the NALSS and forward operating units. An NFLS is typically established at an airfield or seaport close to the main battle area. Like the NALSS, the NFLS is task organized, staffed with whole or modular components of advanced base functional components, and enables Navy and JRSOI operations.

(5) The size and composition of NALSSs and NFLSs are dependent upon the support required and are tailored by Navy logistic planners for the specific operation or contingency. In lesser mobilization scenarios, the Navy component commander may designate an established naval activity to act in this capacity. In either scenario, the Navy component commander coordinates and monitors personnel deployment activities for units and individuals.

d. **US Air Force (USAF).** Some Air Force mobility and SOF have a limited self-deployment capability. However, the Air Force and Air Force SOF rely on common-user transportation to move support forces and sustainment cargo. Within the Air Force forces component, the logistics directorate is the principal coordinator of Air Force logistics. When required, the director of logistics provides centralized direction and control of deployment, reception, integration, employment, and redeployment of logistic and support assets. The USAF inserts all force deployments within a TPFDD using the Deliberate and Crisis Action Planning and Execution Segments (DCAPES) as its primary automated data processing system for operations, logistics, manpower, and personnel. The Air Force Weather Agency (AFWA) produces strategic weather products, including climatological studies, and data to support planning for deployment of US forces. CCDR-focused strategic and operational weather products are provided as outlined in JP 3-59, *Meteorological and Oceanographic Operations.*

e. **Defense Logistics Agency.** DLA is a CSA and is controlled and directed by the Under Secretary of Defense for Acquisition, Technology, and Logistics. DLA provides worldwide logistic support to the Services, CCMDs, other DOD components, USG departments and agencies, foreign governments, and international organizations (through foreign military sales). AV initiatives enable DLA responsibilities such as those listed in Figure II-1. AV provides users with timely and accurate information on the location, movement, status, and identity of units, personnel, equipment, and supplies during force projection operations. DLA manages more than 80 percent of the items and nearly all of the fuel and petroleum products for military usage. During deployment of the joint force, DLA requires common-user transportation to move, stage, and recover its logistic resources in support of joint force operations. Supported CCMD planners are responsible for validating DLA movement requirements entered in the TPFDD for scheduling by USTRANSCOM. DLA has the following logistic responsibilities: integrate materiel management and supply

Defense Logistics Agency Responsibilities

- Integrate materiel management and supply support for subsistence; clothing and textiles; petroleum, oils, and lubricants; construction materials; medical materials; repair parts; and map distribution
- Property and hazardous waste disposal
- Deploy Defense Logistics Agency (DLA) Support Team for command and control of DLA personnel and streamline customer support to supported combatant commander
- Additional support, as required

Figure II-1. Defense Logistics Agency Responsibilities

support for subsistence; clothing and textiles; petroleum, oils, and lubricants (POL); construction materials; medical materials; repair parts; map distribution; property and hazardous waste disposal; deployment of the DLA support team for C2 of DLA personnel; streamlining of customer support to the supported CCDR; and additional support as required.

f. **Defense Intelligence Agency (DIA).** The mission of the DIA is to satisfy the full range of foreign military and military-related intelligence requirements in support of joint military operations. In addition, DIA provides intelligence support for Service weapons acquisition, defense policy making, and the full range of current and long-term military intelligence products. DIA provides military intelligence for counterintelligence, manages and operates the Defense Counterintelligence and Human Intelligence Center (including the Defense Attaché System), manages all-source DOD collection requirements, serves as national functional manager for measurement and signature intelligence, and provides functional management of military intelligence throughout the intelligence community.

g. **Defense Information Systems Agency (DISA).** DISA is a CSA responsible for planning, engineering, acquiring, fielding, and supporting global net-centric solutions to serve the needs of the President, the Vice President, SecDef, and DOD components. DISA core mission areas are communications, combat support computing, information assurance, joint C2, and joint interoperability support. It provides guidance and support on technical and operational communications and information systems issues affecting the Office of SecDef, the Military Departments, the CJCS and the Joint Staff, the unified and specified commands, and DOD. DISA ensures the interoperability of the Global Command and Control System-Joint (GCCS-J), the defense communications system, theater and tactical C2 systems, NATO and/or allied communication systems, and those national and/or international commercial systems that affect the DISA mission. In addition, DISA supports national security emergency preparedness telecommunications functions of the National Communications System.

h. **National Geospatial-Intelligence Agency.** The National Geospatial-Intelligence Agency, a DOD CSA, is a source for imagery intelligence and geospatial information during planning and execution of deployment operations. It provides geospatial information and services support, including safety of navigation and safety of flight information; imagery and geospatial system technical guidance; staff assistance to the Services, CCMDs, and DOD components; and is the focal point for imagery, imagery intelligence, and geospatial information.

For more information see JP 2-01, Joint and National Intelligence Support to Military Operations.

8. Other Government Departments and Agencies

a. **Department of Homeland Security (DHS).** DHS responsibilities include customs, aerial and seaport security, and infrastructure hardening and protection. DHS coordinates and leverages resources with different governmental jurisdictions at the federal, state, and local levels. DHS coordinates the transition of multiple agencies and programs into a single, integrated agency focused on protecting the American people and their homeland. A comprehensive national strategy seeks to develop a complementary system connecting all levels of government without duplicating effort. The DHS agencies that impact DOD deployment/redeployment include:

(1) **Federal Emergency Management Agency (FEMA).** FEMA coordinates the execution of emergency preparedness actions of all USG departments and agencies, including deployment of military support for defense support of civilian authorities' missions. FEMA HQ is located in Washington, DC, and operates with 10 regional and multiple area offices across the country.

(2) **United States Customs and Border Protection (CBP).** The Commissioner of CBP is responsible for maintaining surveillance of illegal goods entering the US through DTS PODs. CBP is also responsible for guarding against potential plant or animal infestations entering the US through DTS PODs. All forces and material redeploying to the US will require CBP agricultural inspections.

(3) **US Coast Guard (USCG)**

(a) The USCG is the primary US maritime agency for waterway safety and security. The USCG, the only military organization within DHS, supports the GCCs. The USCG is unique among US military forces because it has statutory law enforcement authority.

(b) The USCG core competencies include national defense, maritime safety and security, maritime law enforcement, and maritime environmental protection.

(c) During deployment operations supporting joint force operations, the USCG protects military shipping at US seaports of embarkation (SPOEs) and outside the continental United States (OCONUS) PODs by conducting port security and harbor defense operations in conjunction with Navy coastal warfare forces.

(d) Major USCG cutters may be deployed to participate in maritime interception and coastal sea control operations, enforce sanctions against other nations, and conduct theater security cooperation activities. The major USCG cutters, like Navy combatants, are self-deploying in support of joint force operations. However, deploying port security units and stocks for sustainment must be time-phased to support Navy component operations and scheduled for movement on common-user transportation assets.

(e) Supported CCMD planners validate movement data from port security units and sustainment stocks and enter it on the TPFDD.

(f) Port safety responsibilities in the US include the establishment, certification, and supervision of ammunition loading operations, inspection and certification of US flag vessels in the ready reserve fleet, and licensing additional merchant mariners to serve expanded defense shipping needs.

b. **Department of Health and Human Services.** During natural disasters or civil emergencies, the Department of Health and Human Services assists FEMA and other national agencies in caring for the affected personnel. FEMA will coordinate Department of Health and Human Services movement requirements and deployment and/or redeployment support.

For additional information, see JP 3-27, Homeland Defense.

c. **Department of Transportation (DOT).** During national defense emergencies, the Secretary of Transportation has a wide range of delegated responsibilities, including executive management of the nation's transportation resources in periods of crisis. Surge sealift-government owned military useful ships maintained in varying states of readiness/reduced operating status by the MSC and by the Maritime Administration for activation in time of crisis. These ships, under the combatant command (command authority) of CDRUSTRANSCOM, are ordered into service and placed under the OPCON of Commander, MSC, in support of US wartime, humanitarian and disaster relief, or civil contingency operations to offset shortages of commercial US flagged ships. Surge sealift may also be used for routine operations such as sustainment when commercial assets are not available and exercise support.

d. **Department of State.** DOS and DOD are responsible for the operation of the noncombatant evacuation operation (NEO) program. Deployments executed as part of a NEO will require coordination with DOS representatives. DOS representatives may have access to embassy evacuation, marshalling, and security plans for the objective country. DOS embassy personnel should have an estimate of the number of US citizens in the country and their locations for NEO redeployment planning. Additionally, DOS coordinates foreign country overflight and landing rights, diplomatic clearances, and visa and/or passport requirements for all deployment operations.

e. **National Oceanic and Atmospheric Administration.** The National Oceanic and Atmospheric Administration is a Department of Commerce agency that has worldwide aeronautical data available and is capable of providing backup weather services in the event that both the Fleet Numerical Meteorology and Oceanography Center and AFWA are out of service.

f. **US Postal Service.** The US Postal Service supports joint force operations through movement of essential military mail, including small class IX repair parts. Depending on the scope of the deployment, it may require a significant amount of common-user airlift to support forward-deployed forces.

9. Other Transportation Partners

The DTS relies heavily on the commercial transportation industry to perform a multitude of services during deployment operations in peacetime and war. These commercial source capabilities span all modes of transportation and may include the use of contracted US or foreign commercial air and maritime assets as well as HNS within a joint operations area (JOA). Commercial rail, trucking, ITV assets, and other transportation services may also be contracted to support deployment operations. Deployment planners should consider the implications of the employment of these transportation services as they plan deployment and redeployment operations.

CHAPTER III
DEPLOYMENT AND REDEPLOYMENT PLANNING

"To successfully fight and win wars, we must make war planning our central focus. We will develop the best possible plans using the collective wisdom available among all military planning staffs. The products of our planning efforts must be able to stand up to the strongest scrutiny, including the ultimate test: execution."

General John M. Shalikashvili, US Army
Chairman of the Joint Chiefs of Staff, 1993–1997

1. General

a. This chapter describes deployment and redeployment planning within the context of joint operation planning, and more specifically, the JOPP. Planning is the first phase of both the joint deployment and redeployment processes. Figure III-1 and Figure III-2 depict the planning phase of the joint deployment and redeployment processes, respectively. The entire joint deployment and redeployment process maps are shown and described in Appendix B, "Joint Force Development and Joint Reception, Staging, Onward Movement, and Integration and Joint Force Redeployment Process Maps Descriptions."

Deployment Planning Functional Events and Deployment Processes		
Functional Events	Conduct Force and Support Planning	Initiate Deployment Operations
Deployment Processes	Receive Warning Order/Establish Command Relationships Receive TPFDD Guidance Develop Deployment/Redeployment Concept, Identify WRM/PREPO/TPE Requirements Conduct Deployment Analysis (installations) Assess Operational Environment: Supporting Infrastructure Plan Movement Infrastructure; Transportation Mode, Source, Primary/Alternate Ports and Nodes Assess Force/Sustainment Movement Requirements Supported CCDR Conducts JRSOI Planning Plan Force Flow Conduct Transportation Feasibility Analysis Refine Force and Deployment Data	Supporting CCDR Verifies Unit, Force, and Deployment Data Validate Deployment Data for Movement Execute Supporting Plans

Legend

CCDR	combatant commander	TPE	theater provided equipment
JRSOI	joint reception, staging, onward movement, and integration	TPFDD	time-phased force and deployment data
PREPO	pre-positioned materiel	WRM	war reserve materiel

Figure III-1. Deployment Planning Functional Events and Deployment Processes

Redeployment Planning Functional Events and Redeployment Processes		
Functional Events	Conduct Force and Support Planning	Initiate Redeployment Operations
Redeployment Processes	Receive Warning Order/Establish Command Relationships Receive TPFDD Guidance Develop Refine Redeployment Concept Plan WRM/PREPO/TPE Equipment Disposition Identify HN, and Contract Support Requirements and HN Inspection Requirements Plan/Confirm Movement Infrastructure, Transportation Mode/Source, Primary/Alternate Ports and Nodes Assess Force/Sustainment Movement Requirements Supported CCDR or Supporting CDRs Conduct JRSOI Planning Plan Force Flow Conduct Transportation Feasibility Analysis Refine Force and Deployment Data	Supporting CDR or Supported CCDR Verifies and Validates Unit and Force Deployment Data

Legend

CCDR	combatant commander	TPE	theater provided equipment
CDR	commander	TPFDD	time-phased force and deployment data
JRSOI	joint reception, staging, onward movement, and integration	WRM	war reserve materiel
PREPO	pre-positioned materiel		

Figure III-2. Redeployment Planning Functional Events and Redeployment Processes

b. Deployment and redeployment planning are explicitly identified as elements of joint operation planning.

For more information on joint operation planning, see JP 5-0, Joint Operation Planning.

2. Deployment and Redeployment Planning

a. Deployment planning is operational planning directed toward the movement of forces and sustainment resources from their original locations to a specific OA for conducting the joint operations contemplated in a given plan. It encompasses all activities from origin or home station to final destination, specifically including intra-continental US, intertheater, and intratheater movement legs, SAs, and assembly areas.

b. Redeployment planning is operational planning directed toward the transfer of forces and materiel from a JFC to support another JFC's operational requirements, or to return personnel, equipment, and materiel to the home and/or demobilization stations from a JFC's OA for reintegration and/or demobilization. It encompasses all activities from the redeploying unit's location through destination, specifically including intratheater, intertheater, and intra-continental movement legs, SAs, and assembly areas.

(1) In redeployment operations involving further employment of the force in support of another JFC's operation, the planning is conducted by the gaining supported commander in the same way as deployment planning.

(2) For redeployment operations that return forces to home station or demobilization station, when operationally feasible, redeployment planning will be based on guidelines established for tour length, the transfer of authority between inbound and outbound forces, the recovery and reconstitution requirements of supporting commanders and parent Services, and the demobilization of RC forces.

3. The Joint Operation Planning Process and Deployment and Redeployment Planning

JP 5-0, *Joint Operation Planning,* describes the seven steps of JOPP and outlines the information that the commander needs from the deployment/redeployment planners to ensure that the COAs presented are feasible from the force and transportation resource standpoint. Specific deployment considerations are first highlighted in step 2 (Mission Analysis), and the deployment concept as a planning product is first mentioned in step 3 (COA Development). Refined TPFDD feasibility estimates are included in step 4 (COA Analysis, under Wargaming), and are among the key inputs to step 5 (COA Comparison), step 6 (COA Approval), and step 7 (Plan or Order Development). However, in times of crisis, any or all of these steps can and likely will be abbreviated.

a. **Step 1 - Planning Initiation**

(1) Joint operation planning begins when an appropriate authority recognizes a potential for military employment in response to a potential or actual crisis and issues a planning directive, guidance, or order. At this time, the JFC will normally issue initial planning guidance, which could include information on the operating environment and the operational approach for the campaign or operation. Prior to or after planning is initiated by higher HQ, the supported commander publishes instructions for TPFDD development in the TPFDD LOI. The LOI provides operation-specific guidance for utilizing the APEX processes and systems to provide force visibility and tracking, force mobility, and operational agility through the TPFDD and validation process. It provides procedures for the deployment, redeployment, and rotations of the operation's forces. The LOI provides instructions on force planning, sourcing, reporting, and validation. It defines planning and execution milestones and details movement control procedures and lift allocations to the commander's components, supporting commanders, and other members of the JPEC. A TPFDD must ensure force visibility, be tailored to the phases of the CONOPS, and be transportation feasible. A sample TPFDD LOI is at Appendix C, "Sample Time-Phased Force and Deployment Data Letter of Instruction."

(2) **Abbreviated Procedures.** During a rapidly emerging crisis, the authority to begin deployment may be executed based on verbal orders. Verbal authority to deploy forces can be delegated from SecDef for specific operations and/or events. With Joint Staff concurrence, the JFC may relay deployment requirements by phone calls, e-mails, or other expeditious means. The Joint Staff may host conference calls or video teleconferences with the JFC, JFPs, Services, and Service components to abbreviate the validation and staffing

process. Verbal orders, however, do not replace the standard JOPES TPFDD or GFM allocation processes, but are simply the verbal authority to begin the movement of forces and units. The supported JFC enters all force requirements into the JCRM and submits all RFFs moving under verbal orders within the time-frame specified by SecDef and CJCS. Verbal orders are followed up with written orders.

b. **Step 2 - Mission Analysis.** In this step, the JFC's staff analyzes the mission received in step 1 to propose a restated mission for the commander's approval. Mission analysis is used to study the assigned mission and to identify all tasks necessary to accomplish it. The key mission analysis outputs required from the deployment/redeployment planners are an initial deployment staff estimate and, if necessary, inputs to the commander's refined operational approach and commander's critical information requirements (CCIRs).

(1) From a deployment perspective, when a JFC receives a mission tasking in the form of a warning order (WARNORD) or other directive, analysis begins with the following questions:

(a) What deployment tasks must be performed for the mission to be accomplished?

(b) What forces and assets are required/available to support the deployment?

(c) Have any limitations been placed on deploying the force?

(d) What are the command relationships?

(2) During mission analysis, the JFC and the staff examine imposed operational limitations, lift allocation, and other restrictions that limit the JFC's freedom of action, such as diplomatic agreements. Force planners at this stage will begin to conduct initial force analysis, reviewing assigned and reserve forces and force apportionment tables and comparing them to capabilities required to accomplish specified and implied tasks to identify shortfalls. This effort will begin to produce the initial force list used later from COA development and deployment feasibility analysis. These may significantly affect the deployment scheme, and the staff must develop options to minimize the impact. At a minimum, deployment/redeployment planning must consider and document the assumptions, physical and information factors, and any predicted impact enemy/neutral forces may have on the ability to deploy to or redeploy from the OE.

(3) To assist with mission analysis, the JFC develops CCIRs, which are elements of information that the commander considers as being essential to timely decision making. The JFC's staff can recommend deployment-related priority intelligence requirements about the OE that become CCIRs if approved by the JFC.

(4) The JFC's deployment planners in coordination with the development of the logistics staff estimate initiate a deployment staff estimate during mission analysis to inform the commander, staff, and subordinate commands how the deployment scheme supports mission accomplishment and to support COA development and selection. The estimate should identify available transportation capabilities and coordination requirements to support

the time-phased deployment, employment, and sustainment of tentative COAs. It will include requirements for intertheater and intratheater transportation assets and requirements to protect critical transportation nodes and lines of communications (LOCs). Consideration should be given to the requirement to document the transportation of contractors support equipment and the procedures to integrate movement details for these personnel and equipment into the force flow.

c. **Step 3 - COA Development.** A COA is a potential way of accomplishing the assigned mission, and the products of COA development are tentative COAs.

(1) The JFC's staff develops COAs to provide the JFC markedly different choices of achieving the military end state.

(2) A deployment concept for each tentative COA should be developed to determine its feasibility. While the detailed deployment concept will be developed during plan synchronization, enough of the concept must be described in the COA to show the force buildup, sustainment requirements, and military-political considerations. COAs should also include the possible use of war reserve materiel (WRM), pre-positioned stocks and equipment, and theater provided equipment (TPE). COAs may include contingency response group (CRG) requirements to augment or expand transportation infrastructure and/or airfield capabilities.

d. **Step 4 - COA Analysis and Wargaming.** COA analysis identifies advantages and disadvantages of each proposed friendly COA. Deployment planners analyze each COA separately with the primary goal of helping to answer three of the CCDR's primary questions: Is the COA feasible (i.e., can the mission be accomplished within the established time, space, and resource limitations)? Is the COA acceptable (i.e., does it balance cost and risk with the advantage gained)? And, is the COA complete (i.e., does it include who, what, where, when, how, and why)?

(1) Wargaming is the primary means to conduct this analysis, and can be done in any of three methods: a simple, but detailed narrative; a more comprehensive "sketch-note"; and computer-aided modeling and simulation. Each critical event within a proposed COA should be wargamed based upon time available using the action, reaction, and counteraction method of friendly and/or opposition force interaction. This basic wargaming method (modified to fit the specific mission and environment) can apply to the deployment events in the COA.

(2) During the wargame, the deployment planner takes a COA statement and begins to add more detail to the deployment concept. The JFC and the staff may change an existing COA or develop a new one after identifying unforeseen critical events, requirements, or problems affecting deployment.

e. **Step 5 - COA Comparison.** In this step, the JFC and staff evaluate all COAs against established evaluation criteria and select the COA that best accomplishes the mission.

(1) COAs are not compared to each other, but rather they are individually evaluated against the criteria that are established by the staff and the commander.

(2) Deployment planners identify criteria relating to deployment for COA comparison, particularly focusing on the ability to deliver forces in time to meet the commander's phasing and mission essential task schedules.

f. **Step 6 - COA Approval.** The staff briefs the COA comparison results and the analysis and wargaming results to the JFC in COA approval.

(1) The JFC selects a COA or forms an alternate COA based upon the staff recommendations and the JFC's personal estimate, experience, and judgment.

(2) The staff refines the JFC-selected COA into a clear decision statement and prepares the commander's estimate.

g. **Step 7 - Plan or Order Development.** The JFC staff translates the JFC's guidance and intent into a CONOPS and executable plan.

4. Plan or Order Development

While deployment and redeployment were critical considerations in the previous steps of JOPP, it is in step 7 (Plan or Order Development), that the preponderance of the deployment and redeployment planning takes place. During this step, the supported CCDR and staff, in collaboration with subordinate and supporting components and organizations, expand the approved COA into a detailed joint OPLAN/CONPLAN or OPORD by first developing an executable CONOPS. While force, support, deployment/redeployment and JRSOI planning are inextricably linked, the following text provides discussion on each.

a. **Force Planning**

(1) The primary purpose of force planning is to identify all forces needed to accomplish the supported component commanders' CONOPS and effectively phase the forces into the OA. Force planning consists of determining the force requirements by operation phase, mission, mission priority, mission sequence, and operating area. It includes force allocation review, major force phasing, integration planning, force list structure development, and force list development. Force planning is the responsibility of the CCDR, supported by component commanders in coordination with the Joint Staff, JFPs, and force providers.

(2) Force planning begins early during CONOPS development and focuses on applying the right force to the mission while ensuring force visibility, force mobility, and adaptability. The commander determines force requirements, develops a TPFDD LOI or supplement to the standing joint TPFDD LOI specific to the OA, and designs force modules to align and time-phase the forces IAW the CONOPS. Proper force planning allows major forces and elements to be selected from those apportioned or allocated for planning and included in the supported commander's CONOPS by operation phase, mission, and mission priority. Service components then collaboratively make tentative assessments of the specific sustainment capabilities required IAW the CONOPS. Upon direction to execute, the CCDR then submits the refined force requests to the Joint Staff.

(3) The Joint Staff assigns a JFP to each force request and directs the JFP to forward a recommended sourcing solution (execution sourcing). The JFP provides the recommended sourcing solution with the operational and force provider risk for SecDef decision. The allocation decision is published in a modification to the CJCS GFMAP annex that directs the JFP to, in turn, direct the force provider to deploy forces. After the actual units are identified (sourced), the CCDR refines the force plan to ensure it supports the CONOPS, provides force visibility, and enables flexibility. The commander identifies and resolves or reports shortfalls with a risk assessment.

(4) In CAP, force planning focuses on the actual units designated to participate in the planned operation and their readiness for deployment. The supported commander identifies force requirements as operational capabilities in the form of force packages to facilitate sourcing the GFM process. A force package is a list (group of force capabilities) of the various forces (force requirements) that the supported commander requires to conduct the operation described in the CONOPS. The supported commander typically describes required force requirements in the form of broad capability descriptions or unit type codes, depending on the circumstances. The supported commander submits the required force packages through the Joint Staff to the force providers for sourcing. Force providers review the readiness and deployability posture of their available units before deciding which units to nominate to the supported commander's force requirements. Services and their component commands also determine mobilization requirements and plan for the provision of individual augmentee sustainment. The supported commander will normally review the sourcing recommendations through the GFM process to ensure compatibility with capability requirements and CONOPS.

b. **Support Planning**

(1) The purpose of support planning is to determine the TPFDD sequencing of the personnel, logistics, and other support necessary, including contractors and their equipment, to provide mission support distribution, maintenance, engineering, medical support, personnel service support, and sustainment for the joint force IAW the CONOPS. Support planning is conducted in parallel with other planning, and encompasses such essential factors as information operations, strategic communication, lead component identification, responsibility for base operating support, communications and network support, airfield operations, management of individual augmentees, health service support, personnel service support, personnel management and visibility, financial management, handling of prisoners of war and detainees, theater engineering policy, logistics-related environmental considerations, integrated financial operations, support of noncombatant evacuation and other retrograde operations, and nation assistance.

(2) The GCC and the GCC's subordinate commanders review their inter-Service support agreements. The GCC must decide if he desires to delegate directive authority for a common support capability to a subordinate JFC or Service component and determine the function and scope of the specific authority. The GCC must also decide whether to assign specific common-user logistics functions to a lead Service and what size, roles, and functions a JDDOC will have if a common-user logistics lead is assigned. The GCC planning guidance must clearly articulate the degree of reliance on HNS, acquisition and cross-

servicing agreement (ACSA), or contract support within each phase of operations. Finally, the GCC must decide whether or not to establish a joint command for logistics or to delegate the authority to a subordinate Service component.

(3) Support planning is primarily the responsibility of the Service component commanders and begins during CONOPS development. Service component commanders identify and update support requirements in coordination with the Services, DLA, and USTRANSCOM. They initiate the procurement of critical and low-density inventory items, determine HNS availability, determine contractor support requirements and plans, develop plans for AV, and establish phased delivery plans for sustainment in line with the phases and priorities of the CONOPS. They develop and train for battle damage repair, develop reparable retrograde plans, develop container and 463L pallet management plans, develop force and LOC protection plans, develop supporting phased transportation and support plans aligned to the CONOPS, and report movement support requirements.

For further information on planning for and management of intermodal equipment in theater, see Defense Transportation Regulation (DTR) 4500.9-R, Defense Transportation Regulation, *Part VI, Management and Control of Intermodal Containers and System 463L Equipment Mobility, and JP 4-09,* Distribution Operations.

(4) Service component commanders continue to refine their mission support, movement infrastructure, sustainment, and distribution requirements as the force providers identify and source force requirements. During distribution planning, the supported CCDR and USTRANSCOM resolve gross distribution feasibility questions impacting intertheater and intratheater movement and sustainment delivery. If these feasibility questions identify shortfalls due to inadequate resources, then planners must address these shortfalls.

(5) USTRANSCOM and other transportation providers identify air, land, and sea transportation resources to support the approved CONOPS. These resources may include apportioned intertheater transportation, GCC-controlled theater transportation, transportation organic to the subordinate commands, and contracted transportation. USTRANSCOM and other transportation providers develop transportation schedules for movement requirements identified by the supported commander. A transportation schedule does not necessarily mean that the supported commander's CONOPS is transportation feasible; rather, the schedules provide the most effective and realistic use of available transportation resources in relation to the phased CONOPS. (See JP 4-01, *The Defense Transportation System*, for more detailed capabilities and roles and responsibilities of USTRANSCOM.)

(6) Installation planners conduct a deployment analysis based on early information acquired to determine potential scenarios, mission requirements, and COAs. From those assessments, installation planners determine how to best support the deployment.

c. **Deployment and Redeployment Planning.** Deployment and redeployment planning is conducted on a continuous basis for all approved OPLANs/CONPLANs and as required for specific crisis action plans. Planning for redeployment should be considered throughout the operation and is best accomplished in the same time-phased process in which deployment was accomplished. In all cases, mission requirements of a specific operation define the scope, duration, and scale of both deployment and redeployment operation planning. Unity of effort is paramount, since both deployment and redeployment operations involve numerous commands, agencies, and functional processes. Because the ability to adapt to unforeseen conditions is essential, supported CCDRs must ensure their deployment plans for each contingency or crisis action plan support global force visibility requirements. When planning for operations that may be lengthy, consideration must be given to force rotations. Units must rotate without interrupting operations. Planning should consider JRSOI, turnover time, relief-in-place and transfer of authority, and time it takes for the outbound unit to redeploy. This information is vital for the JFPs to develop force rotations in the GFMAP annex schedule if the operation is executed.

(1) **Deployment and Redeployment Concept**

(a) Supported CCDRs must develop a deployment concept and identify specific predeployment standards necessary to meet mission requirements. The Services and supporting CCDRs must ensure unit OPLANs/CONPLANs are prepared, forces are tailored and echeloned, personnel and equipment movement plans are complete and accurate, command relationships and integration requirements are established and identified, mission-essential tasks are rehearsed, mission-specific training is conducted, force protection is planned and resourced, and sustainment requirements are identified.

(b) Careful and detailed planning ensures that only required personnel, equipment, and materiel deploy; unit training is exacting; missions are fully understood; deployment changes are minimized during execution; and the flow of personnel, equipment, and movement of materiel into theater aligns with the CONOPS.

(c) Supported CCDRs must also develop a redeployment CONOPS to identify how forces and materiel will either redeploy to home station or to support another JFC's operation. This redeployment CONOPS is especially relevant and useful if force rotations are envisioned to provide the requisite forces for a long-term operation. CCDRs may not have all planning factors to fully develop this CONOPS, but by using the best available information for redeployment requirements, timelines, and priorities, the efficiency and effectiveness of redeployment operations may be greatly improved. Topics addressed in this early stage of a redeployment CONOPS may include a proposed sequence for redeployment of units, individuals, and materiel. Responsibilities and priorities for recovery, reconstitution, and return to home station may also be addressed along with transition requirements during mission handover. As a campaign or operation moves through the different operational plan phases, the CCDR will be able to develop and issue a redeployment order based on a refined redeployment CONOPS. Effective redeployment operations are essential to ensure supporting services and rotational forces have sufficient time to fully source and prepare for the next rotation.

(2) **Movement Planning**

(a) Movement planning integrates the activities and requirements of units with partial or complete self-deployment capability, activities of units that require lift support, and the transportation of sustainment and retrograde. Movement planning is highly collaborative and is enhanced by coordinated use of simulation and analysis tools.

(b) If deployment operations are initiated and a plan is executed, the supported command forwards force requests in a RFF to the Joint Staff. These force requests are allocated in a modification to the appropriate GFMAP annex. The JFP then publishes the GFMAP annex schedule specifying the LAD and end date of each unit's deployment. These allocated forces begin the process of building the TPFDD and preparing the proper documentation required for the deployment of forces. The individual force requirements and the deployment information are loaded into the execution plan identification number (PID) and further refined.

(c) The supported command is responsible for movement control, including sequence of arrival, and exercises this authority through the TPFDD and the APEX/JOPES validation process. While planning the force flow, the supported CCDR must carefully balance the force mix and arrival sequence of combat forces, combat service support units, and contracted and HNS capabilities to ensure that deployment support and throughput requirements can be met. Supporting CCDRs and Service components responsible for deployment operations must refine and verify unit force and deployment data and validate and continuously review the TPFDD changes that may occur. As with any dynamic process, external changes in the environment, as well as those within the force, necessitate corresponding changes to the flow of forces (personnel, equipment, and materiel). During execution the supported command may sequence movement within the limits specified in the GFMAP by SecDef. The supported commander will use organic and nonorganic lift, common-user, and strategic lift resources made available for planning by the CJCS. Competing requirements for limited strategic lift resources, support infrastructure, and intratheater transportation assets will be assessed in terms of impact on mission accomplishment. If additional resources are required, the supported command will identify the requirements and provide rationale for those requirements in an RFF.

(d) The supported commander's operational priorities and any movement constraints (e.g., chemical, biological, radiological, or nuclear contamination of POE/POD, cargo, or lift assets) are used to prepare a movement plan. The plan will consider en route staging locations and the ability of these locations to support the scheduled activity. This information, together with an estimate of required site augmentation, will be communicated to appropriate supporting commanders. The global force manager and USTRANSCOM, in consultation with the supported CCDR, use the Joint Flow and Analysis System for Transportation (JFAST) model to conduct and assess transportation feasibility analysis and develop recommendations on final POE selections for those units without organic lift capability. During redeployment movement planning, the supported GCC executes this task in place of the global force manager. Movement feasibility requires current analysis and assessment of movement C2 structures and systems; available organic, strategic, and theater lift assets; transportation infrastructure; and competing demands and restrictions.

Refer to JP 3-11, Operations in Chemical, Biological, Radiological, and Nuclear (CBRN) Environments, *for more information concerning mobility planning for operations in CBRN environments.*

(e) After coordinated review of the movement analysis by USTRANSCOM, the supported command, and the JFPs, the supported command may adjust the CONOPS to improve movement feasibility where operational requirements remain satisfied. CDRUSTRANSCOM should adjust or reprioritize intertheater transportation assets to meet the supported commander's operational requirements. If this is not an option due to requirements from other commanders, then the supported commander adjusts the force flow and the TPFDD requirements or is provided additional intertheater and intratheater lift capabilities using (but not limited to) CRAF and/or VISA capabilities as necessary to achieve end-to-end transportation feasibility.

(f) Operational requirements may cause the supported commander and/or subordinate commanders to alter their plans, potentially impacting the deployment priorities or TPFDD requirements. Planners must understand and anticipate the impact of change. There is a high potential for a sequential pattern of disruption when changes are made to the TPFDD. A unit displaced by a change might not simply move on the next available lift, but may require reprogramming for movement at a later time. This may not only disrupt the flow, but may also interrupt the operation. Time is also a factor in TPFDD and force flow changes. Airlift can respond to short-notice changes, but at a cost in efficiency. Sealift, on the other hand, requires longer lead times and cannot respond to change in a short period. These plan changes and the resulting modifications to the TPFDDs must be handled during the planning cycles.

(3) **Joint Reception, Staging, Onward Movement, and Integration Planning.** The supported CCDR conducts JRSOI planning to ensure deploying forces arrive and become operational in the OA as scheduled. Establishing personnel visibility for force protection purposes is necessary for joint forces immediately upon their arrival in the OA, and plans to accomplish this task are issued by the GCC manpower and personnel staff. JRSOI planning is also conducted to ensure forces can be scheduled in the GFMAP annex schedule to rotate without impacting operations. Effective integration of the force into the joint operation is the primary objective of the deployment process.

(4) **Deployment and Joint Reception, Staging, Onward Movement, and Integration Refinement.** The supported command conducts deployment, JRSOI, and TPFDD refinement in coordination with Joint Staff, JFPs, USTRANSCOM, the Services, and supporting commands. The purpose of the deployment and JRSOI refinement is to ensure the force deployment plan maintains force mobility throughout any movements, provides for force visibility and tracking at all times, provides for effective force preparation, and fully integrates forces into a joint operation while enabling unity of effort. The refinement conference examines planned missions, the priority of the missions within the operation phases, and the forces assigned to those missions. By mission, the refinement conference examines force capabilities, force size, support requirements, mission preparation, force positioning/basing, weapon systems, major equipment, force protection, and sustainment requirements. The refinement conference should assess the feasibility of force closure by the commander's RDD and the feasibility of successful mission execution within the time frame established by the commander under the deployment concept. The refinement conference should assess potential success of all force integration requirements.

Transition criteria for all phases should be evaluated for force redeployment including rotation requirements.

d. **Operational Environment.** For a given plan, deployment planning decisions are based on the anticipated OE, which may be permissive, uncertain, or hostile. The anticipated OE dictates the type of entry operations, deployment concept, mobility options, predeployment training, and force integration requirements. Normally, supported CCDRs, their subordinate commanders, and their Service components are responsible for providing detailed situation information; mission statements by operation phase; theater support parameters; strategic and operational lift allocations by phase (for both force movements and sustainment); HNS information and environmental standards; and pre-positioned equipment, WRM, and TPE planning guidance.

e. **Planning Changes. Planning continues during deployment execution.** Tactical and intelligence considerations, force and non-unit cargo availability, availability of strategic lift assets, and POE and POD capabilities may necessitate changes to the original plan.

5. Considerations of Operational Requirements

While conducting deployment planning in JOPP, the following operational requirements should be considered:

a. **Training**

(1) Supported CCDRs develop a deployment concept and identify specific predeployment standards necessary to meet mission requirements. Supporting CCDRs provide trained and mission-ready forces to the supported CCMD deployment concept and predeployment standards.

(2) The Services' predeployment planning and coordination with the supporting CCMD must achieve predeployment standards specified by the supported CCDR, ensure supporting personnel and forces arrive in the theater fully prepared to perform their mission, and eliminate deployment delays caused by duplication of predeployment efforts.

(3) Department of Defense Directive (DODD) 1322.18, *Military Training,* states that "Individual, collective, and staff predeployment training shall be certified to standards by either the mission commander or the commander responsible for the predeployment training." The directive also requires that cultural awareness and language training be embedded in predeployment training.

b. **Protection**

(1) Deployment planners assess the impact of the OE and threats in relationship to the mission. Joint intelligence preparation of the OE must address to what degree a potential threat can interdict, disrupt, or block deployment and redeployment operations. Consequently, force and facility protection is planned and resourced.

(2) Planning the proper balance between deploying the force rapidly with the right mix of combat power and materiel is crucial. The JFC must develop a balance that provides protection, efficient deployment, adequate support, and a range of response options to enemy activity.

(3) Protection resource limitations will probably mean that the staff cannot plan to protect every capability, but rather will look at prioritizing protection for critical capabilities and developing overlapping protection techniques.

(4) Information about the movement of forces may provide an adversary with critical insight they need to defeat a force even before it arrives in its theater of operations. It is crucial that force deployers coordinate with their command's operations security (OPSEC) personnel to develop appropriate countermeasures to mitigate this potential vulnerability.

(5) The protection challenge during deployment will expand in the future as enemies find new ways to attack US forces and resources. Adversaries may increasingly test force protection at home stations before or during deployment.

c. **Communications Systems Supporting Visibility of Deployment Operations**

(1) Visibility of assets moving through DTS or in support of DOD operations is an essential element of the DOD capability and is required by the supported CCDR. A rapidly changing adversary situation or other aspects of the OE may cause the commander to alter the planned arrangement of operations even as forces are deploying. Therefore, ITV and theater AV are critical to maintaining flexibility.

(2) Early on in joint operation planning, the supported CCDR, through the TPFDD LOI, provides operation-specific guidance for utilizing the APEX processes and systems to provide force visibility and tracking. The CCDR's staff, during staff estimate development, should identify and examine the feasibility of providing adequate communications systems support for tentative COAs. The estimate should also address the adequacy and security of networks used to manage, store, manipulate, and transmit operational or logistical data. During deployment and JRSOI refinement, the supported CCDR ensures that the force deployment plan provides for force visibility and tracking at all times.

(3) Communications systems may be a limited resource, which will require detailed planning to provide the appropriate level of communications resource allocations to maintain ITV and AV. Initial phases of a deployment may not have the robust communications network required for extensive use of information systems. Phasing joint and Service communications systems into the force flow early provides a system that allows the JFC to take advantage of the automated tools available for force and sustainment tracking.

d. **Infrastructure Assessment**

(1) Understanding the capabilities of the theater infrastructure and the time when assets become available is crucial for developing successful deployment operations. An infrastructure assessment is essential for understanding the capabilities and limitations of the OA to support deployment operations. The assessment serves as a basis to determine the

forces, equipment, and materiel that must be deployed and the facility upgrades required to enhance operations. Infrastructure consists of the physical network and the resource network.

(2) The type, number, and condition of facilities, transportation networks, real estate, and modes of transportation characterize physical networks. Transportation infrastructure strongly influences deployment operations and a robust network of modern air and seaports, highways, railroads, petroleum distribution, and inland waterways greatly expedite the throughput of forces, equipment, and supplies. A lesser-developed, austere, or damaged infrastructure impedes deployment operations, affects POD or POE alternatives, and may require an early deployment of support capabilities such as joint logistics over-the-shore (JLOTS) or engineer units.

(3) Resource network includes personnel, organizations, materiel, and equipment operating within the physical network and enabling the deployment, JRSOI, employment, sustainment, and redeployment of the joint force. A thorough assessment of the physical network will lead to better understanding of and planning for what is required in the resource network.

(4) The collection and maintenance of infrastructure information is the purview of the Services and numerous agencies that include the DIA, the supported CCDR's joint intelligence operations center, USTRANSCOM's joint intelligence operations center and engineer/analysis functions, as well as Service organic intelligence services and engineer organizations. More detailed infrastructure information collected and available includes information on infrastructure capacity and condition as well as engineering capability (ports, railroads, inland waterways, roads, airfields, bridges, off-road land tractability, power plants, and communications nodes) in most theaters. USTRANSCOM's En Route Infrastructure Master Plan outlines the key en route locations and infrastructure required to enable deployment and redeployment operations. Such information serves as baseline data for planning. For example, the SDDC Transportation Engineering Agency (TEA) compiles unclassified and classified data on many seaports, to include throughput calculations and infrastructure assessments. SDDC TEA also develops and maintains detailed transportation infrastructure networks of various theaters for use in analyzing intratheater transportation capabilities feasibility using the Enhanced Logistics Intratheater Support Tool (ELIST). Infrastructure evaluations may also be augmented by team site surveys such as those conducted by a joint or Air Force assessment team. Figure III-3 provides some items for infrastructure assessment.

e. **Host-Nation Support**

(1) When available, HNS assists in executing deployment operations. Provisions in an HNS agreement can potentially overcome logistical shortfalls and decrease the amount of equipment and cargo that has to be deployed. Elements of the agreement could include basing rights, life support, border and/or diplomatic clearance procedures, construction and engineering, labor force, transit authority, POD services, and transportation assets and infrastructure.

Example of Infrastructure Assessment

Physical Network

- Airports
- Seaports
- Highways
- Railroads
- Bridges
- Tunnels
- Terminals
- Inland waterways
- Storage facilities
- Pipelines
- Communication systems

Resources Network

- Aircraft
- Ships
- Trucks and rail equipment
- Lighterage
- Host-nation support
- Contractors
- Materials handling
  - equipment and cargo
  - handling equipment
- Civilian, government, and military personnel
- Automation

Figure III-3. Example of Infrastructure Assessment

(2) During the COA development and selection, the CCDR's staff examines existing HNS agreements to determine what infrastructure, logistics, capabilities, and procedures are available to support the deployment. If HNS agreements do not exist, or offer limited capabilities, then the CCDR, in coordination with DOS, should immediately start negotiating HNS agreements to obtain necessary support.

(3) Maintaining current, comprehensive base support plans and conducting periodic site surveys are critical for validating HNS agreements required for implementing specific OPLANs and CONPLANs.

f. **Contracted Support**

The CCDR determines whether contracted support is warranted based on mission assessment, available forces, and operational objectives. Factors that warrant consideration for the use of contracted support in contingency operations include the continual introduction of high-tech equipment, force structure and manning limitations, and high operating tempos. These factors may require that military forces be significantly augmented with contracted support. Accordingly, the supported GCC, subordinate JFCs and their staffs, and Service component commanders and their staffs must be familiar with how to plan for and integrate contractors, and contracted support into deployment and redeployment operations. This includes both the deployment of contractor personnel and equipment and the employment of contracted personnel and assets to facilitate deployment and redeployment operations.

For more information regarding operational contract support, see JP 4-10, Operational Contract Support.

Intentionally Blank

CHAPTER IV
PREDEPLOYMENT AND PRE-REDEPLOYMENT ACTIVITIES

> *"To a conscientious commander, time is the most vital factor in his planning. By proper foresight and correct preliminary action, he knows he can conserve the most precious elements he controls, the lives of his men. So he thinks ahead as far as he can. He keeps his tactical plan simple. He tries to eliminate as many variable factors as he is able. He has a firsthand look at as much of the ground as circumstances render accessible to him. He checks each task in the plan with the man to whom he intends to assign it. Then—having secured in almost every instance his subordinates' wholehearted acceptance of the contemplated mission and agreement on its feasibility—only then does he issue an order."*
>
> **General Matthew B. Ridgway, US Army**
> ***The Korean War*, 1967**

1. General

Predeployment and redeployment activities are the second phase in the joint deployment and redeployment process. The activities are functions deploying/redeploying planners and unit commanders must accomplish to successfully complete their movement to the POE. A majority of these functions are performed at the unit level linking the installation, base/unit deployment/redeployment efforts to the overall strategic movement. This chapter addresses the predeployment activities for deployment and redeployment taken by the JPEC and supported and supporting CCDRs to prepare forces to execute a deployment/redeployment operation before actual movement. Figures IV-1 and IV-2 are the process maps for the predeployment and pre-redeployment phase of the deployment/redeployment process. See Annex A, "Joint Force Deployment Process Map Description," to Appendix B, "Joint Force Development and Joint Reception, Staging, Onward Movement, and Integration and Joint Force Redeployment Process Maps Descriptions," for the complete joint deployment and redeployment process maps.

Predeployment Activities			
Functional Events	Prepare the Force	Schedule Movement	Assemble and Marshal Forces
Deployment Processes	Activate deployment command and control, support organizations Conduct movement and support meetings Develop deployment equipment listing, identify shipping/handling requirements Conduct required training	Receive strategic movement schedule Receive/assess movement and lift schedules Receive port call Confirm movement clearances Build and publish schedule of events	Establish support organizations at port of embarkation Assemble/marshal cargo Sequence cargo loads and conduct inspections Assemble and manifest personnel and cargo

Figure IV-1. Predeployment Activities

Pre-Redeployment Activities			
Functional Events	Prepare the Force	Schedule Movement	Assemble and Marshal Forces
Redeployment Processes	Activate deployment command and control, support organizations Conduct movement and support meetings Develop deployment equipment listing, identify shipping/handling requirements Conduct required training Complete equipment disposition actions	Receive strategic movement schedule Receive/assess movement and lift schedules Receive port call Confirm movement clearances Build and publish schedule of events	Establish support organizations at port of embarkation Prepare and conduct customs/agricultural inspections Assemble/marshal cargo Sequence cargo loads and conduct inspections Assemble and manifest personnel and cargo

Figure IV-2. Pre-Redeployment Activities

2. Deployment Prepare the Force Activities

a. Select forces may deploy within hours or days from receipt of a DEPORD while other units may deploy on a timeline of days to several weeks. Regardless of the deployment timeline, a myriad of predeployment activities, actions, and events must be accomplished to deploy the force with their required equipment and supplies. These actions range from the strategic to the tactical level. At the strategic level, TPFDD sourcing/refinement and transportation feasibility may continue well into this phase. At the installation and unit level, activities range from personnel and equipment status confirmed and upgraded to conducting required training. Deployment timelines will dictate available time to conduct *prepare the force activities,* which include:

(1) Activate deployment and C2 support organizations.

(2) Conduct movement coordination and support meetings.

(3) Develop deployment equipment list and identify shipping/handling requirements.

(4) Conduct required training.

(5) Manage Service members' deployment requirements.

b. Since deployment timelines may be short, commanders and their deployment planners at all levels must develop plans for the key activities that a deploying unit must perform to support their timely deployment. These activities will vary based on unit location and deployment mode/node but a key deployment enabler at all levels is the activation of **deployment C2 support organizations.** These organizations play a major role in activating and synchronizing support activities for deploying units. These support activities vary but may include medical and personnel support facilities, supply and maintenance activities, and critical deployment nodes to include railheads, airfields, and seaports.

c. **Conducting movement and support meetings** is a task that encompasses deployment planning and operations at the strategic through tactical/unit level. Identifying and resolving transportation shortfalls or limitations are key areas addressed during this task at all levels. Transportation planners at the strategic level must be prepared to participate in the development of collaborative transportation solutions and offer alternate COAs if transportation feasibility analysis indicates transportation shortfalls and the desired CCDR deployment timelines cannot be met with existing strategic mobility triad assets. Resolving these *shortfalls* may require resolution at the joint staff level so identifying any transportation shortfalls early is critical to obtaining a timely resolution. At the tactical/unit level, identifying and resolving transportation shortfalls and/or limitations must also occur early in these *movement and support meetings.* Requesting and receiving additional transportation assets such as railcars and commercial heavy equipment transporters or containers may be time-consuming and should be done early in this phase. Another key interface required during these *support meetings* is between the deploying units and the C2 elements of the air and sea POEs. A multitude of topics may be discussed *and* coordinated at these meetings. Port support activity (PSA) requirements and availability of ITV infrastructure and processes to be used are two topics that require special consideration. Transportation planners may also find it beneficial to conduct site surveys at the POEs prior to these support meetings. Coordination with local, state, or HN authorities for movement permits for equipment being convoyed to the POEs is another separate but critical task that must occur. Coordination done at these meetings with the POE C2 elements or local/HN authorities provides the foundation for a successful transition to the establishment of PSAs or arrival/departure airfield control group (A/DACG) during the *assemble and marshal* forces activities.

d. **Developing deployment equipment list and identifying shipping/handling requirements** and conducting required training are primarily the responsibility of the deploying unit. Accuracy of the unit deployment list (UDL) is critical as strategic transportation planners commit USTRANSCOM lift assets based on the information within the UDL and as such, incorrect data can lead to inadequate assets available to move deploying units. Not identifying equipment in a timely manner could affect the JOPES validation process.

3. Sustainment

a. Deployment planners should account for concurrent sustainment activities in their overall plans. Activities in the planning phase may capture the basic requirements for the movement of sustainment, but planners will have to finalize sustainment movement plans as part of their predeployment activities. Conducting this planning in a collaborative environment allows USTRANSCOM to gain and maintain visibility on all known strategic movement requirements, facilitating responsive support by the strategic mobility triad. Preplanned sealift supporting sustainment requirements is also a part of predeployment activities. Any preplanned sealift support that occurs is a benefit to the supported commander, as it does not detract from the deployment of forces and capabilities by intertheater airlift.

b. The supported commander establishes the policy, procedures, priorities, and LOC for sustainment activities. Normally, the commander will immediately begin to submit demand-based or "pull" sustainment requirements for Services to resupply their forces in theater. In the absence of the commander's specific guidance and requirements, each of the Services will sustain its forces using Service methodologies, which may include initially "pushing" sustainment to its forces. Sustainment supplies do not always follow the designated deployment LOC since some supplies (POL and ammunition) require special handling facilities and could result in significant disruption of port activities. Optimizing port throughput will be a primary factor in balancing pull and push sustainment procedures.

c. Transportation planners must be aware that **sustainment movement** and required intertheater lift is handled differently than deployment intertheater lift. Time-phased deployment requirements are developed, sourced, refined, and validated in JOPES for USTRANSCOM movement scheduling. Intertheater airlift for deployment operations is requested through JOPES. Normally, some sustainment is planned as part of the deployment TPFDD developed in JOPES. However, as the operation progresses, intertheater sustainment airlift becomes more requirements based. Channel service or express service airlift is the normally planned method for the movement of sustainment by air. This process involves sustainment moving on predetermined channels that are established IAW existing regulations.

For additional information on sustainment movement, see JP 4-09, Distribution Operations.

d. Supply and support requirements of deploying forces consist of two major categories: **unit-related supplies and equipment and non-unit-related supplies and equipment**.

(1) Unit-related supplies and equipment include a unit's organic equipment, basic load, and accompanying supplies. Unit-related supplies and equipment are configured (palletized or containerized) and documented for deployment by the unit. Unit planners enter movement data for unit-related supplies and equipment in the UDL and later into the TPFDD.

(2) Non-unit related supplies and equipment include all supply sustainment support requirements that are not identified for a specific unit. They include pre-positioned war reserve stock, sustaining supplies, and resupply. Non-unit-related supplies and equipment are configured and documented as cargo increment numbers for deployment by the sourcing organization and provided for distribution in theater by DLA and Service component logistic units.

e. **Non-Unit-Related Personnel (NURP). NURP are any active duty personnel from any Service (including RC members accessed onto active duty), DOD civilians, contractors authorized to accompany the force, and Red Cross personnel who deploy as individuals or as a small group of individuals without a unit.** NURP consists of individual augmentees alerted for deployment to serve as individual unit fillers to bring

DEPLOYMENT: WORLD WAR II

"To deploy these forces overseas was another great matter. Although the US merchant marine ranked second only to Great Britain's and the country possessed an immense shipbuilding capacity, the process of chartering, assembling, and preparing shipping for the movement of troops and military cargo took time. Time was also needed to schedule and organize convoys, and owing to the desperate shortage of escort vessels, troop movement had to be widely spaced. Convoying and evasive routing, in themselves, greatly reduced the effective capacity of shipping. Moreover, vast distances separated US ports from the areas threatened by Japan, and to these areas went the bulk of forces deployed overseas during the months immediately following Pearl Harbor. Through March 1942, as a result, the outflow of troops to overseas bases averaged only about 50,000 per month, as compared with upwards of 250,000 during 1944, when shipping was fully mobilized and plentiful and the sea lanes were secure.

There seemed a real danger early in 1942, however, that German U-boats might succeed in reducing transatlantic deployment to a trickle—not so much by attacking troop transports, most of which could outrun their attackers, as by sinking the slow cargo ships on which the forces overseas depended for support. Soon after Germany's declaration of war, the U-boats struck at the virtually unprotected shipping lanes in the western Atlantic, and subsequently extended their attacks to the Gulf of Mexico and Caribbean areas and the mouth of the St. Lawrence. During the spring of 1942 tankers and freighters were torpedoed in plain view of vacationers on east coast beaches..."

SOURCE: *American Military History, Army Historical Series*

undermanned units to authorized manning levels and replace casualties in theater. NURP are normally moved via commercial transportation from losing organizations to designated replacement locations. The Services designate organizations to coordinate strategic lift requirements with USTRANSCOM for movement of NURP from designated origins into theater based upon deployment shelf requirements incorporated into the TPFDD during planning. Shelf requirements are integrated into transportation and reception plans and used to determine the number and location of US replacement centers and APOEs required to support the deployment.

f. For international ports, the GCC will assign waiver and clearance responsibilities to one of the component commands.

For a detailed discussion on the joint process of "prepare the force," see Annex A, "Joint Force Deployment Process Map Description," to Appendix B, "Joint Force Deployment and Joint Reception, Staging, Onward Movement, and Integration and Joint Force Redeployment Process Maps Descriptions."

4. Redeployment Prepare the Force Activities

a. **A successful redeployment requires the planning and execution of the** *prepare the force activities* used in deployments. The execution of these pre-redeployment activities will not be identical to deployment activities due to the OE, available resources, and the force structure of the redeploying units. As such, procedures and unit level activities may vary from those performed during a deployment but these ***activities*** require detailed planning for a successful redeployment operation. Redeployment *prepare the force* activities also has a unique sixth activity, *complete equipment disposition actions.* This activity is only done in the redeployment process and requires a detailed planning effort since this activity may significantly affect the amount of equipment that is redeployed.

b. Within the redeployment activity, *activate deployment and C2 support organizations,* redeployment planners at the **supported CCDR should establish clear C2 channels for redeployment operations.** The CCDR's JDDOC is an organization that may be capable of performing much of this mission, but planners must clearly identify the JDDOC role in redeployment operations.

c. Planners and unit commanders will be required to conduct a multitude of *movement coordination and support meetings* as they plan redeployments. Force protection is a topic that must be addressed throughout this activity and requires a significant amount of planning. Contract or HN security may be used as forces reach staging bases and turn in their equipment and Class V. If contract security is used, planners should work closely with the contracting officer or contracting officer representative to establish the requirement and to ensure that the capability is present throughout the redeployment process. As redeployments continue, there will be fewer military personnel and equipment to execute redeployment tasks. Thus planners should consider the use of HNS or contracted support to provide personnel or cargo handling equipment to resolve transportation shortfalls. As part of this activity, a pre-redeployment site survey (the reverse of the predeployment site survey) may be required for any POE or staging base used. Staging bases used for redeployment operations may be either a Service component operated base or a "joint" base with all Service units passing through. Regardless of the organizational structure of the staging base, redeployment planners should coordinate support to assist units in SAs with actions such as:

(1) Turn-in of excess supply stocks and pre-positioned equipment.

(2) Reconstituting and cross leveling of supplies and equipment.

(3) Identify requirements for loading on pallets, containers, and flat racks.

(4) Repacking and loading for movement.

d. US customs and agricultural requirements are two areas that require special planning considerations and coordination during redeployment *site surveys and support meetings.* Wash rack operations/facilities and secure equipment SAs at the POE are topics dealt with at the unit/tactical level but have a major impact on the overall joint deployment movement phase and movement schedules.

e. The unique sixth activity done during pre-redeployment is *"complete equipment disposition."* Redeployment and sustainment planners must collaborate early in the redeployment planning phase to allow for a cohesive equipment disposition plan for excess materiel turn-in and timeline to be developed and implemented. Equipment earmarked for this disposition action or a foreign military sales program is not included in the deployable equipment list (DEL) or redeployment TPFDL.

f. Redistribution and retrograde of supplies and materiel may play a major role in the activity *complete equipment disposition.* Significant national resources are invested in supplies and materiel to support joint operations. The following are some of the guidelines for redistribution:

(1) Non-unit redeployed equipment and supplies are redistributed according to plans developed by the Joint Staff and the Services with input from the CCDRs.

(2) A significant amount of sustainment material may be in transit when a requirement is reduced. This material must be diverted or redirected as required. Discipline in maintaining ITV will facilitate this part of redeployment planning. Forces waiting for redeployment should consume theater stocks and materiel. Distribution management centers should cease requisitioning from outside the theater, to the extent possible.

(3) Priority of effort is generally for forces committed to approved OPLANs. However, political agreements or commitments in a combined operation may alter redistribution efforts. Other redeployment recipients may include HNs, Service materiel commands, DLA, and General Services Administration distribution centers.

(4) In the redistribution process, equipment may be available for foreign military sales or grant programs, such as excess defense articles, to support national interests and policies.

(5) The safe redeployment or retrograde of equipment with previous or residual contamination should be limited to critical items unless equipment has been assessed to be safe or meets clearance standards. This information allows detailed planning for equipment consolidation sites and contamination mitigation assets required by the CBRN retrograde support element. The safety of service and transport personnel is of foremost concern during the redeployment and retrograde of equipment with potential residual or low-level contamination.

5. Schedule Movement for Deployment

a. Movement scheduling is an iterative process done at every level of supported and supporting commands to transport, move, or deploy the right forces (unit-*related* personnel and equipment) and sustainment (NURP, supplies, and equipment) to the right place at the right time. Transportation planners should become familiar with JOPES and its Web scheduling and movement (Web SM) application as this is the primary source for up-to-date scheduling movement data. *Schedule movement* consists of five activities to include:

(1) Receive strategic movement schedule.

(2) Receive/assess movement and lift schedule.

(3) Receive port calls.

(4) Confirm movement clearances.

(5) Build and publish schedule of events.

b. Supported and supporting CCDRs receive **strategic movement schedules** as they are scheduled and registered in JOPES and the Web SM application. These strategic movement schedules provide critical information for deployment planners and as such, planners should *assess lift schedules* to determine if these schedules support the overall operational timelines of the deployment. Lift shortfalls and other scheduling discrepancies must be reconciled at the earliest opportunity with USTRANSCOM to prevent delays in the overall strategic deployment plan/operation. Once the strategic movement schedules are published, supporting commanders and their units/installations will receive a port call message from SDDC. Installations and commands at the tactical/local level should utilize the port call information to finalize movement planning and coordination.

c. Movement control elements confirm diplomatic and ground movement *clearances* with HN, state, and governmental agencies. This requirement may be a very simple one for local/tactical units involved in the deployment; however, it also may be a strategic level task. Strategic transportation planners may be required to request and confirm multiple HN road/rail and port *clearances* for ground deployments as well as state department coordination for obtaining diplomatic *clearances* for aircraft overflights.

d. Movement instructions are published based on JOPES strategic lift schedules and the supported commanders' movement priority. These detailed instructions allow for installations and commanders at all levels to build and publish a schedule of events for their own deploying timelines. The schedule of events should be based on the date deploying units and equipment arrive at the POD on or before the scheduled ALD shown in JOPES. All supporting commanders and deployment planners must realize that their movement schedules are part of the overall time-phasing of forces and as such, little or no deviation to the published schedule of events is allowed in order to complete the deployment in the timelines planned.

For a more detailed discussion on the five activities for "schedule movement" function, see Annex A, "Joint Force Deployment Process Map Description," to Appendix B, "Joint Force Development and Joint Reception, Staging, Onward Movement, and Integration and Joint Forces Redeployment Process Maps Descriptions."

6. Schedule Movement for Redeployment

a. The *schedule movement activities* discussed for deployment are also applicable to redeployment to include utilization of the APEX process. Normally, redeployment TPFDDs are developed with the redeployment plan during force employment planning and updated and refined during redeployment preparations. Redeploying forces are tailored and prioritized for redeployment based on the supported CCDR's intent expressed in the OPLAN or redeployment plan. During redeployment preparation, it is a Service/unit level responsibility to update unit movement data to reflect changes to the DEL. Subordinate organizations and component commands must verify unit movement data to the supported CCDR for redeployment TPFDD validation. USTRANSCOM develops the redeployment *strategic movement schedule* after receiving the validated TPFDD from the supported CCDR.

b. The supported CCDR has the primary responsibility for redeployment planning and execution. As such, this redeployment plan will be the major driver for *movement schedule* timelines for redeploying forces. Similar to deployment, CCDRs and supporting Services will input their data into JOPES and the scheduling and movement application. These schedules will provide dates for units to arrive at sea and air POEs. Planners should focus on units arriving at the POEs at the ALDs as they develop and publish their internal redeployment *movement schedules.*

For a more detailed discussion on the five joint processes for "schedule movement" function, see Annex A, "Joint Force Deployment Process Map Description," to Appendix B, "Joint Force Deployment and Joint Reception, Staging, Onward Movement, and Integration and Joint Force Redeployment Process Maps Descriptions."

7. Assemble and Marshal Forces for Deployment

a. Assembly and marshalling involve bringing together personnel, supplies, and equipment in preparation for final movement to the POD. It is comprised of four activities to include:

(1) Assemble personnel and cargo.

(2) Conduct unit inspection, load equipment, and prepare.

(3) Sequence loads.

(4) Establish support organization at the POE.

b. Establishing support organizations at the POE is an activity that is coordinated and planned in the earlier pre-deployment activity *"conducting movement and support meetings."* Strategic and tactical/unit interface occurs within this task as support units move to their designated POEs and begin the process of preparing to load cargo vessels and aircraft. Also as part of this activity, units establish support functions such as movement to their POEs.

c. The last three activities of *assembly and marshalling forces* are interrelated and as such may occur simultaneously. A critical task for all units to accomplish within these activities is to ensure proper ITV occurs for deploying equipment and supplies. This entails the writing of radio frequency identification (RFID) tags or the use of license plate tags for deploying organizational equipment and containers prior to movement to the POEs; regardless of whether data rich or license plate RFID tags are utilized, shipment data is uploaded to the radio frequency ITV system server. Timelines to accomplish this critical

ITV task may vary, but for planning purposes, deployment planners should schedule this critical event prior to the completion of *assembly and marshalling forces.* Commanders and deployment planners should refer to port call messages and the DTR and internal Service policies for detailed instructions on RFID data requirements. At a minimum, they should plan to provide content level detail IAW the DTR RFID tag data standards. Correct utilization of RFID tags (data rich or license plate) provides the entire DTS the capability to have timely and accurate information on deploying and redeploying cargo movements.

d. Correctly manifesting deploying personnel is also a critical task that requires planning and proper execution. The DTR requires the manifesting of all deploying personnel. For deployment by air, the passenger terminal or base operations at the POE and en route stops are normally responsible for passenger manifesting. However, the aircraft commander is ultimately responsible for compliance with these procedures. For unit moves, the respective Service deployment automated information system (AIS) will be the primary means to generate and transmit an electronic manifest.

For further information on passenger manifesting, see DTR, Part I, Passenger Movement.

8. Assemble and Marshal Forces for Redeployment

a. A successful redeployment also requires the planning and execution for all the *assembling and marshalling forces* activities. These redeployment activities are the same as those performed during a deployment and may require additional time and locations. There is also an additional redeployment activity; *prepare and conduct customs/agricultural inspections.*

b. *Assembling and marshalling forces* activities may begin at the tactical level with units withdrawing from OAs and moving to tactical assembly areas (TAAs) to begin their preparation for redeployment. Units may then move to a staging base close to their POEs and then to the POE and its supporting marshalling areas. Redeployment planners must plan for the *establishment of support organizations at the POE.* However, planners must understand that redeploying units may not have the assets required to fully support this task or to prepare their equipment for redeployment. Supporting unit assistance or contractor support may be required.

c. The task of *preparing and conducting customs/agricultural inspections* is one that is uniquely linked to pre-redeployment operations. Redeploying forces must meet US or HN customs and agricultural requirements before they can redeploy. Supported commanders are responsible for establishing a military customs inspection program (MCIP) to ensure that redeploying personnel, equipment, and materiel comply with customs and agricultural requirements for their redeployment destination. An approved MCIP must be in place prior to redeployment to clear personnel, cargo, and battle-damaged equipment returning to the US for disposition.

(1) *US customs clearance and CBP inspection* and wash-down of all personnel, equipment, vehicles, and retrograde cargo redeploying to the US is IAW DOD policy.

(2) *Customs/agricultural inspections* requirements for forces returning to home station in a foreign country will be different from those for units returning to the US. *Redeployment* planners should determine these requirements in coordination with their HNs and coordinate inspections with the HN accordingly.

d. Cargo documentation is one of the many activities that will occur during the last three activities of *assemble and marshal forces for redeployment*. Commanders must ensure that cargo documentation follows existing Service and CCDR policies. The rush to return to home/demobilization station may bring about severe problems unless command emphasis is placed on accurately marking and documenting redeploying cargo. Unit movement data provided to TCCs must be correct to document cargo properly to prepare manifests for redeployment. Transportation planners should strive to maintain unit integrity for redeployment as it is as critical to readiness as it is during deployment.

Intentionally Blank

CHAPTER V
MOVEMENT

"The USTRANSCOM [United States Transportation Command] team's approach to building and providing winning logistics solutions starts always by building and leveraging a partnership with those that we serve."

General Duncan J. McNabb, Commander, US Air Force
US Transportation Command
September 2008–October 2011

1. General

a. This chapter describes the movement phase of the joint deployment and redeployment process. During this phase, validated TPFDD movement requirements developed during the planning phase and scheduled for movement during the predeployment activities phase must now be physically moved from origin to the designated aerial ports of debarkation (APODs)/seaports of debarkation (SPODs). The movement phase of the joint deployment and redeployment process includes self-deploying forces and forces requiring lift support and is composed of three segments: Movement from origin to APOEs/SPOEs, POE operations, and movement from the POE to POD. However, in order for joint deployment to produce a seamless, end-to-end deployment movement process, consideration should be given to movement that extends beyond the POD. Refer to Appendix B, "Joint Force Deployment and Joint Reception, Staging, Onward Movement, and Integration and Joint Force Redeployment Process Map Descriptions," for the entire joint deployment and redeployment process maps and accompanying text.

b. This chapter discusses each of the deployment movement segments in greater detail as well as tracking and controlling the movement of forces and materiel through the deployment and redeployment processes. Movement control involves planning, routing, scheduling, and controlling common-user assets and maintaining ITV of forces and materiel executing deployment and redeployment operations. Properly resourced and executed movement control assists commanders in force tracking and provides the capability to adjust the flow as necessary. It enhances JRSOI of personnel, equipment, and supplies moving over LOCs IAW command directives and responsibilities. This chapter also includes important movement reporting requirements to enhance ITV. Force visibility provides AV for deploying units and supplies and allows for a more responsive supply system. Lastly, when employment draws down, this chapter covers redeployment movement of personnel, equipment, and materiel to home and/or demobilization stations or transfer of forces and materiel to support operational requirements of another JFC.

2. Movement Considerations

a. **General.** During deployment or redeployment, forces requiring movement comprise three general categories: self-deploying forces, forces requiring intertheater and intratheater common-user airlift support, and unit movements involving a combination of self-deployment and common-user airlift support. USAF aircraft squadrons routinely require intertheater and intratheater common-user airlift support to deploy a majority of their ground support capability as the flight crews self-deploy. Self-deploying forces, to include contractors, may move directly from origin to a JRSOI or an employment location. Self-deploying forces must still be reflected in the TPFDD and should arrive in theater based on the scheduled EAD/LADs. Lift-supported movements may be divided into three segments: movement from origin to POE (usually the responsibility of the supporting CCDR or Service with planning and coordination support from USTRANSCOM); POE operations; and movement from the POE to the POD. Intratheater common-user airlift that occurs beyond the POD is the responsibility of the GCC or Service, but may be supported by USTRANSCOM using common-user airlift assets.

b. **Management of Change.** Effective deployment execution involves successfully coping with change. More specifically, timely and responsive deployment and redeployment operations are a direct function of the executing command's ability to manage changes in joint force organization, phasing, employment sequence, or circumstance and maintain control of deployment execution. Whenever possible, efficient use of scarce resources should be the goal. Managing change in a dynamic environment is best accomplished in a collaborative manner. Optimizing the deployment process is a combat multiplier that enhances joint force effectiveness.

c. **Deployment and Redeployment Changes.** TPFDD and movement schedule changes during deployment and redeployment execution are inevitable. Changes in mission requirements, operating environment, or unanticipated circumstances may cause the JFC to modify the organization of forces, command relationships, phasing, or sequence of force employment. Late decisions or changes regarding transportation modes or routing, LOCs, or POEs and/or PODs supporting deployment and redeployment may have a significant negative impact on the operation, and may cause delayed satisfaction of requirements, delayed movements, bottlenecks at transportation nodes, and increased transportation costs. More importantly, an impeded deployment may jeopardize mission success.

d. **Managing the Impact.** Since changes during deployment and redeployment execution are inevitable, the JFC's staff must anticipate adjustments and manage the impact of changes to avoid disrupting or impeding the force flow. Prior planning is the key.

OPERATION JOINT ENDEAVOR

"For the first few weeks of the deployment, the time-phased force deployment data changed an average of 14 times per day. The result was confusion about what was to be loaded on the aircraft at the aerial ports of embarkation. Army units showed up unexpectedly at the aerial port of embarkation for air transportation, and aircraft arrived at airfields for units that were not there."

SOURCE: Operation JOINT ENDEAVOR
Description and Lessons Learned
(Planning and Deployment Phases)

Management of change is possible if changes are held to a minimum and require supported CCMD approval. The JFC's staff must also:

(1) Understand and anticipate changes;

(2) Provide resources at critical sites to ensure timely reporting of changes;

(3) Develop flexible, responsive steps, at all levels, to capture and properly document changes;

(4) Synchronize all aspects of the required change (e.g., adjusted force flow may require different staging or support); and

(5) Ensure that requested changes are consistent with the commander's intent and CONOPS.

e. **Movement in Support of Homeland Defense and Defense Support of Civil Authorities.** Deployment operations within the homeland follow the same processes as outlined in the preceding paragraphs; however, the timelines can be extremely compressed. The national importance of these missions is reflected in the elevated movement priorities that can be invoked by the President or SecDef. USTRANSCOM can quickly assemble aircraft and flight crews for operations where expedited passenger movement is required. Surface transportation (commercial and organic) can be a viable option in those situations where the distance between the home station and the OA is relatively short.

For more information on deployment within the homeland, see JP 3-27, Homeland Defense, *JP 3-28,* Defense Support of Civil Authorities, *and Chairman of the Joint Chiefs of Staff Instruction (CJCSI) 4120.02,* Assignment of Movement and Mobility Priority.

3. Movement Control

a. **General.** Movement control involves planning, routing, scheduling, and controlling common-user assets and maintaining ITV of forces and materiel moving through the deployment and redeployment processes. Successful employment of military forces depends on assured and timely deployment and support. Movement control coordinates transportation resources to enhance combat effectiveness and meet the deployment/redeployment and sustainment priorities of the supported CCDR. Effective movement control during deployment operations provides the JFC with the capability to monitor and manage movement execution, and adjust the flow of forces and materiel as necessary. It provides for mechanisms to coordinate and deconflict movements and priorities for limited road space, constrained common-user airlift assets, and cross boundary/activities. In such conditions, the commander and staff should anticipate requirements to identify demands for joint support, prioritize among operations or force element, and communicate extensively with other affected components. Visibility of deploying forces and materiel is established by AV systems such as IGC, Global Decision Support System (GDSS), single mobility system (SMS) and the common operational picture (COP) provided by GCCS-J. USTRANSCOM facilitates this effort by providing movement summaries of TCC and organic movements from departure to final destination in theater in coordination with the supported and supporting commanders. USTRANSCOM provides analysis of movement execution to the Joint Staff, supported CCMDs, and supporting commands and agencies. This analysis includes progress reports, status, problems, port workloads, daily movement statistics, and resolution of problems encountered with intertheater and intratheater common-user transportation means. In addition, movement control must be coordinated and synchronized with JRSOI and a TD plan that describes the in-theater network and system for distribution management. JRSOI focuses on building mission-capable forces as quickly as possible. TD focuses on establishing a distribution management structure and battlefield architecture to maintain visibility and control over forces and materiel arriving for employment in theater.

b. **Organization for Movement Control.** The supported CCDR has a wide range of options for performing movement control. These options include directing subordinate JFCs and Service components to perform their own movement control or creating a fully integrated joint organization. Regardless of the movement control option selected, the GCC should task organize the movement control function commensurate with the mission, scope of operations, and geography of the OA. Normally, the GCC delegates OPCON of the various parts of the transportation system to the most capable Service components, but retains the authority to set priorities and apportion and distribute resources and makes the final determination of transportation mode and sources. The GCC exercises this authority through a theater - joint transportation board or JDDOC or assigns the responsibility to a staff element (normally the command's senior logistic staff officer) who coordinates closely with the operations staff.

c. **Strategic Movement Control. Effective strategic movement control requires the coordinated efforts of USTRANSCOM, supporting CCDRs, the supported GCC, and their components.** Strategic movement control begins with identifying total joint force movement requirements and translating those requirements into logistic terms (e.g., barrels, short tons [STONs], square feet, passengers [PAX]). These movement requirements are documented in the appropriate TPFDD and scheduled for movement in the sequence and priority validated by the supported GCC. Deliberate planning focuses on time-phasing movements and assigning transportation resources to support operations for a set period. CAP follows the basic process of deliberate planning. The fundamental difference is the reduced amount of time available to reach allocation, scheduling, identification of threats to transportation assets en route to the debarkation ports, en route access or overflight status, and other execution decisions. Early identification of the force and its movement requirements in a collaborative environment are key to rapid crisis action movement planning and execution.

(1) **USTRANSCOM uses the TPFDD to analyze the flow of forces and materiel from their points of origin to final destination in theater.** They distribute the apportioned strategic transportation resources and make adjustments, as necessary, to ensure the unimpeded flow of forces and materiel to the final destination in theater. During this process, CDRUSTRANSCOM follows CJCS guidance and coordinates major decisions with the supported CCDR.

(2) **Time-Phased Force and Deployment Data Execution.** Upon initial execution of an OPORD's TPFDD, and until the situation stabilizes or the theater matures, CDRUSTRANSCOM and the supported GCC may have to exercise direct control of movement operations. Repetitive or cyclic validations of projected movement requirements (both mode and destination) may be necessary. In addition, ascertaining transportation asset availability through an accurate TPFDD is critical to optimizing strategic mobility resources and keeping the chain of command apprised of deployment progress.

For additional information on TPFDD analysis and transportation planning, see JP 5-0, Joint Operation Planning, *and CJCSM 3122.01,* Joint Operation Planning and Execution System (JOPES) Volume I, Planning Policies and Procedures.

(3) **US Transportation Command Deployment and Distribution Operations Center (DDOC).** The DDOC directs the global air, land, and sea transportation capabilities of the DTS to meet national security objectives provided by DOD. The DDOC fuses capabilities of multimodal deployment and distribution operations, intelligence, force protection, capacity acquisition, resource management, and other staff functions to collaboratively provide distribution options to the warfighter. C2 of the majority of intertheater lift forces and logistic infrastructure is accomplished through the DDOC, which tracks the movement requirement from lift allocation and initial execution through closure at final destination through their support teams. The support team construct provides better upfront planning through collaboration with the supported commander and other key stakeholders. This allows the process to stay in step with commander's intent as the operation unfolds and increases visibility of all movement requirements. The geographical orientation of support teams enables a holistic view of all warfighter requirements, provides an opportunity to conduct a thorough transportation analysis, reduces correspondence management, leverages collaboration technologies, and enables aggregation of requirements within movement windows.

(4) **Joint Deployment and Distribution Operations Centers.** The integration of intertheater and intratheater movement control is the responsibility of the supported CCMD and USTRANSCOM. The JDDOC is a GCC movement control organization designed to synchronize and optimize national and theater multimodal resources for deployment, distribution, and sustainment. The JDDOC is normally placed under the control and direction of the logistics directorate of a joint staff at the CCMD level, but may also be placed under other command or staff organizations. The JDDOC's strength is the ability to reach back to the national partners (USTRANSCOM, DLA, Army Materiel Command, Joint Munitions Command, and the individual Services) to address and solve issues for the supported commander. The DDOC and JDDOC collaborate to link strategic deployment and distribution processes to operational and tactical functions in support of the warfighter. This improves the speed and agility of deploying forces, increases effectiveness and efficiency of distribution, and enhances the ability to meet constantly changing requirements.

d. **Barge.** In some cases, unit equipment is moved to the POE by commercial barges operating over inland and coastal waterways. The unit movement officer forwards requirements for commercial transportation to the installation transportation officer (ITO) (US Army)/ traffic management office (US Air Force)/transportation management office (US

Marine Corps/US Navy) who reviews the movement requirement, determines if barges are an option, and coordinates barge transport with SDDC. Unit movement officers coordinate with SDDC (or its forward stationed elements) for specific requirements at the barge loading and discharge sites.

(1) **Joint Movement Center (JMC).** The JMC may be established at a subordinate unified or JTF level to coordinate the employment of all means of transportation (including that provided by allies or HNs) to support the CONOPS. This coordination is accomplished through the establishment of theater and JTF transportation policies within the assigned OA, consistent with relative urgency of need, port and terminal capabilities, transportation asset availability, and priorities set by a JFC. The JTF JMC will work closely with the JDDOC.

(2) **Theater Movement Control.** The supported GCC controls intratheater movement. Theater movement control plans should provide the supported GCC with the highest practicable degree of influence or control over movement into, within, and out of theater. The same movement control functions used for strategic movement control should be applied to perform theater movement control. Regardless of the option selected, the theater movement control system must allow the supported GCC the capability to plan, apportion, allocate, coordinate, deconflict transportation requirements, and track the movement of forces and materiel in theater. Moreover, the theater movement control plan must coordinate incoming strategic movements with the TD plan and theater JRSOI operations.

For additional information on theater movement control and TD, see JP 4-09, Distribution Operations.

4. Movement

The movement phase of the deployment/redeployment process is divided into three segments; **movement from origin to POE, POE operations,** and **movement from POE to POD.**

a. Movement from Origin to Port of Embarkation

(1) Validated movement requirements developed during the deployment planning phase and scheduled for movement during predeployment activities phase must now be physically moved, by some mode of transportation, from point of origin to the designated APOEs/SPOEs (when not colocated). USTRANSCOM and its components select APOEs/SPOEs based on the mission, port capabilities, location, and mode characteristics in coordination with the supported and supporting CCDRs. Airlift and sealift schedules are prepared by USTRANSCOM and coordinated with the supported CCDR. SDDC provides call forward instructions to the base/installation transportation or traffic management offices using a port call file message for deployment movements via sealift using procedures outlined in the DTR.

(2) Equipment of deploying forces may either self-deploy or be transported to the POE by commercial rail, truck, or barge. Using the planning factors developed in the earlier

stages of the deployment process, the base/installation transportation office requests the necessary DOD and/or commercial transportation assets (e.g., railcars, trucks, containers) to meet validated movement requirements.

(3) **Surface Movement**

(a) **Military Convoy**

1. Units may convoy to the POE. The unit reviews policy and guidance for public highway use in CONUS and convoy procedures that apply during peacetime, mobilization, and deployment. Procedures for highway movement OCONUS (to include Hawaii and Alaska) are found in local command regulations and policies.

2. Organic convoy operations are not visible to USTRANSCOM during peacetime movement. US convoy movements are the responsibility of the respective Service and must be scheduled consistent with SDDC call forward instructions or AMC published strategic lift schedules to ensure correct arrival times at assigned POEs.

For further information on organic convoy operations, see DTR 4500.9-R, Defense Transportation Regulation, Part III, Mobility, *Appendix F,* Permits for Military Movements on United States Public Highways and Army Convoy Operations and Procedures.

(b) **Commercial Movement.** Unit vehicles and equipment that are not convoyed to the POE using military transport normally move by commercial rail or truck.

(c) **Rail.** In the US, the deploying unit determines its movement requirements and submits them through command channels to the ITO or traffic/transportation management office. The ITO or traffic/transportation management office, in coordination with SDDC, can obtain both commercial and military rail assets based on unit requirements. ITO or traffic/transportation management office personnel validate railcar requirements based on unit rail load plans and the shipping configuration of the items to be deployed. The ITO or traffic/transportation management office maximizes the available loading space to efficiently use rail assets and to reduce the carrier's transportation charges.

(d) **Commercial Truck.** The unit movement officer forwards requirements for commercial trucks to the ITO or traffic/transportation management office who reviews the movement requirement and coordinates the commercial transport with SDDC.

(e) **Commercial Vessels.** All ocean cargo authorized for movement in DTS during wartime, peacetime, and contingencies will be reported to USTRANSCOM then routed to the SDDC who will evaluate the cargo to determine the most cost-effective and expeditious commercial vessel options. SDDC considers relevant factors such as vessel schedules, customer requirements, cost, and capacity. Other factors include the nature of the cargo, the capabilities of and restrictions at proposed load and discharge ports, the capabilities and limitations of available vessels to meet strategic sealift requirements. These considerations should not be construed as an all-encompassing list. USTRANSCOM maximizes the use of commercial vessels already under charter and activated organic sealift vessels. Should neither be available, USTRANSCOM's intent is to offer cargo first to scheduled commercial ocean liner service provided it cost-effectively meets DOD requirements IAW DOD polices. Scheduled commercial ocean liner service is acquired through one of USTRANSCOM's ocean liner contracts, most commonly the Universal Services Contract, but occasionally under the Regional Domestic Contract or other, smaller contracts. Such contracts are used to satisfy strategic sealift requirements. When liner service is not reasonably available, or there is a documented negative critical mission impact, USTRANSCOM may utilize commercial charters. If commercial sealift is otherwise unavailable, a government-owned asset may be activated.

For further information on commercial movement, see DTR 4500.9-R, Defense Transportation Regulation*, Part II, Cargo Movement, Chapter 201, General Cargo Movement Provisions, and Chapter 203, Shipper, Transshipper, and Receiver Requirements and Procedures.*

b. **Port of Embarkation Operations**

(1) **Aerial Port of Embarkation.** AMC is the DOD-designated SPM for all worldwide common-user/commercial aerial ports. APOE operations are divided into four areas: marshalling area, alert holding area, call-forward area, and ready line/loading ramp area. Operating within these areas is the deploying unit, the A/DACG and mobility forces to include the contingency response element, and the load teams. Movement and documentation of equipment and personnel to the APOE may be in preparation for movement by commercial charter aircraft. If this is the case, actions at the APOE will be IAW commercial carrier instructions and Joint Federal Travel Regulations. USSTRATCOM requirements will stress air movement capabilities. Many USSTRATCOM requirements are more time-sensitive than other CCMDs, so sea or land transportation normally cannot provide movement support to meet specified OPLAN timeline requirements.

For further information on activities at the APOE, see DTR 4500.9-R, Defense Transportation Regulation*, Part III, Mobility, Chapter 303, Deployment Activities, and JP 4-01.5,* Joint Terminal Operations.

(2) **Seaport of Embarkation**

(a) SDDC is the DOD-designated SPM for all worldwide common-user/commercial seaports. Units deploy equipment and supplies by sea through a port that is generally commanded or contracted by SDDC. Where SDDC does not have a transportation terminal battalion or other contractual agreements, an SDDC deployment support team may temporarily manage cargo at the SPOE.

(b) USTRANSCOM, through SDDC, directs the deployment of units and sustainment through SPOEs according to the TPFDD. The port call message identifies the earliest/latest dates the unit must arrive at the SPOE for movement processing and vessel loading and gives the unit special instructions for a successful movement to the SPOE. USTRANSCOM's responsibilities include evaluate movement requirements and coordinate vessel selection between SDDC and MSC; prepare and issue port call messages; receive PSAs and direct their activities; receive, stage, and tranship unit equipment in the port;

establish and direct port communications; enforce safety and physical security policies and procedures; develop stow plans, supervise vessel loading, inspect vessel readiness, and provide documentation. The cargo manifest is documented in Global Air Transportation Execution System (GATES) so the receiving organizations at the SPOD and installation can be prepared to receive the equipment. For movements originating in foreign countries, supporting commands and the Service transportation component coordinate with the JDDOC and SDDC forward operating elements to plan and execute the movement of forces to the POE.

For further information on sealift movements, see DTR 4500.9-R, Defense Transportation Regulation, *Part III, Mobility, Chapter 303, Deployment Activities, Chapter 305, Redeployment, and Appendix C, Sealift Sources, and JP 4-01.5,* Joint Terminal Operations.

c. **Movement from Port of Embarkation to Port of Debarkation.** From the APOE/SPOE, deploying forces now move to the APOD/SPOD. In situations that require rapid response or joint integration, traditional Service port opening/operating forces may not be sufficient. While all Services have the organic capability to execute theater opening functions, USTRANSCOM's joint task force-port opening (JTF-PO) provides the supported GCC rapid port opening capability to facilitate crisis response in austere environments. The task force is designed to be in place in advance of a deployment of forces, sustainment, or humanitarian/relief supplies. JTF-PO deploys with seven days of supply. APOD forces are ready to deploy within 12 hours; SPOD forces within 36 hours; and both are designed to operate for 45-60 days and then redeploy or be relieved by follow-on forces. Transit times and other limitations associated with movement to POD differ by port, mode, and cargo type. Each has to be evaluated during planning and managed closely during execution. A smooth and coordinated flow of requirements through ports is essential. USTRANSCOM can provide planning assistance for transload and transshipment operations and factors.

5. Force Visibility

a. The integrated use of C2 systems and innovative information technology makes force tracking through the deployment and redeployment processes possible. The key data that enable force tracking are the force module tracking number, the FTN, and the ULN. Visibility of deploying forces and materiel is established through the logistics management construct of AV and the GCCS-J COP. AV is possible through integration of the capabilities provided by automated identification technology (AIT) (also called automatic identification technology), ITV, and the information systems and decision support tools comprising the IGC, GCSS-J, SMS, and the Web SM of JOPES. Control of the deployment and redeployment processes is exercised through the C2 capabilities of GCCS-J. See Figure V-1 on force visibility. C2 systems should expect degradation during a nuclear exchange. Electromagnetic pulse can have a negative impact on C2 systems and their connectivity links.

For additional information on the COP, see CJCSI 3151.01, Global Command and Control System Common Operational Picture Reporting Requirements.

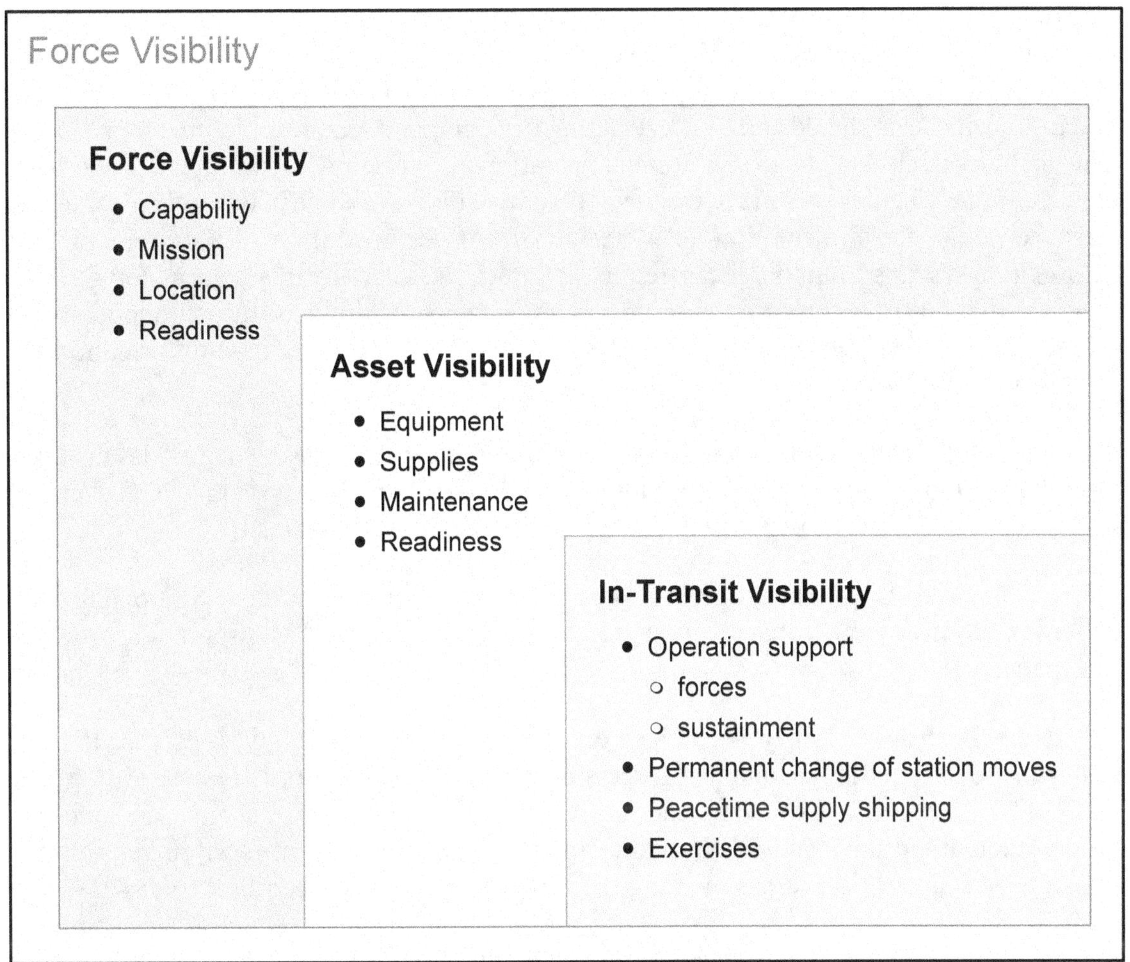

Figure V-1. Force Visibility

b. **Unit Movements.** For non-self-deploying forces, unit moves involve various combinations of assets to transport personnel, unit-related supplies, and equipment. Force tracking is focused on maintaining visibility of these separate unit shipments from origin to destination and through redeployment. Force tracking includes monitoring the elements of a unit until they are reassembled under the commander's control as a mission-capable force. It continues until all units that constitute the specified force assemble and authority transfers back to the supported commander. It further continues through redeployment. The supported CCDR assigns each force requirement a unique FTN. The FTN is included in each ULN in the TPFDD, to allow end-to-end tracking from the generation of the force requirement to the deployment and redeployment.

c. **Asset Visibility.** AV provides the capability to determine the identity, location, and status of forces, equipment, and supplies by class of supply, nomenclature, and unit. It includes the ability to determine the status of personnel and patients. It provides visibility over equipment maintenance and retrograde actions. It also includes the capability to act upon that information to improve the overall performance of the DOD logistic practices supporting operations. AV requires horizontal integration of supply and transportation activities and one-time data capture. AV includes in-process, in-storage, and ITV. The function of performing AV is a shared responsibility among deploying forces, supporting commands and agencies, USTRANSCOM, and the supported CCDR. DLA and USTRANSCOM developed and implemented IGC to work collaboratively to ensure supply and in-transit data is shared and fused, resulting in a complete seamless picture for end-users. This includes deployment and sustainment operations. Through AV, commanders and staffs can determine whether specific items of supply are readily available in the logistic system or must be deployed with the unit. AV results from the integration of requirements and information systems from four areas: requisition tracking, visibility of assets in-storage or in-process, visibility of assets in-transit, and asset management within the theater of operations. In each case, a specified "data repository" serves as a central hub for asset information and visibility.

(1) **Requisition Tracking.** The logistics online tracking system provides visibility over the status of requisitions. This system also provides status information to IGC to enable it to provide accurate status information when a requisition is in-transit.

(2) **Assets In-Storage or In-Process.** The AIS of each inventory control point will provide visibility of assets that are in-storage or in-process (defined as assets being procured or repaired).

d. **In-Transit Visibility.** ITV, as a component of force visibility, preserves the link between the in-transit force and that force's mission within an operation phase through the ULN. ITV is the ability to track the identity, status, and location of DOD units, and non-unit cargo (excluding POL), and PAX, medical patients, and personal property from origin to consignee or destination across the range of military operations as part of AV.

(1) The transportation tracking account number (TTAN) is a non-editable 13-digit random number generated by JOPES and links unclassified transportation schedules, movement and manifest information with classified force plans without compromising OPSEC.

(2) IGC is the designated DOD system for ITV during the movement phase of deployment and redeployment. IGC collects ITV information from distribution source systems, Service systems, and commercial systems and then distributes ITV information to customer, Service, and joint systems. The provision of initial carrier manifest information is the responsibility of supported and supporting commands through their commanders of deploying and redeploying forces. IGC provides this information to Web SM. In conjunction with the use of force modules, this permits the JPEC to monitor and subsequently influence common-user and non-common-user lift as well as self-deploying units. Data quality is directly linked to data collection and entry at the POE and POD and requires appropriate commander emphasis to ensure its accuracy.

(3) A TPFDD identifies all the movements associated with a specific operation. Operation/force ITV, phase and mission ITV, and force requirement visibility are provided by a well-structured TPFDD. Structuring the TPFDD to provide ITV at this level is the responsibility of the supported commander. This level of visibility is required to monitor and project force closure. This level of visibility is enabled by accurate and timely

movement reporting; compliance with transportation procedures and schedules; and properly prepared personnel/cargo accompanied by accurate shipping documents. Effective interfaces between JOPES, Service deployment systems, and transportation systems are essential. During execution of a crisis action deployment, all deviations should be reported to the Service, global force manager, and the supported commander immediately to minimize operation impact and to ensure rapid resolution of process, training, or interface failures. See Figure V-2 on ITV.

(4) **Accurate Data.** Use of JOPES is directed. ITV begins with the use of JOPES and depends upon accurate, disciplined adherence to TPFDD movement validation, allocation of scheduled lift, and manifesting procedures. Deploying forces are responsible for confirming accurate force data via the TPFDD verification and validation process. The supported CCDR ultimately validates the force flow and data to USTRANSCOM. Shipper services are responsible for ensuring accurate and timely submission of data for strategic lift IAW the DTR and GATES. Accurate ITV is enabled by accurate movement reporting, compliance with transportation procedures and schedules, properly prepared personnel manifests and cargo accompanied by accurate shipping documents including TTAN and transportation tracking number.

(5) **Movement Reporting.** Accurate and timely reporting begins with the deploying force. However, ITV involves many participants who must follow designated procedures to ensure accurate source data, timely updates, and shipment status information.

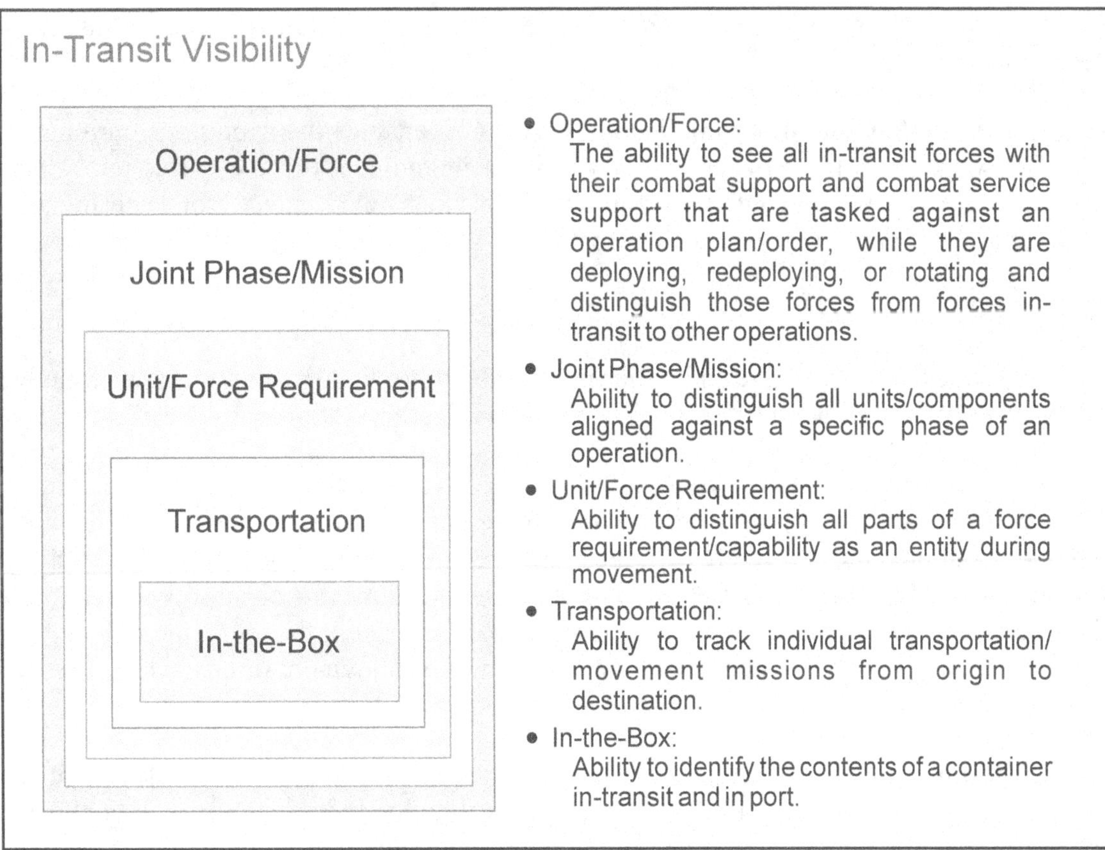

Figure V-2. In-Transit Visibility

Those participants include, but are not limited to deploying units, port operators, commercial transportation service providers, contractors, installations, depots, and contingency locations. Each has a key role in ensuring relevant, accurate, timely, usable, complete, precise, and secure data is provided to support ITV. Required data includes passenger, cargo, schedule and movement information to IGC. IGC receives movement data from various systems from the point of origin, through the POE and POD, within the US and theater. Generation of DTR compliant deployment data is the unit responsibility. GATES is the single POE and POD system for sealift and airlift manifesting.

(6) **Force Tracking.** Force tracking during deployment and redeployment is vital to overall joint force readiness. Unit integrity should be maintained, to the maximum extent possible, and commanders must have the capability to determine the exact location of unit personnel, equipment, and materiel in the event the deploying or redeploying force must be diverted en route to another mission. USTRANSCOM is responsible for tracking forces and equipment embarked on common-user strategic lift using ULNs and transportation control numbers. IGC is the central repository for visibility of assets in-transit from origin to destination, including all military, government, and vendor documented shipments. The IGC database contains shipment status information, booking information, passenger reservation information, aircraft and ship manifests, personal property data, medical patients' information, and vessel and aircraft scheduling data. IGC provides the capability to track unit movements and sustainment operations globally by integrating the automated movement control systems used by the Services, DOD agencies, and USTRANSCOM. IGC integrates the automated movement control systems used by the Services, DOD agencies, and USTRANSCOM, providing the capability to track unit movements and sustainment operations globally.

e. **Automated Identification Technology.** AIT enables the capture of current and accurate source data through the use of various technologies such as; bar codes, optical memory cards, RFID, and satellite/communication links. AIT integration with logistics information systems is key to the AV effort.

6. Redeployment

Movement in support of redeployment moves forces to support a new mission in another JFC's OA or to return them to their home or demobilization station.

a. **Force tracking during redeployment operations** is vital to joint force readiness. Redeployment is not complete until the joint force has completed movement through the redeployment pipeline and emerged at the prescribed destination. Unit integrity should be maintained, to the extent possible, and commanders must have the capability to determine the exact location of unit personnel, equipment, and materiel in the event the redeploying force has to be diverted en route for another mission. Redeployment force tracking uses the same systems and procedures discussed for deployment operations.

b. **Requirements Validation.** Movement execution begins with validation of the movement requirements in JOPES. Requirements validation for redeployment is conducted using the same process used during deployment operations. Redeploying units confirm readiness, movement available dates, PAX, and cargo details to their higher commands that verify total unit movement requirements to the GCC. The supported CCDR receives component redeployment data, merges this data into the redeployment TPFDD, and makes adjustments to the redeployment flow as necessary. Once adjustments are complete, the supported CCDR validates the lift requirements within the specific TPFDD movement window for USTRANSCOM movement scheduling by confirming that the TPFDD accurately reflects current movement requirements. USTRANSCOM conducts a transportation feasibility review and coordinates unresolved transportation conflicts with the supported CCDR for resolution. The end result of this process is a supported CCDR approved redeployment TPFDD that units use to prepare for movement.

c. **Schedule Movement.** Movement scheduling is an iterative process conducted at every level of command with the objective of getting the right personnel, equipment, and materiel to the right place at the right time. Once validated TPFDD requirements are received from the supported CCDR, strategic lift assets are scheduled and registered in JOPES. These movement schedules are also utilized by commands supporting redeployment operations for movement planning, coordination, and execution. After strategic lift schedules are developed, units and/or installations receive call forward messages from USTRANSCOM elements in theater directing movement to SPOEs in designated time windows. Airlift schedules are published and are visible in JOPES, GDSS, and SMS. Instructions are issued which generally require the redeploying cargo to arrive at the designated aerial port 24 hours prior to scheduled lift. Redeploying commands assess their ability to meet strategic lift schedules, make adjustments, and plan unit moves accordingly. Lift shortfalls and available lift are identified to the TCCs. Prior to redeployment, movement control elements confirm movement clearances with HN agencies.

d. **Redeployment movements** are governed by the supported CCDR's redeployment plan and policies and the theater movement control plan. As with deployment, there are three distinct segments during the movement phase of the redeployment process.

(1) **Movement to POEs.** Some units may move to the POE with organic lift assets. However, the majority of redeploying units may require a combination of organic and theater transportation assets. Organic lift movements are normally coordinated by the redeploying unit and controlled by the established theater movement control organization. The theater movement control organization is responsible for management of common-user movements to the POEs as well as synchronization and integration of intertheater lift with intratheater movements to ensure an optimum flow of forces and sustainment into and out of the theater.

(2) **Conduct POE Operations.** Activities at the POE focus on marshalling, capturing ITV data, and loading individuals, unit equipment, and materiel on designated transportation assets. POE operations begin the strategic leg of the redeployment process and are managed by USTRANSCOM. Essential actions are performed at the POE to complete unit movement responsibilities. Unit personnel, equipment and materiel are staged and sequenced in the unit marshalling areas. Inspections are conducted in the alert holding area and/or call forward areas IAW the DTR and the redeployment plan. Aircraft and vessels are loaded and manifests are documented in the appropriate automated system to

allow receiving APODs, SPODs, and installations to prepare for their arrival. Throughout the movement phase of the redeployment process, movement reporting is required and essential.

(3) **Movement to PODs.** Strategic movement from POE to POD for non-self-deploying units is controlled by USTRANSCOM. Force tracking during redeployment operations is vital to assessing joint force readiness. If specified in the redeployment plan, unit integrity should be maintained to the extent possible and commanders should have the capability to determine the exact location of unit personnel, equipment, and materiel in the event the redeploying force needs to be diverted en route for another mission. The tracking of units during redeployment uses the same systems and procedures discussed for deployment operations.

*For more information on redeployment JROSI, see Chapter VI, "*Joint Reception, Staging, Onward Movement, and Integration.*" For more information on redeployment responsibilities, see CJCSM 3122.02,* Joint Operation Planning and Execution System (JOPES) Volume III, Time Phased Force and Deployment Data Development and Deployment Execution.

Intentionally Blank

CHAPTER VI
JOINT RECEPTION, STAGING, ONWARD MOVEMENT, AND INTEGRATION

"Future force projection missions, like those throughout history, will demand well-developed operational and logistical planning, force mix, appropriate sequencing into and out of a theater, and a constant requirement for soldier and unit versatility. Such missions will require leaders and units that can operate in ambiguity and have the agility to adapt and adjust. Set piece thinking does not fit force projection. All of these requirements will occur in a joint or combined environment."

General Frederick M. Franks, Jr., US Army
Commander, VII Corps, Gulf War
August 1989–June 1991

1. General

a. This chapter presents an overview of the final phase of deployment and redeployment, JRSOI. It defines the segments, describes the principles, and identifies the essential elements of JRSOI as they support and enhance the JFC's ability to achieve desired outcomes. JRSOI is a set of dynamic and complex activities involving numerous organizations requiring training, continuous coordination, and collaboration. One common element of JRSOI is a change in command relationship. During an initial deployment, responsibility for planning and executing JRSOI belongs to the supported CCDR. During redeployment, the responsibility for JRSOI operations is determined by the post-redeployment mission of the redeploying force (forces may be redeploying to a new OA or returning to home/demobilization station).

(1) Redeployment for further employment will involve JRSOI in the new OA. During deployment or when a force is redeploying to support another JFC's operational requirement, the OPCON or tactical control (TACON) of the deploying force will change from the losing commander to the gaining commander with SecDef approval through the RFF process.

(2) When redeployment is to home station or demobilization station the supported commander relinquishes OPCON/TACON to the supporting commander. This supporting commander is typically the original parent (gaining) command for assigned forces or a Service for non-assigned forces. Redeployment to home and/or demobilization station will involve POD JRSOI coordinated and executed by the Services and USTRANSCOM for common-user PODs and by the respective Service or unit for forces redeploying by organic assets to non-common-user PODs.

(3) Process seams and friction may occur at functional or organizational interfaces when physical resources and information are transferred. JRSOI, like the deployment process itself, requires continuous planning. The JRSOI activities described in this chapter apply to both deployment and redeployment; however, there are significant differences depending on whether the force is deploying or redeploying into a new JFC's OA or

redeploying back to home or demobilization station. These activities are listed in the tables below; however, these *functional events* and *deployment activities* along with descriptive text of each process can be found in Appendix B, "Joint Force Deployment and Joint Reception, Staging, Onward Movement, and Integration and Joint Force Redeployment Process Maps Descriptions."

b. **Segments of Joint Reception, Staging, Onward Movement, and Integration**

(1) JRSOI is the essential process that transitions deploying or redeploying forces, consisting of personnel, equipment, and materiel into forces capable of meeting the CCDR's operational requirements or returns them to their parent organization or Service. The four segments of JRSOI are described below.

(a) **Reception** operations include all those functions required to receive and clear personnel, equipment, and materiel through the POD.

(b) **Staging** assembles, temporarily holds, and organizes arriving personnel, equipment, and materiel into forces and capabilities and prepares them for onward movement, tactical operations, or Service reintegration.

(c) **Onward Movement** is the process of moving forces, capabilities, and accompanying materiel from reception facilities, marshalling areas, and SAs to TAAs and/or OAs or onward from the POD or other reception areas to the home/demobilization station.

(d) **Integration** is the synchronized transfer of capabilities into an operational commander's force prior to mission execution or back to the component/Service.

c. **The supported CCDR is responsible for JRSOI during deployment and redeployment, when the redeployment is to support another JFC.** This includes all actions required to make arriving units operationally ready and integrated into the joint force. During redeployment to home station, the designated command, Service, or agency assumes responsibility for returning units and personnel when OPCON is relinquished IAW an appropriate order. The receiving command then establishes the command relationships and plans and executes JRSOI. The latter task is normally assigned to a Service component or the Service itself.

(1) During JRSOI, the capability of strategic lift to move personnel, equipment, and materiel to reception points (e.g., the PODs) must be matched by the capability to receive and process the force. The CCDR must have visibility of both deployment and redeployment flows to control the rate as well as the sequencing and processing of deploying and redeploying forces.

(2) Although the CCDR is responsible for JRSOI and other facets of logistics support, this does not relieve supporting commanders of responsibility for detailed oversight of both the deployment and redeployment flow and coordinating changes with the supported commander, when appropriate.

d. JRSOI is an integral part of an operation that enables the assembly of required capabilities for application by the JFC. Successful JRSOI requires command emphasis in planning, training, and synchronization in a collaborative environment. Even self-sustaining units that arrive in-theater are heavily dependent on external support until they are reunited with their equipment and become operational. As deploying units assemble, efforts focus on preparing for future operations and integrating into the joint force.

e. JRSOI provides a common framework to focus joint and Service component capabilities on land, at sea, and in the air into a coherent operation. The context of each JRSOI process may vary, reflecting the nature of the operation, mission, enemy, terrain and weather, troops and support available-time available (METT-T), and civilian considerations. However, deploying forces or non-unit personnel, whether affiliated with a Service or a contractor, normally undergo some form of reception, staging, onward movement, and integration. For example, a fighter squadron and other self-deploying forces may complete JRSOI in a few hours at the reception point or aerial port. Other units may require days or weeks to complete the entire process.

2. Principles of Joint Reception, Staging, Onward Movement, and Integration

a. There are three overarching principles of JRSOI as depicted in Figure VI-1. These principles can assist commanders and their staffs in the planning and execution of JRSOI. CCDRs should consider these principles when planning JRSOI operations.

b. The purpose of **unity of command** is to ensure **unity of effort** under one responsible commander for every objective. In the context of deployment and redeployment operations, this is the supported CCDR. The CCDR adjusts resources based upon the deployment flow into the theater. The CCDR also controls the movement of forces in the AOR, provides support to personnel arriving into the theater, and centrally coordinates the efforts of all other key players in the JRSOI process to include supporting CCDRs.

c. **Synchronization links deployed personnel, equipment, and materiel in a timely manner.** A well-synchronized flow expedites buildup of mission capability and avoids saturation at nodes and along LOCs, thereby enhancing survivability. Synchronization requires detailed joint planning, timely and predictable airflow and seaflow, visibility of assets moving through the pipeline, and the ability to adjust movement schedules.

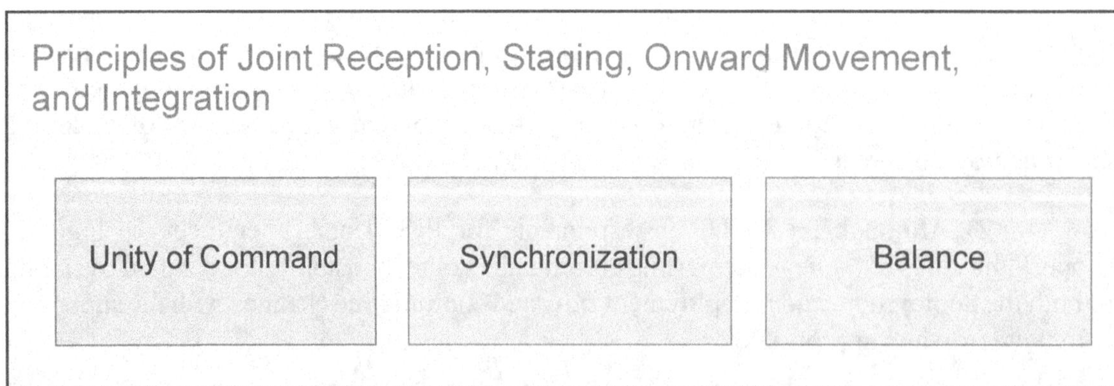

Figure VI-1. Principles of Joint Reception, Staging, Onward Movement, and Integration

UNITY OF COMMAND

"Unity of command means all forces operate under a single commander with the requisite authority to direct all forces employed in pursuit of a common purpose."

JP 1, *Doctrine for the Armed Forces of the United States*

Synchronization occurs when the right units, equipment, supplies, and capabilities arrive in the correct order at the appropriate locations, and supporting activities are coordinated in such a fashion to operate in consonance with one another so that the tempo of force deployment, planning, and execution is uninterrupted. This enhances C2 and helps maintain unit integrity. Managing the timing of the TPFDD flow up to the point of movement is a key activity for ensuring that the arrival time of personnel, equipment, and materiel coincide. Force planners and supporting TCCs must ensure that unit integrity is a dominant consideration when planning unit and equipment deployment and/or movement increments to their supporting transportation load plans and movement schedules.

d. **Balance** applies to managing the TPFDD flow. Managing the TPFDD allows the supported CCDR to adjust the movement schedule for units as mission requirements or conditions change. AV further provides users with timely and accurate information on the location, movement, status, and identity of units, personnel, equipment, and supplies.

SYNCHRONIZATION

"DESERT STORM synchronization required detailed joint planning, timely and predictable airflow and seaflow. In December, the primary cause of overcrowding (in the vicinity of [ports of debarkation]) was a lack of unit integrity in the sea flow. Property of individual units was frequently dispersed among multiple ships. An analysis of 19 randomly selected combat arms and combat support battalions indicate that, on average, a battalion's equipment arrived on seven vessels over a period of 26 days. On average, combat service support battalions came into port on 17 vessels over a period of 37 days. As an example of one extreme, all the equipment of the 121st Signal Battalion of the 1st Infantry Division (M), one of the lead units from [the continental United States], arrived on two ships within three days of each other. At the other extreme, gear belonging to the 143d Signal Battalion and 1st Maintenance Battalion from Europe was spread over 17 and 26 ships respectively, docking over periods of 25 and 45 days respectively. The disruption of throughput operations caused by dispersion of unit property on multiple ships was further exacerbated when single ships were loaded with partial unit sets bound for two different ports. The failure to synchronize airflow and sea flow and not maintain unit integrity contributed to excessively long stays in port by soldiers awaiting equipment. The consequent over concentration in the staging area strained available reception capability and provided the enemy a vulnerable target over an extended period."

SOURCE: 1st Infantry Division (Forward)
DESERT SHIELD/STORM After Action Report, 30 May 1991

Balance is especially relevant to the relationship between deployment and TD. To achieve balance, the flow through the intertheater pipeline and the intratheater network must be regulated and integrated to allow a continuous and controlled flow of forces and sustainment into and within the AOR. Supported CCDRs regulate the transportation flow by ensuring that adequate support and reception assets, effectively coordinated through a theater reception plan, are available or deployed early in the movement schedule to facilitate JRSOI. Continuous flow (balance) is improved by minimizing handling, the number of transfer points, and the number and variety of carriers. Past experience shows the more points of entry into the OA, the more difficult it is to maintain accurate personnel accounting and strength reporting. The JFC can avoid saturation, enhance survivability, and achieve balance by directing personnel, equipment, materiel, and information flow at a rate that can be accommodated at every point along the entire network, from origin to destination. The OE, CONOPS, and available infrastructure are major considerations in determining how to balance the transportation flow and sequence the arrival of combat, combat support, and force sustainment assets in theater.

3. Elements of Joint Reception, Staging, Onward Movement, and Integration

a. JRSOI relies on the essential elements in Figure VI-2 to achieve unity of command, synchronization, and balance. These elements combine in various ways under differing circumstances to make the operations associated with JRSOI possible.

b. **Communications systems are the means by which the CCDR maintains unity of command to balance and synchronize joint force activities and achieve mission success.** Joint forces operate in diverse environments and conduct a variety of operations as part of multinational or interagency teams. Rapid deployment, extended LOCs, and potential forcible entry prior to establishing operations in logistical bare-based areas require a communications system infrastructure (to include AV information) that is interoperable, flexible, responsive, mobile, disciplined, survivable, and sustainable.

(1) JRSOI operations require effective communication systems with responsive leaders and managers. Communication systems must link the supported CCDR, supporting CCDRs, Service components, deploying units, JRSOI support organizations, and the tactical commanders who will integrate the deploying forces and capabilities into their commands. **Reporting and information systems must provide accurate, relevant, and timely**

Elements of Joint Reception, Staging, Onward Movement, and Integration

Essential Elements	Enabling Elements
• Communication systems	• Host-nation support
• Force protection	• Multinational support
• Support organizations and structures	• Contract support

Figure VI-2. Elements of Joint Reception, Staging, Onward Movement, and Integration

information to the appropriate staffs and leaders to plan, integrate, direct, and execute their assigned part of the JRSOI operation.

For more information, see CJCSM 3150.16, Joint Operation Planning and Execution System Reporting Structure (JOPESREP), Volume 1.

(2) Effective communication systems must be responsive to the supported CCDR for deployment and JRSOI management. The supported CCDR should be able to influence the outcome of the deployment. To do this, the commander must know what force capabilities are available and what capabilities will be available in the future. METT-T influenced changes may cause certain units to be in high demand or needed for immediate employment. Communication systems must enable JRSOI C2 elements to locate these units and divert resources to expedite their onward movement.

For additional information on joint communication systems planning guidance, see JP 6-0, Joint Communications System.

c. **Commanders must ensure that requisite protection measures are enforced consistent with the threat.** For JRSOI, the challenge is to protect those forces configured for deployment that are geographically dispersed and possess limited self-protection capability. Risk must be assessed and comprehensive protection plans developed to address vulnerabilities and to counter potential threats to forces, infrastructure, and information systems. Effective and efficient JRSOI operations can reduce force vulnerability by ensuring that units quickly complete the process. Balance and synchronization ensure that forces do not remain static in vulnerable situations and are facilitated by:

(1) Coordinating the flow (achieving balance) so personnel, equipment, and materiel arrive nearly simultaneously;

(2) Minimizing the force footprint by time-phasing units so that those elements required to conduct JRSOI deploy initially;

(3) Synchronizing theater reception, staging, and onward movement capabilities to prevent bottlenecks;

(4) Exercising the ability to control and adjust the TPFDD flow and movement schedules; and

(5) Coordinating with the commands' OPSEC personnel to develop appropriate countermeasures to protect the information related to the movement of forces.

For additional protection information, see JP 3-10, Joint Security Operations in Theater, *JP 3-13.3,* Operations Security, *and JP 3-07.2,* Antiterrorism.

d. Elements of JRSOI can consist of one or more combinations of the following: US forces, HN forces, contractors, or multinational forces. These enablers are force multipliers because they provide the means to expedite buildup of forces in the AOR. Normally, US forces are deployed to support JRSOI operations if the required capability does not exist in the AOR. The necessity to deploy US forces may be reduced if reliable support can be obtained through one of the other sources. To execute JRSOI operations, planners should be aware of the considerations associated with JRSOI support requirements shown in Figure VI-3, and integrate required forces and capabilities early into the deployment process. As units arrive in the OA, they are in a deploying status with little or no operational capability and will most likely require support. Their requirements should be met until the units assemble and become operational and have been integrated into the gaining command. The list in Figure VI-3 is self-descriptive; however, other services encompass life support requirements such as meals, water, shelter, sanitation, trash removal, and support elements for operating marshalling areas and SAs, and reporting movements to the DOD ITV system. Support during JRSOI is provided by organizations such as Army sustainment brigades, Air Force aerial port squadrons and contingency response elements, MAGTF logistics combat element, Navy advanced base functional components and DLA's support teams, or via contracted services. Another important consideration is that organizations with JRSOI support functions may perform other functions simultaneously (e.g., sustainment, retrograde).

e. **Host nations can provide valuable resources to support JRSOI operations.** HNS may include support operations at reception facilities, air and naval operating bases, staging facilities, and support areas, and may encompass a wide variety of commodities and services concerning supplies, medical, transportation, facilities, communications, rear area operations, petroleum, military police, detainees, and civil labor. HNS can reduce the need for early arriving forces and materiel to support JRSOI, shrink strategic lift requirements, and minimize the in-theater logistic footprint. In addition to established HNS agreements normally limited to use in war, declared crisis, or emergency, support can also be arranged through existing ACSAs or, at the local level, by directly contracting for support and services. HN capabilities should be assessed and validated as early on in the deployment process as possible. In contingency operations, an enormous saving in manpower, units, and equipment is possible by maximizing HNS. This is particularly true in the areas of transportation and specialized equipment.

f. **Multinational support has been a traditional strong point for successful JRSOI.** Historically, the US has relied upon its allies to assist during major worldwide contingencies and smaller regional emergencies. Complementary and unique multinational capabilities

Joint Reception, Staging, Onward Movement, and Integration Support Considerations

- Supply
- Maintenance
- Transportation
- Security
- Civil Engineering Support
- Health Services
- Personnel Services
- Other Services

Figure VI-3. Joint Reception, Staging, Onward Movement, and Integration Support Considerations

should be considered during planning.

g. **Contracted support is another force multiplier and, like HNS, should be planned and coordinated in advance of an actual deployment.** Normally, HNS will be considered first before a decision is made to contract for required support. The supported CCDR should ensure the early deployment of contracting, financial management, and legal personnel to enable necessary contracting actions. In the context of JRSOI, contract support is the use of foreign or US civilian personnel and/or equipment to perform a function, such as off-loading vessels or transporting supplies forward. Using contractor personnel reduces the need for US military personnel.

For further information on contracted support, see JP 4-10, Operational Contract Support, *JP 4-0,* Joint Logistics, *and JP 4-08,* Logistics in Support of Multinational Operations.

4. Reception

a. This section describes reception operations at theater PODs and other reception nodes. Reception is the process of receiving, off-loading, marshalling, and transporting of personnel, equipment, and materiel from strategic and/or intratheater deployment phase to a sea, air, or surface transportation point of debarkation to the marshalling area.

b. Reception must be considered in the planning and CONOPS development. Reception begins with the arrival of deploying forces and equipment into an OA. During major strategic deployment, the preponderance of personnel arrive in-theater via intertheater airlift and most equipment and materiel arrives by strategic sealift. Exceptions to this rule include time-sensitive equipment such as C2 assets and other items identified as critical combat capabilities.

c. **POD Operations**

(1) During deployments or when a force is redeploying to a new OA, POD operations will vary depending on whether the reception is occurring at an established APOD/SPOD within a JFC's OA. Effective interface at the POD during reception is crucial to the overall success of the JRSOI process. Forces are received; equipment, cargo, and

DESERT SHIELD RECEPTION

Although personnel were usually flown to the Gulf, most equipment and supplies were sent by sea. Close coordination among the entire transportation network was necessary to ensure that airlifted personnel reached the theater near the date their equipment was scheduled to arrive. Arrival of personnel before their equipment would increase the burden on the Saudi infrastructure. It also would expose troop concentrations in the port areas to possible enemy attack by ballistic missiles, aircraft, and terrorists.

SOURCE: ***Conduct of the Persian Gulf War***
Department of Defense Final Report to Congress, April 1992

vehicles are arranged at the POD and managed/marshalled in preparation for movement to the SA. Ultimately, POD and reception activities are focused on rapidly moving the force from the port to the SA and eventually integrating them into the JFC's mission. During redeployment to home station or demobilization station, POD operations will in most cases occur at a major port (APOD/SPOD) in either CONUS or OCONUS. In either case, activities are focused on receiving personnel and equipment and returning them to their home stations or other facilities.

(2) Overall reception capacity should include, at a minimum, personnel accounting capabilities, strategic lift and delivery capabilities, and the overall throughput capabilities of the port. This enables the port to be cleared in an efficient manner. The transition to theater responsibility can be facilitated by USTRANSCOM TCCs in conjunction with the Services and/or joint forces operating the air and sea PODs. Although the primary focus of reception is to receive, off-load, marshal, and transport deploying forces, the reception process inevitably shifts from receiving sustainment materials, replacement equipment, and personnel to ultimately supporting redeployment operations of in-theater forces. At PODs, these activities may occur simultaneously with two-way traffic into and out of the theater. In all cases, detailed planning, force tracking, and the principles of movement control as described in Chapter V, "Movement," of this publication are essential to the overall success of reception.

d. **Command Relationships.** During deployment or redeployment to a new OA, the supported CCDR is responsible for JRSOI planning and execution. During redeployment to home station or demobilization station, the supported commander retains overall responsibility for the planning and execution of the redeployment operation. However, supporting Services or Service components, in coordination with the supported commander, plan and execute the JRSOI phase. The designated command, Service, or agency assumes responsibility for units and personnel when OPCON is relinquished IAW an appropriate order. Upon arrival at POD or other designated time and place, the unit changes OPCON to the designated commander. The supported CCDR relinquishes the OPCON or TACON over the deployed unit and the unit is transferred back to the designated command or Service. The receiving command establishes the command relationships and plans and executes JRSOI. The latter task is normally assigned to a Service component or to a Service itself.

e. Seaport and aerial port capacities and throughput capabilities significantly influence the speed with which forces can be deployed, the order in which forces must be deployed, and, to a large extent, the types of units that can be deployed. Port efficiency or throughput is a function of the OE and the level of port modernization (developed versus undeveloped). Some instances may necessitate improving or constructing port facilities to meet operational requirements. In addition to the PODs and nodes, several other facilities and areas support the reception process.

f. Marshalling is another essential component of the reception process that facilitates port clearance. The timely movement of personnel, equipment, and materiel to a common assembly or holding area, preferably outside the port, gives the commander the first opportunity to reassemble mission capability. This very important task of assembling forces is often complicated by the fact that units may arrive in-theater at separate PODs and at different times. To further enhance port clearance, the CCDR must designate marshalling areas that support unit re-assembly without impeding the arrival ports for follow-on units.

g. DOD uses the SPM approach for most APOD and SPOD operations. As outlined in the UCP, USTRANSCOM provides worldwide common-user aerial and seaport terminal management and may provide terminal services by contract. Thus USTRANSCOM, through AMC and SDDC, will normally manage common-use aerial ports and seaports, respectively, for the CCDR. In areas not served by a permanent USTRANSCOM presence, USTRANSCOM will deploy an AMC mission support element including aerial port or seaport expertise. If mobile C2 is also required, a mission support team or CRG will deploy as well as the SDDC port management portion of JTF-PO to manage the ports in concert with the designated port operator. Based on availability of fixed-port terminals or OEs or requirement, the port manager may also serve as the port operator.

For more information on redeployment POD operations, see CJCSM 3122.02, Joint Operation Planning and Execution System (JOPES) Volume III, Crisis Action Time-Phased Force and Deployment Data Development and Deployment Execution.

h. **Aerial Port of Debarkation Operations.** The APOD serves as the primary port of entry for deploying personnel, as well as for early entry forces and capabilities airlifted into theater. APODs may be operated in conjunction with the HN.

(1) **APOD Functions.** Numerous operational and support functions occur at the APOD. Primary operational functions are to receive, off-load, marshal, provide essential field services, and transport deploying forces and capabilities. Tasks include off-loading cargo (both equipment and materiel), arriving personnel in theater via personnel accounting systems, clearing personnel through air terminals, accomplishing movement control, and maintaining ITV. In addition to operational functions, there are APOD support functions as listed in Figure VI-4.

(2) **APOD Service Capabilities.** Various organizations provide the operational capabilities needed for APOD reception. For example, AMC, through its air mobility squadrons and/or aerial port flights and CRGs, provides much of the operational and logistic support needed to receive arriving aircraft. Navy overseas air cargo terminal units unload

Aerial Port of Debarkation Support Functions

- Personnel
- Airfield management
- Materials handling equipment
- Maintenance
- Transportation resources
- Security
- Hazardous cargo handling
- Medical
- Transient aircraft servicing
- Air defense
- Command and control
- Equipment refueling

Figure VI-4. Aerial Port of Debarkation Support Functions

aircraft and operate air cargo and passenger airheads. Through its cargo transfer capability, the Army provides the required support to interface with the CRG and begins the staging and onward movement phases for the deploying personnel, equipment, and materiel. When performing this mission, the Army element is often referred to as the A/DACG. Marine Corps units may also be given the A/DACG mission. In addition, HNS, provided under the provisions of an existing agreement or contracted port services, may be used to free up finite reception assets and minimize the logistic footprint at the APOD. Close coordination with HNS activities is necessary to balance the operational requirements of all organizations competing for limited resources.

(3) **APOD Infrastructure Optimization.** Several factors can impede APOD reception. However, the overriding considerations for any airfield operation are parking maximum (aircraft) on ground (MOG) and working MOG. Parking MOG is the number of aircraft that can fit, or be parked, on the ground. Working MOG pertains to how many parked aircraft can be worked based on available personnel, materials handling equipment (MHE), and ramp space. Optimally, working MOG equals parking MOG. But this is seldom the case, since parking MOG usually exceeds working MOG. An airfield's MOG may not remain constant if it lacks a dedicated explosives pad. In these cases, the parking or working MOG will decrease as otherwise available adjacent aircraft parking spaces are removed while explosive cargo is off-loaded from another aircraft. Service and HN operators must ensure that their activities do not reduce MOG capacities.

(4) **APOD Joint Use.** Another consideration is ownership and management of the APOD facility. The APOD may be controlled and/or operated by various HN military and civilian organizations. Additionally, other military and commercial activities may compete for limited facilities. These competing requirements may complicate unity of command and may limit or reduce facility throughput capacities available for reception of forces. To overcome this obstacle, clear C2 relationships must be established by the JFC for all APODs and JRSOI functions.

i. **Seaport of Debarkation.** The SPOD is perhaps the most important because of its enormous throughput potential as it receives deploying forces and sustainment from surface vessels. Historically, 90 percent of a deploying force's equipment and materiel are delivered to the theater via strategic sealift. Three types of seaports can function as a SPOD: **fixed**, which are improved, world-class ports like Dammam, Saudi Arabia, or Pusan, Korea; **unimproved or degraded** ports such as those found in Somalia and Haiti; and **bare beaches** where fixed facilities are unavailable.

(1) **SPOD Functions and Responsibilities.** Responsibility for essential SPOD functions is shared between HN seaport organizations and US DOD organizations such as MSC and SDDC, military terminal service units, and contractors. Shown in Figure VI-5 are examples of SPOD functions.

(2) SPOD operations are normally conducted at established fixed maritime terminal facilities such as a sea or inland maritime port. Pre-positioned port opening packages are an option available to the CCDR through the different Services' pre-positioned equipment

Seaport of Debarkation Functions

- Seaport management
- Cargo offloading, documentation, and clearance
- Berthing and chandler services
- Ship arrival and departure coordination
- Coordination for transportation for onward movement
- Movement control from seaport of debarkation to marshalling area
- Hazardous cargo handling
- Port support activity
- Transient ship services
- Field services
- Medical support
- Contract and demurrage
- Holding area operations
- Maintenance and logistic support for arriving forces
- Port security and force protection

Figure VI-5. Seaport of Debarkation Functions

located either in-theater or afloat. Pre-positioned port opening packages may be capable of operating a maritime terminal and providing the necessary capability to receive forces.

(3) SPOD maritime terminals include both seaports and inland water facilities capable of receiving deep draft vessels, coastal vessels, and barges. Many established terminals have a transportation infrastructure in place such as railways, highways, inland waterways, and adjacent airfields. Although terminal facilities vary, many are already equipped to handle roll-on/roll-off vessels, containers, general and bulk cargo, and lighterage.

(4) JLOTS is an option available to receive the force when debarkation at an established port is impractical or not available. In addition, JLOTS may also provide increased capability to operational fixed ports. In JLOTS operations, Navy and Army logistics over-the-shore (LOTS) forces conduct LOTS operations together under a JFC. JLOTS operations are conducted over unimproved shorelines, through fixed ports not accessible to deep draft shipping, and through fixed ports that are inadequate without the use of JLOTS capabilities. JLOTS operations should be considered when port throughput capacity or reception capability is inadequate to support planned joint force operations, or to augment port reception capability to handle the surge of major combat forces during the early stages of deployment operations. The magnitude of JLOTS operations extends from the reception of ships for off-load through the onward movement of equipment and materiel to inland marshalling areas and SAs.

For further information on JLOTS, see JP 4-01.6, Joint Logistics Over-the-Shore.

(5) The SPOD will contain facilities and organizations, both military and civilian, to perform many of the APOD functions described earlier. One of the key organizations for SPOD operations is the PSA and/or port operations group (POG). It is a temporary organization that aids the port commander in receiving, processing, and clearing cargo. The PSA is under the OPCON of the SPM at common-user seaports. For seaports not designated as common-user seaports, the GCC will designate the port manager, whereas the POG remains under the OPCON of the logistic combat element and/or landing force support party. PSA and POG functions are shown in Figure VI-6.

j. Transportation systems are crucial to the timely and efficient reception of deploying forces at the SPOD. The supported commander should consider all available resources, geography, transportation capabilities, climate and seasonal changes, and distance between LOC nodes as well as projected requirements for movement of the forces from the SPOD. When selecting a SPOD, the supported commander should consider the transportation infrastructure as well as the capacity of the port to handle potential throughput and surges of deploying forces. A robust rail, road, air, and inland waterway (where available) system will be vital in efficiently receiving and moving the force to SAs.

k. **Reception Considerations.** To support operations at the APOD and SPOD, conditions that support the JRSOI process should be considered. The CCDR should determine the type of support units and the composition and/or method of sustainment support necessary to carry out reception. The CCDR may consider most capable Service or predominate user options when configuring the support structure. Figure VI-7 illustrates some reception planning considerations.

(1) **Economy of Resources.** CCDRs should tailor their reception operations to provide efficiency and economy as well as eliminate duplication of limited resources among the Services. The decision by the JFC to establish a joint reception center maximizes use of scarce resources. Efficient resource management of limited transportation assets and reception facilities assists in optimizing reception throughput. Discharge workload should

Port Support Activity and Port Operations Group Functions

- Receiving and staging unit equipment in marshalling areas
- Correcting configured equipment and cargo deficiencies
- Serving as vehicle operators
- Assisting in the servicing of self-deploying aircraft
- Providing necessary maintenance and recovery capability
- Assisting the port commander with cargo accountability
- Providing for security of sensitive and classified cargo

Figure VI-6. Port Support Activity and Port Operations Group Functions

Reception Planning Considerations

- Economy of resources
- Command and control
- Communications
- Force protection
- Transportation
- Supply and services
- Host-nation support
- Contractor support

Figure VI-7. Reception Planning Considerations

not exceed POD throughput capacity. A time-phased build-up of reception capabilities may accomplish this. At the same time, however, the JFC must configure reception forces to handle potential surge capacities of strategic deployment and provide intermodal services for transshipment of arriving cargo and supplies.

(2) **Command and Control.** C2 functions are essential to the successful reception of forces into an OA and are the responsibility of the supported CCDR. Prior to commencement of deployment and reception operations, the JFC should develop an in-theater structure for executing C2 of JRSOI operations. This structure must address the integration of USTRANSCOM assets into the overall C2 for JRSOI to be an efficient operation. Some C2 assets may be pre-positioned in theater, geographically in close proximity to the region, or afloat on MSC or maritime pre-positioning force vessels. Successful execution of a reception operation involves a centralized C2 structure (unity of command), a decentralized execution strategy, and disciplined (synchronized and balanced) movement control. Monitoring and control of deployment operations will be ongoing throughout all segments of JRSOI and will involve joint and theater movement control organizations using joint ITV systems. The following C2 functions (mission and situation dependent) are examples of what may be required to successfully execute reception functions at APODs and SPODs:

(a) Maintain unity of effort for all primary and secondary LOC nodes.

(b) Coordinate, control, and monitor US airlift and sealift operations into APODs and SPODs.

(c) Designate marshalling area.

(d) Provide personnel and cargo clearance of arriving forces.

(e) Provide for personnel, equipment, and materiel accountability.

(f) Determine whether a security risk category is to be designated as a joint risk category.

(g) Provide movement control of arriving personnel, equipment, and materiel.

(h) Provide visibility over arriving and departing personnel and cargo by input of AV source data into appropriate AIS.

(i) Liaise with HN military and civilian officials to obtain required clearances and support.

(j) Coordinate and control loading and off-loading from aircraft and ships.

(k) Coordinate and control personnel and cargo movements from PODs via surface and air to planned holding areas.

(l) Monitor and manage the TPFDD.

(m) Coordinate and control movement of noncombatants.

(n) Provide clearance for intratheater airlift cargo movements.

(o) Provide distribution management for the theater and arriving unit command structures of all arriving personnel, equipment, and materiel.

(p) Provide intermodal services for transshipment of arriving cargo and supplies.

(q) Provide, coordinate, and control construction in support of personnel and cargo movement.

(r) Provide life support facilities.

(3) **Communications.** Effective communications and collaboration, vertically and horizontally, is essential for JRSOI due to the complexity of the operation. Timely and reliable communications should be continuous among all JRSOI participants, both supporting and supported. The following communications functions may be required to successfully execute JRSOI operations:

(a) Establish links between LOC nodes.

(b) Use automation technology. Communications should utilize advanced technologies that will be both an enabler and force multiplier of the reception process. The AISs and the COP described in Appendix A, "Enabler Tools," are crucial to ensure that the commander has access to interactive decision quality information (integrated, real-time, AV, etc.) on personnel, installations, finances, and equipment/material. The entire JRSOI process, especially reception, should leverage the power of automation. Through Global Combat Support System (GCSS)/IGC programs, commanders can obtain AV as well as manage the flow of forces in-theater and through the numerous PODs. Establishing a reliable network to disseminate this valuable information to all Services involved in the reception phase must be a priority for those units with GCSS and IGC capabilities.

(c) Provide LNOs. Effective liaison among the Service components and with HN agencies is paramount in order for effective communication to occur during the entire reception operation.

(d) Monitor IGC and JOPES to provide real-time force tracking information of deploying forces and non-unit replacement personnel. Monitor AV using IGC to provide near-real-time tracking of non-unit sustainment items for all organizations and activities.

(e) Provide for reliable and compatible two-way communications between joint forces.

(4) **Protection.** Deploying forces as well as intertheater airlift and sealift assets may be the most vulnerable during loading or discharge. The threat must be considered in light of the concentration of forces within the limited confines of a POD. As units move forward to secondary LOC nodes, they remain vulnerable until fully integrated into a mission-capable force. Protection capabilities and/or measures should be integrated into the reception plan. The CCDR is responsible for providing the assets needed to protect the force throughout the entire reception process. Protection functions should include but are not limited to:

(a) Providing theater air defense.

(b) Maintaining coastal, harbor, and inland waterway defense.

(c) Providing APOD and SPOD facility defense.

(d) Providing military police support.

(e) Establishing joint security coordination center for security oversight.

(f) Preparing for the effects of NEO on JRSOI operations.

(g) Providing protection against weapons of mass destruction threats.

(h) Protect LOCs.

For further information on security operations, see JP 3-10, Joint Security Operations in Theater.

(5) **Transportation.** All three elements of a transportation system (mode operations, terminal operations, and movement control) should be integrated early into the TPFDD flow to provide adequate reception capabilities for the deploying forces. These elements may be RC assets that must be mobilized and flow early in the TPFDD. Essential to any JRSOI mission is an executable plan that facilitates intratheater transportation between nodes. The primary transportation nodes and the extended LOCs should be mutually supportive of the principle of unit integrity. To transition from strategic intertheater deployment to in-theater reception, the following transportation functions may be required:

(a) Place port opening force packages at PODs providing hand-off of deploying personnel, equipment, and materiel.

(b) Employ movement control principles. Movement control coordinates all aspects of transportation; modes, nodes, and terminals. It includes Service-organic capabilities, HNS, and supporting commands.

(c) Have a support element for off-loading of arriving forces.

(d) Provide intratheater air and surface transportation assets.

(e) Manage and monitor the TPFDD.

(f) Establish theater LOC nodes and links required to meet the anticipated transportation and throughput capacities. Allow for sufficient coordination to ensure timely movement of cargo and equipment through the port to minimize port congestion.

(g) Identify, assess, and provide for required physical transportation capacities and capabilities (ports, airfields, rail and road networks, littoral and inland waterways, and communications infrastructure).

(6) **Supply and Services.** Supply and services compete for limited strategic lift resources as the priority is on receiving and moving the force forward into the theater. However, sustainment of the force while transitioning into the theater cannot be forgotten, and neither can the resources that will be required to sustain reception. The CCDR must provide arriving personnel, equipment, and materiel with required life support and field services until unit personnel are reunited with their supplies and equipment and become self-sufficient. These services may be RC assets that must be mobilized and flow early in the TPFDD. The following are typical categories of support that may be provided to sustain newly arriving forces in-theater:

(a) Field and life support services such as food, water, lodging, and sanitation.

(b) Maintenance and operator support for deploying equipment, vehicles, helicopters, and aircraft.

(c) Munitions storage and handling.

(d) Petroleum products storing and handling.

(e) Medical support and evacuation.

(f) Mortuary affairs services.

(g) Frustrated cargo storing, handling, and processing.

(h) Postal support.

(7) HNS as a potential force multiplier should be planned and coordinated well in advance of an actual deployment. This can best be accomplished through coordination with the US country team (ambassador and staff), if one exists within country. The effect of a well-planned HNS agreement should be a reduction of the US military logistic footprint in-theater and a concurrent reduction in the need for early deployment of supporting units. Some HNS considerations include:

(a) Augmenting reception capabilities early in the deployment cycle with dedicated units if civilian or military HNS are not available at APODs and/or SPODs to quickly throughput combat forces.

(b) Analyzing the PODs' and in-theater transportation infrastructure's capacity.

(c) Anticipating limited materiel, key services, and HNS in-country.

(8) **Contractor support** for materiel requirements is another force multiplier and, like HNS, should be planned and coordinated in advance of an actual deployment. Normally, HNS will be considered first before a decision is made to contract for required support. When contact support is anticipated, the following considerations apply:

(a) The supported CCDR should ensure early deployment of contracting, financial management, and legal personnel to accomplish the contracting actions. Contracts will not be without cost, nor should deploying forces expect to have unlimited access to local facilities and resources.

(b) In most cases, military forces will have to share and compete with HN military, civil, and commercial operations for scarce resources and facilities.

(c) Contractors and their equipment may be deployed with US forces on DOD provided lift, or they may deploy using commercial assets.

(d) JFCs, Services, and their contractors must coordinate to ensure they are not competing for the same lift or space during JRSOI operations.

"As we have learned many times, the US can ship supplies and materiel to an objective area much more effectively and efficiently than the objective area can unload and distribute those supplies."

Lieutenant General (Ret.) Joseph M. Heiser, US Army
***A Soldier Supporting Soldiers*, 1992**

5. Staging

a. **General.** This section describes the staging process and the activities that may be performed in theater SAs during deployments and redeployments to a new OA, or at SAs designated near CONUS or OCONUS PODs during redeployments to home or demobilization station. Regardless of where staging occurs, the activities associated with staging will generally include assembling, temporary holding, and organizing of arriving personnel, equipment, and materiel into units and forces, and preparing them for onward movement and employment by the JFC. Operability checks will need to be performed on equipment and vehicles to ensure their combat readiness, and loads will need to be sequenced and loaded in preparation for onward movement. During staging, deploying forces have limited mission capability and may not be self-sustainable. The CCDR must provide facilities, sustainment, life support, and protection until deploying units regain their combat or mission capability. Redeployment back to home or demobilization station will largely be a Service responsibility as forces and equipment are processed back into their respective Service and are reset. Three essential force-related activities that occur during staging are depicted in Figure VI-8.

b. During deployment or redeployment to a new OA, a major focus of JRSOI specifically during staging is building capabilities required by the JFC. Mission success requires:

(1) Defining combat capability.

(2) Defining logistic capability and sustainability.

(3) Defining how to track and visualize combat power.

(4) Establishing an incremental building of combat power.

(5) Prioritizing and adjusting the flow as needed.

(6) Managing and supervising the unit's progress.

(7) Developing a complementary tracking system that applies to combat operations as well as JRSOI.

c. **Deployment force tracking** aids in predicting the unit's arrival time in theater and incremental build of mission capability. The supported CCDR's staff supports the operational commander in force tracking by providing visibility of deploying forces and materiel. Force tracking includes the following steps:

Staging Force-Related Activities

- Units assemble into a mission-capable force.
- Units of the force prepare to conduct their missions.
- The force prepares for onward movement (if required) and subsequent integration into the theater operation.

Figure VI-8. Staging Force-Related Activities

(1) Elements are monitored until they are reassembled.

(2) Unit commander reestablishes control of the unit.

(3) Unit becomes capable of sustaining itself.

(4) Unit can perform assigned missions.

(5) Unit completes onward movement and integration.

d. **Staging Areas.** SAs are specific locations along the LOC. The CCDR usually designates specific locations for staging in order to provide space and focus resources to support staging operations. SAs provide the necessary facilities, sustainment, and other support to enable units to become mission-capable. The size of the deployment or redeployment and location of the PODs and marshalling areas may necessitate multiple SAs.

(1) In selecting the location of the SAs, the CCDR plans where forces will be strategically concentrated to enter the OA. The CCDR evaluates the location of TAAs or OAs, geographic constraints, availability of organic and HN assets, transportation infrastructure, distance to the ports, and protection considerations. These factors, along with the physical dimensions of the theater, ultimately determine the location of the theater SAs.

(2) The size of the SA is influenced by numerous variables, including the anticipated flow of forces in-theater, space available, and threat. The TPFDD is an important tool for the CCDR to use in understanding the requirements for SAs.

(3) **Intermediate Staging Base.** During deployment, the theater operational situation may necessitate the establishment of an ISB outside of the combat zone or JOA prior to inserting the forces. If established, the ISB is an initial theater staging facility. Deploying forces debark from strategic lift, reassemble, and prepare to accomplish assigned missions. The theater may not have the physical infrastructure to support JRSOI and will require the use of air and sea bases outside the region. ISBs serve as a principal staging base in order to secure a lodgment to project the force for the rapid delivery of combat power to an AOR and can perform selected operational-level tasks. In some instances, an ISB is also used to transition from intertheater lift to intratheater lift to increase the number of points of entry available to the force to mitigate anti-access measures.

(4) During redeployment to home or demobilization station, staging activities will be different. Since forces and equipment are being staged in preparation to being assimilated back into their respective Services, these activities will focus on assembling and processing

> *"Movement is the essence of strategy. This is true even though strategy is not confined to the military art: the implementation of every political decision requires movement. It may be messages that move, or men, or money or munitions."*
>
> **Stephen B. Jones**
> **"Global Strategic Views" in *The Impact of Air Power,* 1959**

personnel, receiving WRM and other equipment and coordinating their onward movement, performing any necessary operation checks, and reporting status to facilitate ITV.

6. Onward Movement

a. **General.** This section describes systems and processes for accomplishing the onward movement of deploying or redeploying forces. Onward movement is the process of moving forces and sustainment from reception facilities and marshalling or SAs to TAAs or other operating areas. Rail, road, inland or coastal waterway, and/or air can be used to accomplish this movement. Challenges associated with onward movement during a deployment or redeployment to a new OA may include establishing distribution networks, limited LOC capacity, degraded LOC conditions, the potential for enemy interdiction, and reporting and movement control procedures. Onward movement during redeployment to home station or demobilization station will be planned and executed by the owning Service and focus on moving returning units from the POD. Transportation from the POD may be arranged for by a Service or USTRANSCOM depending on mode selected to move the returning forces.

b. The deployment and redeployment processes share most of the activities associated with onward movement particularly during a redeployment into another GCC's AOR. However, in the case of redeployment to home or demobilization station, efforts are largely focused on conducting movement control operations as units and equipment make their way to their destinations. These destinations could be the home station or in the case of equipment, a depot maintenance facility for refurbishment or remanufacture. Some challenges to onward movement are illustrated in Figure VI-9.

c. Efficient onward movement of personnel, equipment, and materiel requires a balanced, integrated system of node operations, movement control, mode operations, and cargo transfer operations. The onward movement process encompasses support to all Service components of a joint operation, and often includes HNS. As in all JRSOI activities, onward movement of personnel, equipment, and materiel is prioritized according to the CCDR's needs. Onward movement is complete when force elements are delivered to the designated location at the designated time.

d. **Enablers of Onward Movement.** Key elements of the onward movement process are speed of movement and information flow. Speed of movement is vital for protection and

Onward Movement Challenges

- Establishing the distribution network
- Enemy interdiction
- Reporting procedures
- Movement control

Figure VI-9. Onward Movement Challenges

mission accomplishment. Information flow encompasses locations and capabilities of forces, projected and actual arrival times at en route and final destinations, and component commands' ability to affect the movement. Successful onward movement of deploying/redeploying forces can be viewed in the context of eight onward movement enablers as depicted in Figure VI-10 and explained below.

(1) **Movement Control.** Establishing and maintaining effective movement control is essential during the onward movement segment. JP 4-0, *Joint Logistics,* describes a variety of options available to the CCDR to execute and control joint logistics to include coordinating and synchronizing movement control. To ensure a fully integrated and responsive transportation system, the CCDR should consider assigning responsibility for theater transportation movement control to the JDDOC. The JDDOC must be equipped with sufficient communication and automation capability to ensure adequate interface between strategic and theater transportation systems and the CCDR's staff. Service components also have capabilities to coordinate and synchronize movement control. The Army has various movement control organizations while the Marine Corps has movement control centers (MCCs) planned for all deploying units from the Service component level down to the battalion and squadron level. They are the MDDOC, the MAGTF MCC, and the unit MCCs.

(a) **If a joint movement control organization is established using assets from multiple Services, then the CCDR must conduct joint training to ensure that personnel understand and can operate movement control equipment and C2 processes.** The CCDR should task-organize the movement control functions commensurate with the mission, size, and geography of the OA.

(b) The ITV systems provide a capability vital to coordinated onward movement. They provide a means to track units, personnel, equipment, and materiel en route from reception areas to SAs and forward to the assembly areas. The physical capabilities and limitations of the distribution network, along with the effects of combat, can limit the ability to execute onward movement as planned. Thus, connectivity is essential to provide ITV information to enable successful execution of onward movement to include location, characteristics, and capacities of roads, aerial ports, and rail lines, combined with current status of highway regulation, traffic circulation and surface distribution plans, and movement programs.

Enablers (or Elements) of Onward Movement

- Movement control
- Host-nation support
- Communications/automation
- Acquisition and cross-servicing agreements
- Transportation
- Contract support
- Supply and services
- Force protection

Figure VI-10. Enablers (or Elements) of Onward Movement

OPERATION JOINT ENDEAVOR

"At the time of execution, the rail deployment plan was based on an invalidated deployment rate (20 trains per day). At the planned rate of movement, the division could deploy the bridge opening package, open the ground lines of communications, accomplish the transfer of authority, and begin enforcement of the ZOS [zone of separation] by D+30. As the deployment began, it rapidly became apparent that the rail LOC [line of communications] would only throughput about half of the planned deployment rate. As a result, ad hoc force tailoring decisions had to be made to compensate for the reduced rail lift capacity."

SOURCE: Initial Impressions Report
Operation JOINT ENDEAVOR, 1995

(2) **Communications/Automation.** Movement control elements must be equipped with sufficient communication and automated systems to ensure adequate interface between strategic and theater transportation systems and the CCMD's staff. They should be skilled in coordinating and directing theater transportation operations in support of unit movements and/or logistic resupply operations.

(3) **Transportation.** Nodes, main supply routes (MSRs), and HN assistance should be coordinated to maximize the speed of movement. Close coordination is essential for minimizing congestion because in most cases the Services, multinational units, and HN populace will be using the same networks. It is essential that capacities and capabilities of the transportation network are balanced against the movement requirements so that nodes and routes are neither saturated nor underutilized. As previously explained, the designated movement control element is responsible for coordinating the use of all theater transportation resources with USTRANSCOM and its TCCs, other CCMDs, and the HN.

(4) **Supply and Services.** During deployment or redeployment to a new OA, en route support nodes along the theater LOCs provide security, life support, refueling, limited vehicle maintenance, and vehicle recovery. The size of the support centers will be based upon the available facilities, length of route, and volume of equipment and personnel transiting the sites. Various types of en route facilities that support onward movement include:

(a) Aircraft en route support sites.

(b) Convoy support sites.

(c) Trailer transfer points.

(d) POL transfer points.

(e) Pre-positioned equipment sites.

(f) Pre-stock supply points.

(g) Railheads.

(h) Of the above listed facilities, convoy support sites are among the most critical and provide the bulk of en route support during onward movement. Services provided by convoy support sites may be tailored based upon such factors as distance between LOC nodes; number and location of support bases; and MSRs' congestion, condition, and protection. Convoy support sites usually provide support in the following areas:

1. Administration and communications.

2. Refueling.

3. Dining and billeting.

4. Latrines.

5. Laundry and showers.

6. Vehicle recovery and maintenance.

7. Medical.

8. MHE and cargo-handling equipment.

9. Security (force protection).

(5) **Force Protection.** Protection is critical to onward movement because it minimizes enemy opportunities to inflict serious losses and delays. The threat of enemy interdiction to onward movement of forces presents a special challenge to the commander. The CCDR must assume that interdiction of the LOCs will form an integral part of enemy strategy and must plan operations to preclude them from impacting onward movement.

(a) GCCs are faced with many asymmetrical threats as they conduct tactical convoy operations on today's nonlinear, noncontiguous battlefield. Recent combat operations have evolved by introducing diversified threats that range from vehicle-borne improvised explosive devices (IEDs) to complex ambushes employing IEDs, rocket-propelled grenades, and small arms.

(b) Tactical convoys are combat operations. Although contact with enemy organized/uniformed ground forces may not be anticipated, security against anti-US forces, enemy sympathizers, and IEDs must be maintained and the convoy must be prepared to take immediate action against an enemy threat. To accomplish this, tactical convoys require additional planning and coordination beyond normal line-haul operations. One of the main enemy tactics of the nonlinear OE is to target the convoy LOCs, supplies, and other government resources. To defeat this tactic, each tactical convoy must be prepared to take the necessary actions in the face of ambush and defeat enemy forces once contact is gained, thus retaining the initiative and deterring future attacks.

For further information, see Field Manual (FM) 4-01.45, Marine Corps Reference Publication 4-11.3H, Navy Tactics, Techniques, and Procedures (NTTP) 4-01.3, Air Force Tactics, Techniques, and Procedures (Interim) 3-2.58, Multi-Service Tactics, Techniques, and Procedures for Tactical Convoy Operations.

(c) **Protecting the LOCs.** The JFC is responsible for LOC security. It may be necessary to commit combat capabilities to secure LOCs to ensure that the incremental build of combat power is not interrupted. In addition, alternatives such as rerouting or mode substitution may be required (i.e., air and sea LOCs to replace or supplement ground LOCs) if preventive and preemptive measures fall short.

(6) **HNS resources and facilities** are important to the successful employment, deployment, and redeployment of forces. HNs can often provide a variety of services through their national agencies and can support onward movement in a wide range of categories. Some of these categories are shown in Figure VI-11.

(7) **Acquisition and Cross-Servicing Agreements. ACSAs** provide US pre-negotiated support for contingency operation potential war scenarios. ACSAs provide the legal authority for the US military and armed forces of other nations to exchange logistic goods and services. Transactions under this program must be reimbursed, replaced in kind, or exchanged for equal value, which may not always be the case with HNS agreements.

(8) **Contract Support.** Contractor support for onward movement is another force multiplier which should be planned and coordinated in advance of an actual deployment. There are several benefits in relying on commercial industry to provide equipment and manpower to move unit equipment. The redeploying unit does not have to convoy its equipment from the POD to its TAA/forward operating base, nor does it need to provide a PSA. In addition, the theater requires fewer transportation units as transportation assets are provided by the commercial carrier. This is a valuable service in cases where US forces are unavailable or may not be allowed entry into a country where US cargo must transit. An example of this is the Afghanistan ground LOC operations.

Host-Nation Support to Onward Movement

- Combat service support (food, water, lighting, billeting, showers, and latrines)
- Security
- Communications
- Materials and cargo handling
- Ground transportation (buses, line haul, and heavy lift)
- Convoy, road, rail, and diplomatic clearances

Figure VI-11. Host-Nation Support to Onward Movement

> *"When the enemy assesses our forces, he values only those forces which the logistics community has ready for combat, or can get ready in time, and then sustain for a requisite period of time."*
>
> **General Felix M. Rogers, US Air Force**
> **In *Military Air Power, The CADRE Digest of Air Power Opinions and Thoughts,* 1990**

7. Integration

a. **General.** This section describes the integration process and key integration activities to successfully unite deploying forces into the theater command structure or return them to their home or demobilization station.

b. During deployment or redeployment to a new OA, integration is the synchronized transfer of mission-ready forces and capabilities into the CCDR's force and based on the complexity of the operation, may take hours or days to complete. The complexity and time required for integration depends on the size, contingency conditions, coordination and planning, C2 communications, and security available to manage the deploying or redeploying force. Integration is complete when the receiving commander establishes C2 over the arriving unit and the unit is capable of performing its assigned mission. Force tracking culminates in force closure as reported by the commander of the unit. In deployment operations, force closure occurs when the supported commander determines that the deploying force has completed movement to the specified OA/destination with sufficient resources and is ready to conduct its assigned mission. In redeployment operations, force closure occurs when the designated commander or Service determines that the redeploying force has returned to home station or other follow-on destination. The designated commander or Service will report force closure during redeployment to home/demobilization station or other follow-on destination based on Service guidelines.

ARAB-ISRAELI WAR

During the 1973 Arab-Israeli War, an Israeli commando team of 12 men and a jeep-mounted recoilless (RCL) rifle were inserted at 2400 hours along the Baghdad-Damascus Highway about 100 km north of Damascus, near a bridge crossing a deep ravine. The bridge was rigged for demolition, ambush positions were laid out covering the bridge approaches, with hasty minefields covering the ambush positions. At dawn, an Iraqi tank brigade, moving on transporters, began crossing the bridge. After several vehicles had crossed, the bridge was destroyed, and the exits from the bridge approaches interdicted by the RCL, thus isolating the convoy on the road. The immobilized vehicles were then destroyed by aircraft on-call, and by commandos using satchel charges. In this manner, approximately 50 Iraqi tanks were destroyed, and the road remained closed for several days (during a critical part of the war), due to fear of additional ambushes.

SOURCE: 1973 War Lessons Learned

(1) During execution, the deploying force commander reports that the levels of readiness prescribed by the supported CCDR have been achieved and that integration into the higher HQ is imminent. The supported CCDR is concerned with the following:

(a) Location of the forces.

(b) Capability of the forces.

(c) Projected and actual arrival time at destination.

(d) Commander's capability to affect the movement.

(e) Additional transportation needed (modes, quantities).

(2) By definition, integration is the final element of JRSOI and is normally accomplished concurrently with other deployment and JRSOI tasks. It can occur anywhere along the JRSOI continuum and is normally the last JRSOI segment to be completed. During deployment or redeployment to a new OA, integration has two major prerequisites: the unit must be mission-capable and must be integrated into the C2 processes of its higher HQ. To achieve these requirements, deploying forces must be organized back into operational units, integrate their C2 systems and combat support systems with the supported command, conduct any final requisite training or mission rehearsals, confirm their mission readiness, and finally report force closure.

(3) Tracking the components of building mission capability as a precursor to integration is essential for overall mission success. In order to track mission capabilities, the components of mission capabilities must be known.

c. Monitoring mission capability, early and continuous coordination, and planning can help reduce integration time. Units can establish predeployment liaisons to exchange information, standard operating procedures (SOPs), and communication networks, as well as plan for and prioritize an in-theater incremental buildup of combat power. Once established, the liaison is maintained to update information (intelligence, situation, mission, deployment timeline) to expedite the in-theater integration.

d. **Integration Functions.** Unlike the functions described in reception, staging, and onward movement, the emphasis during integration is on C2 and communications of personnel, equipment, and materiel as they enter the theater and prepare for integration. Critical to this is the COP as described in Appendix A, "Enabler Tools." Force tracking of mission capability components helps predict when integration can begin and how long it will take to complete. Protection is still critical but may be easier as security forces reestablish their military capability during staging and onward movement. However, to accomplish integration of the force, the logistic support should be transferred from JRSOI supporting organizations to the gaining command.

(1) Upon notification of deployment or redeployment, a liaison between the deploying/redeploying unit and receiving HQ should be established to enhance integration. This liaison is conducted through formal liaison teams attached to the arriving and receiving

HQ (the preferred method) or remotely through communication channels. The size and makeup of the liaison teams are based on the mission and operational conditions.

(2) Effective liaison enhances the commander's confidence in planning, coordinating, and executing integration. Subordinate commanders may use an LNO to obtain necessary information such as common coordination measures; tactics, techniques, and procedures; SOPs; rules of engagement; terms; symbology; and exercises.

APPENDIX A
ENABLER TOOLS

Within Figure A-1, the following is provided for the column headings:

Tool: Automated system title

Joint Personnel Accountability Reconciliation and Reporting

Purpose: Short description of what the system does

Provides reconciliation and reporting of personnel from multiple DOD sources.

Features: Unique capability of the system

Defense Manpower Data Center quality controls and consolidates daily feeds from several personnel tracking systems: Army-Deployed Theater Accountability System, Marine Corps-Secure Personnel Accountability, Air Force-DCAPES, CPMS-Defense Civilian Personnel Data System, Contractors-Synchronized Predeployment and Operational Tracker.

Users: At what level is the system used

Service components, JTFs, CCDRs, Joint Staff, intermediate HQ.

Enabler Tools			
Tool	**Purpose**	**Features**	**Users**
Analysis and Mobility Platform Proponent – USTRANSCOM Training – USTRANSCOM	Provides end-to-end modeling and simulation.	Federation of models linked by a runtime infrastructure which allows the models to pass data.	USTRANSCOM planners.
BRACE Proponent – USTRANSCOM Training – USTRANSCOM	Model military air terminal operations.	Estimate throughput capacity, validate maximum on ground.	Airlift planners.
COMPASS Proponent – DISA Training – USFORSCOM	Provides strategic transportation data from units with the US Army commands.	Supports deployments, redeployments, mobilization planning, and execution of military operations.	US Army planners.
COP Proponent – DISA Training – JDTC	Provides a graphic disposition of friendly and enemy forces.	An application of GCCS-J. Graphic display of friendly, hostile, and neutral units, overlays, and tracks.	JTF, CCDR, intermediate headquarters planners.
ELIST Proponent – SDDC Training – USTRANSCOM	Planning and modeling system for deployment analysis.	Rapid planning and re-planning of intertheater transportation.	USTRANSCOM planners.
GCCS-J Proponent – JCS Training – JDTC	DOD system of record for strategic command and control functions. Provides procedures, outlines processes and suite of information system for planning, executing, and managing operations.	Provides guidance, procedures, and information systems architecture.	JTF, CCDR, JS, intermediate headquarters, Service Planners.

Enabler Tools			
Tool	**Purpose**	**Features**	**Users**
GCSS-J Proponent – DISA Training – DISA	Gateway to Web-based resources.	Uses a Web COP to display objects.	JTF, CCDR, intermediate headquarters planners, combat support agencies, and Service planners.
GDSS Proponent – AMC Training – USTRANSCOM	Command and control system for execution of strategic airlift and air refueling.	Track aircraft and aircrew movement.	Airlift planners.
IGC Proponent – USTRANSCOM Training – USTRANSCOM	Provides global transportation management and in-transient visibility.	Organize and display transportation asset information.	JTF, CCDR, intermediate headquarters planners.
I3 Proponent – JCS Training – JDTC	Improves situational awareness pictures of intelligence provided to joint force commanders. Standard set of integrated, linked tools and services.	An application of GCCS-J. Fuses data from multiple sensors and intelligence sources to enable situational awareness.	JTF, CCDR, intermediate headquarters planners.
ICODES Proponent – USTRANSCOM Training – DTF	Develop ship stow plans.	Generate ship manifests, produce customized reports.	JTF, CCDR, intermediate headquarters planners.
JCRM Proponent – JCS Training – JDTC	Enables the Global Force Management allocation process.	Facilitates documentation of emergent and rotational operational force requirements. Provides data for historical analysis.	JTF, CCDR, intermediate headquarters planners, and Service planners.
JET Proponent – JCS Training – JDTC	Create, add, modify, and generate deployment information.	An application of JOPES. Retrieve records using ULN data characteristics.	JTF, CCDR, intermediate headquarters planners.
JFAST Proponent – USTRANSCOM Training – USTRANSCOM and JDTC	Determines transportation requirements, performs course of action analysis, and performs delivery profiles by air, land, and sea.	Rapid planning and re-planning of intertheater ELIST transportation.	JTF, CCDR, intermediate headquarters planners.
JFRG II Proponent – USMC Training – USMC	Build force structure.	Modify and update reference data, interface with JOPES, TC-AIMS II and MDSS II.	JTF, CCDR, intermediate headquarters planners.
JOPES Permissions Manager Proponent – JCS Training – JDTC	Allows the JOPES functional manager to create accounts and assign roles.	An application of JOPES. JOPES functional managers grant permissions, restrict access to operation plans on the database, and perform periodic reviews of user IDs and the content of the JOPES database to ensure outdated plans and accounts are removed when no longer required.	JTF, CCDR, intermediate headquarters planners.
PORTSIM Proponent – SDDC Training – US Air Force	Determine seaport reception, staging, reception, staging, clearance, and throughput capabilities.	Identifies infrastructure constraints, interfaces with ICODES and ELIST.	JTF, CCDR, intermediate headquarters planners.

Enabler Tools			
Tool	**Purpose**	**Features**	**Users**
RAS IT Proponent – JCS Training – JDTC	Input and analysis of Global Status of Resources and Training System data.	An application of SORTS. Provides data input areas for personnel, training, equipment on-hand, and equipment condition.	JTF, CCDR, intermediate headquarters planners.
RAS JT Proponent – JCS Training – JDTC	Provides one stop location for viewing and editing reporting data.	An application of SORTS. Provides unit identification and registration, location, and overall information on personnel, equipment, and training.	JTF, CCDR, intermediate headquarters planners.
RAS OT Proponent – JCS Training – JDTC	Retrieval and analysis of Global Status of Resources and Training System data.	An application of SORTS. Provide personnel and equipment readiness information.	JTF, CCDR, intermediate headquarters planners.
RQT Proponent – JCS Training – JDTC	Develop user defined formatted reports.	An application of JOPES. Ability to save reports as data files and emailing those files.	JTF, CCDR, intermediate headquarters planners.
SMS Proponent – USTRANSCOM Training – USTRANSCOM	Provides visibility of common-user air, sea, and land transportation assets.	Collect aircraft, ship, and ground transportation movement data from other systems.	JTF, CCDR, intermediate headquarters planners.
TMT Proponent – JCS Training – JDTC	Supports management of multiple TPFDDs.	An application of JOPES. Provides ability to create, copy, manage, and delete TPFDDs.	JTF, CCDR, intermediate headquarters planners.
TRAC2ES Proponent – USTRANSCOM Training – USTRANSCOM	Decision support tool for command and control in the movement of patients.	Provides visibility of in-theater patients requiring evacuation, available transportation assets, available hospital bed and in-transient visibility.	JTF, CCDR, intermediate headquarters medical planners. Service medical planners.
Transportation Visualizer Proponent – USTRANSCOM Training – USTRANSCOM	Transportation requirements and plan analysis tool.	Provides user full access to real-time JOPES data and provides a clear visual environment.	
Turbo Planner Proponent – JCS Training – JDTC	Reduce administrative time in developing, reviewing and adjudicating adaptive plans for the JOPES.	An application of JOPES. Allows the planner to focus on content instead of format by providing a template and automatically assembling all the elements of a plan for printing.	JTF, CCDR, intermediate headquarters planners.
Web SM Proponent – JCS Training – JDTC	Supports management of transportation carrier assets.	An application of JOPES. Provides the ability to add, review, update, and delete carrier information.	JTF, CCDR, intermediate headquarters planners.

Legend	
AMC	Air Mobility Command
BRACE	Base Resource and Capability Estimator
CCDR	combatant commander
COMPASS	Computerized Movement Planning and Status System
COP	common operational picture
DISA	Defense Information Systems Agency
DOD	Department of Defense
DTF	United States Army Training and Doctrine Command Deployment Training Facility
ELIST	enhanced logistics intratheater support tool
GCCS-J	Global Command and Control System - Joint
GCSS-J	Global Combat Support System - Joint
GDSS	Global Decision Support System
I3	Integrated Imagery and Intelligence
ICODES	integrated computerized deployment system

ID	identification
IGC	Integrated Data Environment (IDE)/Global Transportation Network (GTN) Convergence
JCRM	Joint Capabilities Requirements Manager
JCS	Joint Chiefs of Staff
JDTC	Joint Deployment Training Center
JET	Joint Operation Planning and Execution System editing tool
JFAST	Joint Flow and Analysis System for Transportation
JFRG II	Joint Force Requirements Generator II
JTF	joint task force
JOPES	Joint Operation Planning and Execution System
JS	the Joint Staff
MDSS II	Marine air-ground task force (MAGTF) Deployment Support System II
PORTSIM	port simulation model
RAS IT	readiness assessment system input tool
RAS JT	readiness assessment tool joint tool
RAS OT	readiness assessment system output tool
RQT	rapid query tool
SDDC	Surface Deployment and Distribution Command
SM	scheduling and movement
SMS	single mobility system
SORTS	Status of Resources and Training System
TC-AIMS II	Transportation Coordinator's Automated Information for Movement System II
TMT	time-phased force and deployment data management tool
TPFDD	time-phased force and deployment data
TRAC2ES	United States Transportation Command Regulating and Command and Control Evacuation System
ULN	unit line number
USMC	United States Marine Corps
USFORSCOM	United States Army Forces Command
USTRANSCOM	United States Transportation Command

Figure A-1. Enabler Tools

1. General

Commanders and staffs at the JTF level and above must have the capability to successfully conduct deployment operations; i.e., to plan, execute, and monitor each deployment. The CCDR uses a variety of enablers including processes, systems, and equipment to manage movement flow, obtain AV, and achieve balance and synchronization (see Figure A-1). Deployment enablers provide that capability in the form of processes, systems, and equipment, providing commanders with the flexibility in adapting to changing situations. **Enablers are processes, systems, and equipment that facilitate accomplishment of the assigned mission.** Rapid force projection operations require enablers that improve deployment and redeployment planning and execution, thereby improving overall mission response time, and also possess the necessary flexibility to adapt to changing situations. Deployment and redeployment enablers required to support joint force operations include interoperable joint and Service systems and procedures, robust supporting facilities and infrastructure, and agile information management and communications systems. This appendix describes select enabling tools that allow the commander to:

a. Conduct situational awareness and maintain accurate deployment and redeployment information during the execution phase. (Situational Awareness)

b. Conduct planning. (Planning)

c. Conduct execution and provide C2 over deploying and redeploying forces. (Execution)

2. Automated Information Systems

The goals of AISs are to provide the CCDR with increased situational awareness. Automated C2 systems are used to exchange information among the CCDRs, national partners, the Service HQ, and Service and functional component commands. The exchange, processing, and analysis of data and information are continuous throughout mission execution. Necessarily the systems must be interoperable. **Interoperability is the condition achieved when information or services can be exchanged directly and satisfactorily between user systems and equipment.** It is a function of commonality, compatibility, and standardization of equipment and systems and standardization of procedures.

See JP 6-0, Joint Communications System, *for additional information on interoperability.*

3. Adaptive Planning and Execution

Joint operation planning occurs within APEX which is the DOD level system of joint policies, processes, procedures, and reporting structures, supported by communications and information technology that is used by the JPEC to monitor, plan, and execute mobilization, deployment, employment, sustainment, redeployment, and demobilization activities associated with joint operations.

For additional details on APEX, see JP 5-0, Joint Operation Planning, *or CJCS Guide 3130,* Adaptive Planning and Execution (APEX) Overview and Policy Framework.

4. The Global Command and Control System - Joint

a. GCCS-J is the DOD's computerized system of record for strategic C2 functions. GCCS-J enables warfighters to plan, execute, and manage military operations. The system helps JFCs synchronize the actions of air, land, maritime, space, and SOF. It has the flexibility to be used in a wide range of operations ranging from actual combat to humanitarian assistance. GCCS-J provides CCDRs a complete picture of the OE and the ability to order, respond, and coordinate communications system information. GCCS-J is a comprehensive automated communications system designed to improve the JFC's ability to manage and execute joint operations. GCCS-J interoperates with Service and agency communications systems, providing a global network of military and commercial communications systems that the JFC uses to send and obtain critical information. GCCS-J supports the exchange of information from the President/SecDef to CCDRs and their components. GCCS-J incorporates procedures, reporting structures, AIS, and communications connectivity to provide the information necessary to effectively plan, deploy, sustain, employ, and redeploy forces.

b. The three GCCS-J baselines are described below:

(1) Global - The GCCS-J global release focuses on applications that are fielded in CCMD local environments, such as the COP, and integrated imagery and intelligence; in addition, the GCCS-J global release provides enhanced functional capabilities in such areas as the theater ballistic missile defense as well as increased horizontal integration and access of intelligence capabilities with the Modernized Integrated Database. Specific global applications include:

(a) **Common Operational Picture.** COP provides a graphical display of friendly, hostile, and neutral units, assets, overlays, and/or tracks pertinent to operations, and is a key tool for commanders in planning and conducting joint operations. The GCCS-J COP may include relevant information from the tactical to the strategic level of command. COP provides commanders an understanding of the disposition of friendly and enemy forces. It is a tool to help predict force movement in combat. The purpose of COP is to provide common data and associated information to the appropriate levels of command. This includes every level, up to and including the National Security Council. The GCC has control of the data and information overlays within the GCC's AOR.

(b) **Global Command and Control System - Integrated Imagery and Intelligence** improves rapid development of situational awareness pictures of intelligence provided to joint forces commanders. This system offers users a standard set of integrated, linked tools and services which give immediate access to imagery and intelligence directly from a COP.

(2) JOPES is an integrated joint C2 system used to support military operation monitoring, planning, and execution activities procedures for JOPES, and automated data processing systems are the mechanisms for submitting movement requirements to USTRANSCOM for joint operations and exercises. Specific JOPES applications include:

(a) **JOPES Editing Tool.** The JOPES editing tool provides the capability to create, add, modify, delete, and generate deployment-related information contained in a TPFDD. It offers the ability to retrieve records using any characteristics that exist in the ULN details. It does not provide the ability to view non-TPFDD DTS movements. The JOPES editing tool can perform TPFDD editing on multiple ULNs based on information retrieved.

(b) **Rapid Query Tool (RQT).** The RQT provides a powerful, relatively quick, read-only capability to develop many user-defined formatted and tabular reports that focus directly on TPFDD related issues. It cannot track any non-TPFDD movements in the DTS. The RQT offers the ability to save the full report and its format as a data file, retrieving it in another application or e-mailing it to any SECRET Internet Protocol Router Network (SIPRNET) recipient as a Word document, Excel spreadsheet, or ASCII file.

(c) **TPFDD Management Tool (TMT).** TMT allows JOPES functional managers the ability create, manage, and delete TPFDDs within their assigned series. The tool also provides copy file, download, and upload utilities to allow requirements to be transferred between various TPFDDs or from external systems.

(d) **JOPES Permissions Manager.** The JOPES Permissions Manager allows the JOPES functional manager the ability to create user accounts and assign roles for JOPES applications as well as permissions for various TPFDDS either individually or by series.

(e) **Web Scheduling and Movement.** Web SM provides the capability to add, review, update, and delete carrier information. Carriers may be created and linked to TPFDDs complete with itinerary information. Itinerary information includes planned and reported arrival and departure times at itinerary routing locations. Additionally, TPFDD requirements may be allocated and manifested on carriers and linked with specific carrier onload and off-load locations. Obsolete information may also be deleted.

(3) **Status of Resources and Training System (SORTS).** SORTS is an integrated, automated reporting and assessment toolset providing vital readiness information needed to make timely resource allocation and force commitment recommendations to decision makers. Specific SORTS applications include:

(a) **Readiness Assessment System - Output Tool.** The Readiness Assessment System - Output Tool is a SIPRNET application providing query-based access to readiness data. It provides decision type information on the status-of-force readiness. The query functionality supports retrieval, analysis, and export of current or historical information on the total force, status of each Service in the areas of personnel, equipment readiness and condition, and select JOPES data. It also provides the means to generate reports in four views: summary, graphic, tabular, and pipes.

(b) **Readiness Assessment System - Input Tool.** The Readiness Assessment System - Input Tool is a SIPRNET application providing four measured areas for data input consisting of personnel, training, equipment on-hand, and equipment condition. It provides three basic functions to units: unit identification registration, viewing and updating unit database information, and enter unit readiness data into the SORTS database.

(c) **Readiness Assessment System - Joint Tool.** The Readiness Assessment System - Joint Tool is a SIPRNET application providing both view and editing for unit registration and unit reporting data for all Service and reporting entities to include joint entities. The tool provides for unit identification and registration, organizational location, reporting structure information, and overall information on personnel, equipment supply and condition and training.

5. Global Combat Support System - Joint

GCSS-J is the system of record for the joint logistics warfighter as identified in JP 4-0, *Joint Logistics*. GCSS-J currently includes a portal and Web-based applications that deliver enhanced visibility to the joint logistician (e.g., essential capabilities, functions, activities, and tasks necessary to sustain all elements of operating forces in theater at all levels), and facilitates information interoperability across and between combat support and C2 functions. In conjunction with other DOD information network elements and CCMDs'/Services'/agencies' information architectures, GCSS-J will continue to provide capabilities required to move and sustain joint forces throughout the spectrum of military operations (e.g., maps, reports, and watchboards).

6. Other Joint Applications

a. **Global Force Management**

(1) **Joint Capability Requirements Manager.** JCRM is a secure tool that enables the GFM allocation process. CCDRs can electronically document emergent and rotational operational force requirements and forward them to the Joint Staff for validation, prioritizing, and assignment to a JFP. The tool also enables the JFPs and their assigned Service components to provide sourcing recommendations and generate the GFMAP annexes for SecDef approval. During execution, the tool enables the JOPES TPFDD to be compared to the GFMAP annexes to validate execution in JOPES as per SecDef order. JCRM enables CCDRs to generate DEPORDs based on the GFMAP annexes. The tool provides CCMD planners the ability to generate, store, and share force requirements in support of plans, as operational capability packages (OCPs), based on force structure from authoritative databases. These OCPs can be rapidly transitioned to operational force requirements as well as populate a JOPES TPFDD if the plan were to be executed. JCRM also allows a TPFDD or OCPs to be contingency sourced and the sourcing provided back to JOPES. JCRM provides a capability to output desired current and historical data for follow-on analysis.

(2) **GFM Logbook.** GFM Logbook is the collaborative staffing application used by the JFPs staff actions associated with determining the sourcing solutions for emergent and rotational operational force requirements from JCRM.

b. **Joint Transportation Support and Analysis**

(1) **Global Decision Support System.** GDSS is the worldwide C2 system for execution of airlift and air refueling. GDSS contains essential information used to monitor and manage all in-progress DOD air mobility missions throughout the world, including all active duty, Air Force Reserve, Air National Guard, and contracted commercial airline aircraft on AMC airlift missions, plus all operational DOD air-refueling missions. GDSS has automated tools to track aircraft and aircrew movement and aid the decision-making process. In addition, GDSS provides the control center with C2 information from the AMC Deployment Analysis System and Command and Control Information Processing System, the wing-level C2 planning and execution system.

(2) IGC establishes common integrated data services providing CCMDs, Services, DOD, and other USG departments and agencies a cohesive solution for the management of supply, distribution, and logistics information with a global perspective. IGC integrates information from a variety of DTS AISs to provide consolidated ITV and C2 data support. IGC feeds shipment status to Service and agency systems and provides joint force movement tracking and closure. IGC integrates automated data processing and information systems, electronic commerce, and electronic data interchange to track the identity, status, and location of DOD unit and non-unit cargo, PAX, patients, forces, and military and

commercial air mobility, sealift, and surface assets from origin to destination across the range of military operations.

The classified IGC home page is located on the SIPRNET at https://www.igc.ustranscom.smil.mil/igc. The unclassified IGC home page is located at http://www.dla.mil/InformationOperations/Pages/IGC.as.px.

(3) **Single Mobility System.** SMS is a Web-based application, both SIPRNET and Non-Secure Internet Protocol Router Network that provides visibility of common-user air, sea, and land transportation assets and provides aggregated reporting of cargo and passenger movements. SMS collects plane, ship, and truck movement data from other computer systems such as IGC, Consolidated Air Mobility Planning System, and GDSS. SMS provides requirements planners and unit schedulers visibility of planned and scheduled air missions, MSC ship schedules, commercial liner service, seaport reference data, and movement of US security risk category cargo. There are three phases in SMS: air mobility, sea mobility, and land mobility.

(a) **Air Mobility.** The air mobility phase of SMS is a Web-based tool that provides visibility of scheduled air mobility missions and requirements early in the planning process. All command levels of all DOD units, wings, and HQ can use SMS as a tool to display missions.

(b) **Sea Mobility.** The sea mobility phase provides visibility over sealift requirements through SDDC's Integrated Booking System and GATES, and MSC's Integrated Command, Control, and Communications reporting system. SMS also offers a sealift assets database, a voyage finder, port locator, and a shipping cost calculator.

(c) **Land Mobility.** The land mobility phase provides visibility over hazardous materials (HAZMAT). The arms, ammunition, and explosives (AA&E) movement link in SMS allows access to the database that tracks and records positions for movement of high-risk cargo in the US, inclusive of AA&E.

(4) **Joint Flow and Analysis System for Transportation.** JFAST is an analytical tool for making detailed estimates of resources required to transport military forces (including cargo, personnel, and sustainment). JFAST is used by the CCMDs as a planning and forecasting tool for deployment planning. The system determines the transportation feasibility of the TPFDD (from origin through arrival at the POD) and generates summary data via charts, tables, maps, and other visual aids. JFAST determines closure dates, congestion points, lift utilization, and shortfalls. JFAST products include delivery profiles and lateness analysis, required lift by day versus lift available, and port workload by level of activity based on capacity. JFAST has five major capabilities: TPFDD analysis, air/land/sea movement simulation and analysis, sustainment calculation, TPFDD construction from scratch, and several useful utilities. The JFAST model contains separate air, land, and sea schedulers and operates in either a stand-alone or networked environment.

(a) **TPFDD Analysis.** TPFDD analysis is used to review a TPFDD to determine which records qualified for analysis, analyze records that did not qualify, and identify requirements that missed the LAD.

(b) **Notional Requirements Generator.** The Notional Requirements Generator provides the capability to create notional movement requirements when no plan currently exists. Force selection and CONOPS can be recorded along with expected levels of activity, climate, and days of supply. This capability allows a planner to execute ad hoc queries and perform "what if" analysis.

(c) **Transportation Analysis.** The transportation analysis function includes model setup, execution, and output analysis for land, air, and sea modes of military transportation.

(5) **Enhanced Logistics Intratheater Support Tool.** ELIST is a feasibility planning and modeling system for deployment analysis. ELIST performs detailed intratheater deployment studies to analyze effects of force modernization and new force structures and changes to DTS and to check transportation feasibility of contingency operations. ELIST enables planners to explore and model the impact of theater infrastructure limitations (through combat loss, weather, or limited HN access) and make adjustments to infrastructure and assets at any point in time in the flow. Through ELIST, planners have the ability to accurately define the infrastructure and consider the throughput capability available for a specific plan.

(6) **Transportation Visualizer** is a transportation requirements and plan analysis tool. It can give users full access to real-time JOPES data and provide a clear visual environment to explore. It is a client/server based software application that provides transportation requirements in a graphical depiction of the JOPES TPFDD data. It allows the transportation analyst to identify and address potential movement issues and enhances the validation and scheduling process by allowing sharing and manipulation of TPFDD data to aid in movement issue resolution and analysis.

(7) **Port Simulation Model (PORTSIM).** PORTSIM is a time-stepped, discrete event simulation of SPOE and SPOD during a force deployment. PORTSIM provides scenario-specific, force clearance profiles and reports on the use of port assets. PORTSIM can determine a port's reception, staging, clearance, and throughput capabilities. The model identifies systems or infrastructure constraints and provides port-specific, time-phased force clearance profiles. PORTSIM interfaces with the integrated computerized deployment system (ICODES), calculates the impact of JLOTS, incorporates two- and three-dimensional visualization for training, and interfaces with ELIST to facilitate theater analysis.

(8) **Integrated Computerized Deployment System.** ICODES is a decision support system for developing ship stow plans. It assists in developing stow plans by matching vessel characteristics against cargo being offered for shipment. ICODES develops stow plans for up to four specific ships concurrently and checks for access and hazard violations. ICODES can automatically attempt to maintain unit integrity in stow plans it develops. Once stow plans are completed, ICODES automatically generates ship manifests

and templates cargo items onto ship drawings. ICODES can produce customized reports which detail both the process of constructing stow plans and results of the process, and builds a database that provides details on the availability of external ship ramps and the facilities for ports around the world.

(9) **Base Resource and Capability Estimator (BRACE).** BRACE is the planning tool to model military air terminal operations. BRACE simulates airfield onloading, off-loading, en route, and recovery base operations, including ground activities such as cargo handling, refueling, maintenance, and aircraft parking. The model can be used to: estimate airfield throughput capability; estimate air, ground, and other resources required to support a given level of throughput at an airfield; and validate MOG values used in existing air transportation models such as JFAST.

(10) **USTRANSCOM Regulating and Command and Control Evacuation System.** TRAC2ES is an automated decision support tool that functions as a single C2 system that can be used in peacetime and contingencies. It provides visibility of in-theater patients requiring evacuation, available transportation assets, available hospital beds (by medical specialty), and patient ITV. TRAC2ES accommodates three modes of operation: deliberate planning, forecasting, and reactive planning at both the intertheater and intratheater level.

(11) **Analysis of Mobility Platform.** The Analysis of Mobility Platform is an end-to-end modeling and simulation environment that supports programmatic analysis, planning, execution analysis, and peacetime operations. It is a federation of models linked by a runtime infrastructure which allows the models to pass data to one another in parallel during model execution. The Analysis of Mobility Platform has two port analysis tools:

(a) **Airport Simulation Tool.** The Airport Simulation Tool provides a graphical depiction of the process and capabilities for cargo and passenger handling to include flight line activities; aircraft parking; cargo yard; MHE; fuel reception, storage and delivery; and reception and onward movement.

(b) **Seaport Simulation Tool.** The Seaport Simulation Tool provides a graphical depiction of the process and capabilities for cargo and passenger handling at a single seaport to include dock activities; ship berths and unloading; cargo processing and handling; MHE (including crane usage and types); onward movement of cargo (railheads and gateways).

(12) **Joint Force Projection.** Joint force projection retrieves and presents essential force projection information to support decisions of the JPEC throughout the force projection process. Joint force projection provides read/view access to multiple systems enabling the end user to quickly grasp the status of requirements, deployment, TPFDD status, and reception, staging, onward movement and integration without having to log on to each system individually.

c. **Service Systems Supporting JOPES**

(1) **Transportation Coordinator's Automated Information for Movement System II (TC-AIMS II).** TC-AIMS II provides detailed equipment sourcing to Computerized Movement Planning and Status System (COMPASS) for US Army units. TC-AIMS II passes UDL and roster data back to COMPASS. The data is then rolled up to a level four TPFDD ULNs in COMPASS and exported back to JOPES.

(2) **Joint Force Requirements Generator II (JFRG II).** JFRG II is an automated, personal computer-based planning tool designed to support deliberate and crisis action plans. It supports tactical and administrative planning by providing the following capabilities: rapid force list creation, lift analysis, and interface capabilities with JOPES, TC AIMS II, and MAGTF Deployment Support System II (MDSS II), logistics factors file, and war reserve and the JFRG II reference files. JFRG II operates in a stand-alone configuration on standard IBM-compatible microcomputer hardware. JFRG II passes unclassified force deployment requirements to TC-AIMS II and MDSS II for detailed sourcing. TC-AIMS II and MDSS II pass UDL and roster data back to COMPASS. The data is then rolled up to a level four TPFDDs/ULNs in COMPASS and exported back to JOPES.

(3) **Computerized Movement Planning and Status System.** COMPASS provides strategic transportation data from units within Army commands to DOD, Joint Staff, and DA planners. COMPASS also provides the Joint Staff with cargo data from notional units. COMPASS is designed to support deployments, redeployments, mobilization planning, and execution of military operations. COMPASS extracts data from unit movement data contained within COMPASS to update OPLANs with nonstandard level four cargo data.

(4) **Deliberate and Crisis Action Planning and Execution Segments.** DCAPES supports the deliberate planning and CAP and execution functions for the mobilization, deployment, employment, sustainment, redeployment, and demobilization of Air Force forces. Global Command and Control System-Air Force DCAPES provides four strategic server enclaves. Throughout the entire planning and execution process, DCAPES provides users the capability to create and maintain unit type codes to support the build of TPFDD for resource movement. DCAPES also produces standard and ad hoc reports and processes feedback reports. DCAPES is built on the JOPES foundation and extends the JOPES functionality to support USAF lower-level detail planning and execution capabilities.

(5) **MAGTF Deployment Support System II.** MDSS II is a stand-alone system used by Marine Corps operating forces to support force deployment planning and execution. It is the database and interface hub for unit deployment. Through the use of extensive reference files, the system provides actual data to JFRG II to create an executable TPFDD. It reads/writes standard military shipping labels and active RFID tags. It collects and formats data for transmission to the ITV server and exchanges information with Marine Corps, other Service and joint logistics, movement, and distribution systems.

APPENDIX B
JOINT FORCE DEPLOYMENT AND JOINT RECEPTION, STAGING, ONWARD MOVEMENT, AND INTEGRATION AND JOINT FORCE REDEPLOYMENT PROCESS MAPS DESCRIPTIONS

Intentionally Blank

ANNEX A TO APPENDIX B
JOINT FORCE DEPLOYMENT PROCESS MAP DESCRIPTION

1. Conduct Force and Support Planning

Military operations begin with an event that requires movement of forces to somewhere in the world. This can be a planned or no-notice movement. The process begins with development of COAs, includes selection of the desired COA, and ends with the development of orders and their transmission.

a. **Receive Warning Order (WARNORD) and Establish Command Relationships.** Formal notification is received which directs deployment planning and preparation. Units receive notification of impending operations via a WARNORD that describes the situation, allocates forces and resources, establishes command relationships, provides other initial planning guidance, and initiates subordinate unit mission planning. Command relationships are also determined. The Joint Staff confirms supported CCDR, supporting CCDR, and agency relationships by message for a given operation.

b. **Receive TPFDD Guidance.** The supported CCDR publishes AOR specific or mission specific TPFDD LOI as necessary to plan and execute a TPFDD for the operations within the AOR or for a specific mission. Supported CCDR will publish supporting information via a TPFDD LOI or newsgroup messages that provide specific theater/operationally focused information to those in support. This information will provide additional detail including ULN, force module numbering conventions, refined TPFDD guidance, and other specific directions to forces deploying or redeploying.

c. **Develop Deployment/Redeployment Concept.** Supported CCDRs develop a deployment concept and identify specific predeployment standards necessary to meet mission requirements. The Services and supporting CCDRs ensure that predeployment standards specified are achieved and forces and supporting personnel arrive in the supported theater fully prepared to perform their mission. Supported CCDRs also develop a redeployment CONOPS to identify how forces and materiel will either redeploy to home station, to mobilization station, or to support another JFC's operation. The redeployment CONOPS is especially important when force rotations are envisioned for a long-term operation. In addition, planners should consider what WRM, pre-positioned, and/or TPE or supplies may be available or required for forces deploying or redeploying into the OA.

d. **Conduct Deployment Analysis.** Installation planners determine based on early information acquired, potential scenarios, mission requirements, and COAs. From those assessments, installation planners access and determine what local procedures and equipment may be required to prepare forces to deploy.

e. **Assess Operational Environment: Supporting Infrastructure.** Deployment installations assess the projected operational tempo, movement requirements, facilities, equipment, and deploying force support requirements to meet the timeline of the deployment or redeployment. In addition, deployed location requirements and capabilities will need to be evaluated to collect intelligence on theater terrain, weather, and infrastructure.

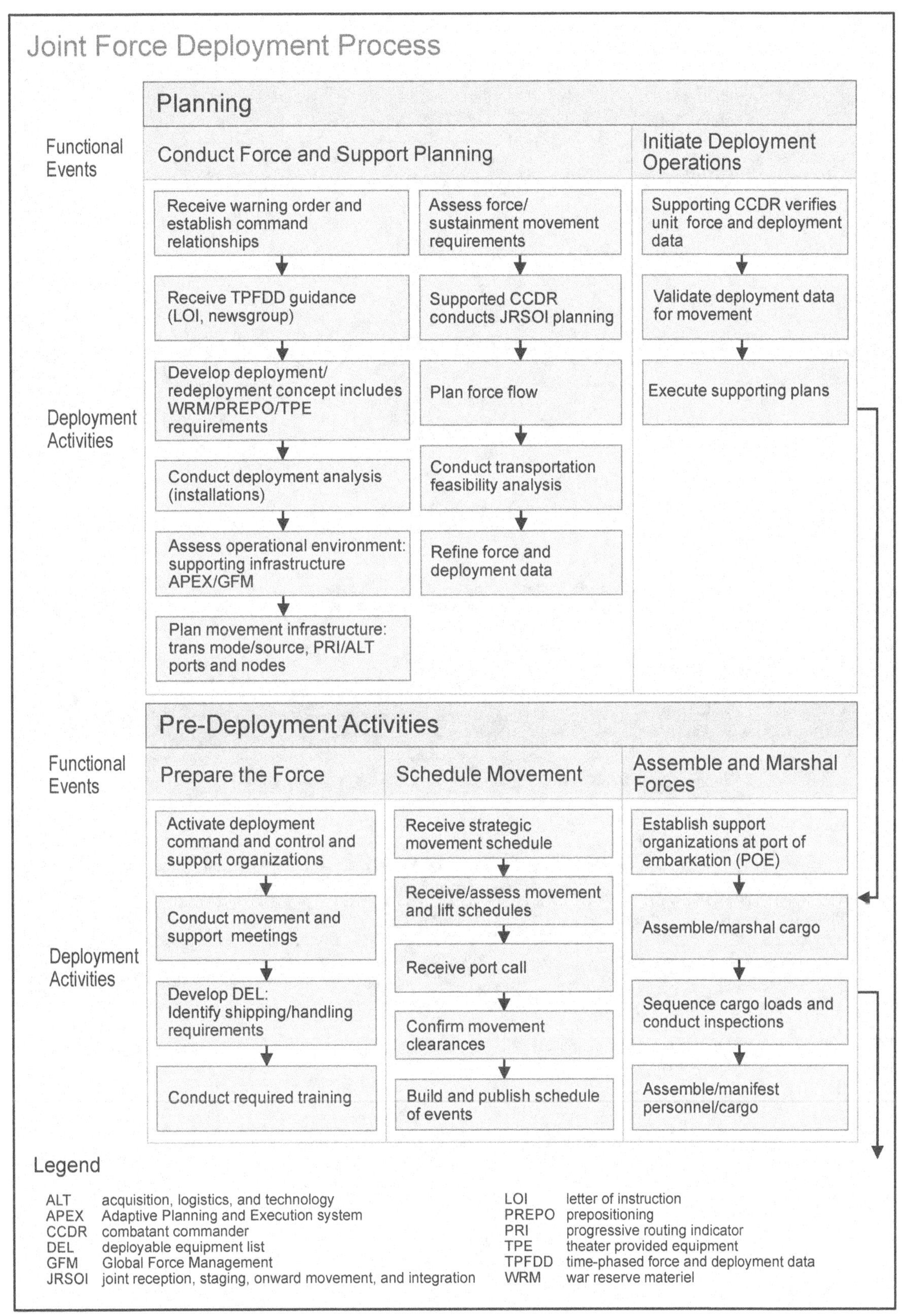

Figure B-A-1. Joint Force Deployment Process

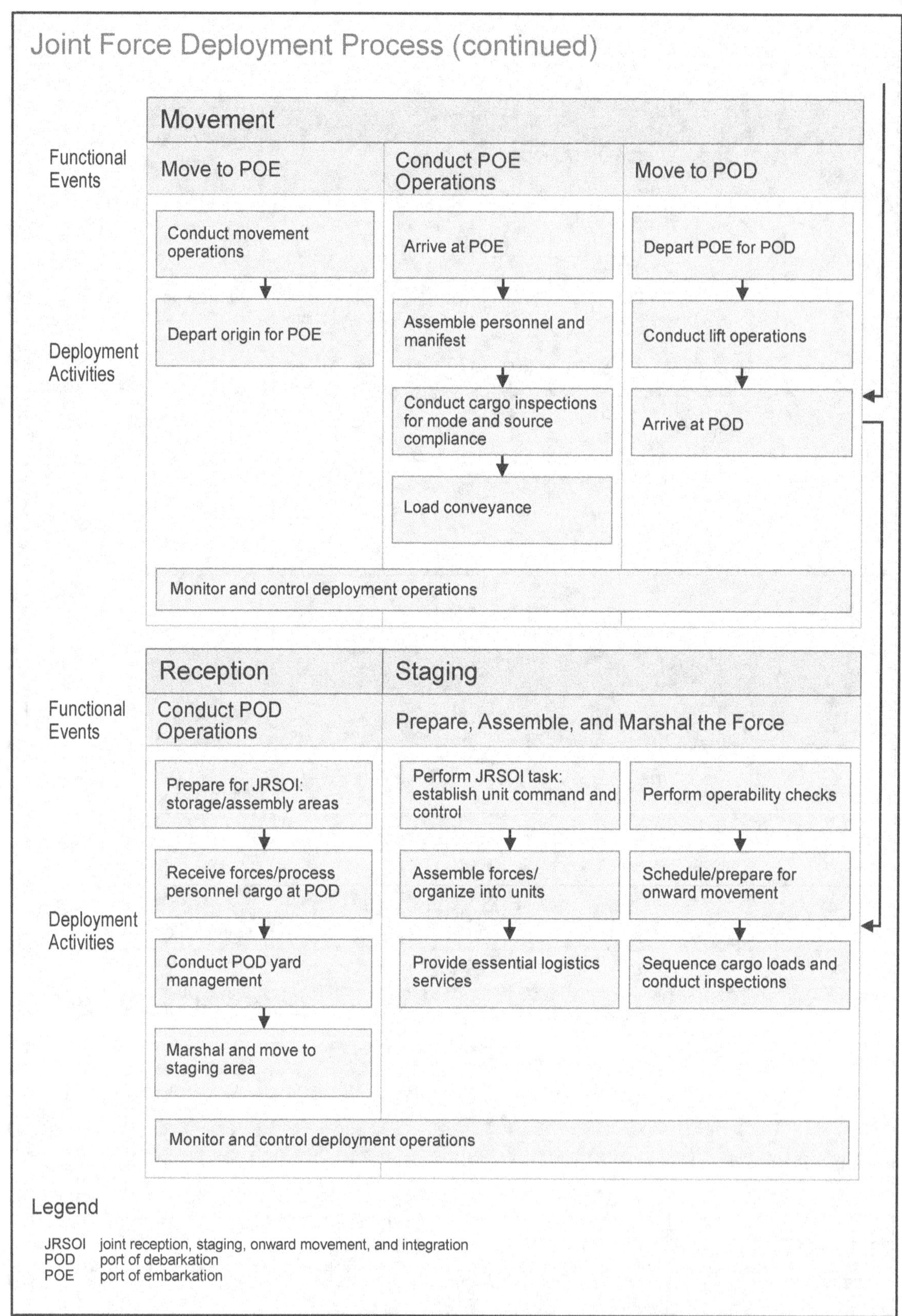

Figure B-A-1. Joint Force Deployment Process (continued)

f. **Plan Movement Infrastructure.** Supported commander plans transportation modes and sources, establishes primary and alternate nodes to include air and sea ports of debarkation, plans for port operations, and establishes MSRs. Additionally, supporting commanders and lift providers conduct similar planning in preparation for movement of forces by the mode and source requested and determine their special handling cargo requirements.

g. **Supported CCDR Conducts JRSOI Planning.** It is imperative early in the deployment process that the supported CCDR begins the planning to receive forces. Early planning will ensure there are appropriate reception forces, material, and equipment available to quickly and effectively process personnel and cargo through the APOD/SPOD and move them to the SA. In addition, the supported CCDR may designate a lead service to plan and execute the intratheater movement of forces, sustainment, and materiel from the APOD/SPODs to destination.

h. **Plan Force Flow.** JFPs and force providers source and task organize allocated force requirements filling JFC or supported component force requirements. JFCs or supported components prioritize force flow within the TPFDD based on operational needs and strategic lift limitations. Proper planning will permit the time needed to develop transportation COAs.

i. **Conduct Transportation Feasibility Analysis.** Based on the supported CCDR's RDD, the lift provider will determine if the supported CCDR's planned force flow requirements are transportation feasible given available strategic lift assets.

j. **Refine Force and Deployment Data.** Force providers tailor the deploying units' passenger and cargo information in the TPFDD and will ensure that units identify planned accompanying supplies.

2. Initiate Deployment Operations

Deployment operations will commence once TPFDD verification and validation is complete. Verification and validation procedures are used by CCMD components, supporting CCDRs, and providing organizations to confirm to the supported commander and USTRANSCOM that all information in TPFDD records are not only error-free for automation purposes, but also accurately reflect the current status, attributes, and availability of units and requirements. Unit readiness, movement dates, PAX, and cargo details should be confirmed with the unit before verification or validation occurs. Finally, supporting plans will be executed.

a. The supporting CCDR verifies unit force and deployment data.

b. The lift provider validates the deployment data for movement to meet the RDD.

c. Execute supporting plans.

3. Prepare the Force

Multiple actions, events, and activities must be accomplished to get the force ready to deploy. Planned requirements (represented by the TPFDD) are communicated to tasked units and supporting agencies, which take actions to prepare and organize the actual people, supplies, and equipment for movement. This process also includes getting support organizations prepared to conduct deployment operations. Specific activities within this phase include:

a. **Activate/Confirm Deployment C2 and Support Organizations.** These C2 organizations play a major role in activating and synchronizing support activities for deploying units. These support activities may vary but may include medical and personnel support facilities, supply and maintenance activities, as well as critical deployment nodes such as railheads, airfields, and seaports.

b. **Conduct Movement Coordination and Support Meetings.** A multitude of topics may be discussed and coordinated at these meetings, but PSA requirements and availability of ITV infrastructure and processes to be used are two topics that require special consideration. Coordination with local, state, or host county authorities for movement permits for equipment being convoyed to the POEs is another separate but critical task that must occur. Coordination done at these meetings with the POE C2 elements or local/HN authorities will lay the groundwork for a successful transition to the establishment of support activities (PSA or A/DACG) in the *assemble and marshal* forces functional events.

c. **Develop Deployable Equipment List.** Many activities occur simultaneously at all levels from the Service, force provider to the supported CCDR to enable the movement of forces. These activities include identifying/assembling RFID requirements and tags, containers, flat racks, MHE, pallets, nets, and arranging local transportation requirements. Supporting activities receive container and/or 463L pallet requirements from units, assess capability to meet these requirements, and determine MHE and/or cargo handling equipment requirements to move containers and pallets from storage sites to unit areas. Based on DTR Parts II and III, *Cargo Movement* and *Mobility*, for units moving between CCDRs, all RFID layer 4 shipments (e.g., 20/40 foot seavan, 463L pallet with net, large engine container) and all major organizational equipment, must have either data rich or license plate RFID tags written and applied at the point of origin by all activities (including vendors/contractors subject to contract requirements). Additionally, initial load and/or stow plans are developed; for movement planning purposes, airlift aircraft load planning considerations are characterized as either administrative-loading or combat-loading. The deployment concept will provide guidance on combat- or administrative-loading based on the supported CCDR's requirements and the TPFDD.

(1) **Administrative-loading** gives primary consideration to using airlift assets most efficiently. Administrative-loading maximizes use of volumes and weight capacities of airlift aircraft and their allowable cabin load without regard to ground force tactical considerations. Routine air movement is usually unopposed and uses secure airfields or well-established landing zones; the majority of these missions involve the administrative-loading of troops and equipment.

(2) **Combat-loading** arranges personnel and materiel to arrive at their intended destination in an order and condition so they are ready for immediate use. Combat-loading maximizes the combat readiness of the organizations and equipment being moved and stresses effectiveness. Airlift forces can move combat-loaded units to maximize their readiness for immediate combat operations. Given the assumption of immediate combat, user requirements should dictate scheduling and load planning.

d. **Conduct Training if Required.** SecDef and CCDRs routinely require deploying forces to execute individual or unit training prior to deployment; these may include self-aid, weapons qualification, and vehicle/equipment certification.

4. Schedule Movement

Movement scheduling is an iterative process at every level of supported and supporting command to deploy the right people, supplies, and equipment to the right place at the right time.

a. **Receive Strategic Movement Schedule.** As received from validated TPFDD requirements, strategic lift assets are scheduled and registered in JOPES and shown in the Web SM tool. These movement schedules are utilized by commands in support of movement planning, coordination, and execution.

b. **Receive/Assess Movement and Lift Schedules.** Commands assess their ability to meet strategic lift schedules. Allocation of ULNs to carriers is accomplished in JOPES. ULN lift shortfalls and available lift are identified to the TCCs.

c. **Receive Port Call.** As strategic sealift schedules are being developed, units and/or installations receive SDDC call forward messages directing movement to SPOEs in designated windows. For amphibious operations and other self-deploying units, SDDC port calls do not apply.

d. **Confirm Movement Clearances.** Movement control elements confirm movement diplomatic and ground movement clearances with HN, state, and governmental agencies.

e. **Build and Publish Schedule of Events.** Movement instructions are published IAW JOPES carrier schedules and priority of force movement.

5. Assemble and Marshal Forces

Assembly and marshalling involves bringing together people, supplies, and equipment in preparation for final movement. Support functions are established and positioned to expedite and control the movement and throughput of the force through the deployment pipeline.

a. **Establish Support Organizations at POE.** POE deployment support organizations, identified in subparagraph 4a, "Receive Strategic Movement Schedule," are established in support of movement operations.

b. **Assemble/Marshal Cargo.** Unit inspections, equipment loading, and process documentation are conducted at home station and/or at intermediate marshalling areas in support of movement preparations. Preparations and inspections for movement operations are completed prior to departure from home station or an intermediate marshalling area. Documentation is married up with cargo and equipment. Note: This also includes the labeling of cargo/equipment with proper military shipping labels and affixing RFID tags and/or other AITs. Planners must ensure that RFID tags have been applied by this stage of the process.

c. **Sequence Loads.** Loads are staged and sequenced in support of movement to POEs based upon priority of force movement schedules.

d. **Assemble/Manifest Personnel and Cargo.** Manifesting is accomplished for both cargo and PAX according to their sequence for movement.

6. Move to Port of Embarkation

In addition to forces, movements to the SPOE/APOE may include materiel from the installation, vendor or supplier, storage activity, or depot. GCC visibility of these movements enables adjustments to the flow of materiel prior to the loading of strategic lift assets. For materiel originating in OCONUS supporting commands, the Service transportation component coordinates with the JDDOC and SDDC forward operating elements to plan and execute the movement of materiel to the POE.

a. **Monitor and Control Deployment Operations.** These activities focus on monitoring deployment operations and achieving and maintaining movement control. Deployment coordination centers like the USTRANSCOM DDOC and the supported CCDR's JDDOC or JMC work to balance and regulate the force flow from origin to destination. Along the way elements coordinate, monitor, and report movement IAW movement instructions, ITV is achieved and maintained, deployment progress and status reports are produced, and changes to the force flow are managed. Force closure will also be reported through these channels. IGC is the designated DOD system for ITV during the strategic movement phase of deployment. IGC collects ITV information from distribution source systems, Services systems, and commercial systems, and then distributes ITV information to customer, Service, and joint systems. A primary control mechanism is the TPFDD, since it specifies the priority of movement and the dates by which cargo and PAX must arrive at the POEs for loading on strategic lift assets. Movement control elements coordinate, monitor, and report movement IAW movement instructions.

b. **Conduct movement operations.** Validated movement requirements developed during deployment planning and scheduled during predeployment activities now must physically move (by some mode of transportation) from origin to the designated APOEs/SPOEs. Equipment of deploying forces may be transported to the POE by commercial rail, truck or inland waterway. Using the planning factors developed in the earlier stages of the deployment process the base/installation transportation office requests the necessary DOD and commercial transportation assets (i.e., railcars, trucks, and containers) to meet movement requirements.

7. Conduct Port of Embarkation Operations

Port operations begin the strategic leg of the deployment pipeline. Essential actions are accomplished at the POE to complete and finalize all unit movement responsibilities. The result is the load and launch of the strategic conveyance. Critical information is provided to C2 and forward support elements to facilitate efficient movement of the force to the POD.

a. **Arrive at POE.** Forces and equipment arrive at their designated departure POEs. Arrival reporting is done by the deployment support organizations and unit as directed.

b. **Assemble Personnel and Manifest.** Personnel, cargo, and equipment are staged, sequenced, and manifested at the departure POE.

c. **Conduct Cargo Inspections for Mode/Source.** Vehicle and equipment are required to complete and pass movement inspections tailored to the mode and source of lift they will move on. For example vehicles and equipment must be clean and their fuel tanks filled to specified levels appropriate to the mode and source. These inspections are conducted within the departure POE alert holding area and/or call forward areas IAW the DTR and joint procedures and policies.

d. **Load Conveyance.** PAX and cargo are physically loaded aboard their scheduled mode of conveyance. Status reports are conducted within the departure POE loading ramp areas. Load lift reports are submitted as directed between the POE support agencies, unit, and component forces. The provision of initial carrier manifest information is the responsibility of both supported and supporting commands. IGC provides this information to the JOPES Web SM tool.

8. Move to Port of Debarkation

Deploying forces physically depart the POE bound for their planned POD.

a. **Conduct Lift Operations.** Movement to the designated PODs is conducted IAW movement instructions. Lift operations entail forces moving via one of three modes: airlift, sealift, or self-deploying. Assignment of lift for each deploying ULN is accomplished during the TPFDD validation process, and can be queried through the JOPES Web SM tool. The DTR requires all deploying individuals be manifested. For deployment by air, the passenger terminal or base operations at the POE and en route stops are normally responsible for passenger manifesting. However, the aircraft commander is ultimately responsible for compliance with these procedures. If there is no passenger terminal, base operations, or other agency responsible for filing the manifest or if PAX do not process through such an agency, the aircraft commander will file a copy of the passenger manifest with the most responsible on-scene agency. For unit moves, the respective Service deployment AIS will be the primary means to generate and transmit an electronic manifest. The deploying force commander is responsible for ensuring accurate manifest data. The lift provider is responsible for entering actual manifested passenger and cargo information in JOPES Web SM tool via GATES. In the case of exercises, the commander who was assigned lead agent responsibilities for a specific exercise as tasked in joint training plans is responsible for using the appropriate feeder systems to ensure data is entered. USTRANSCOM or the actual lift provider will be responsible for entering actual manifest (carrier onload/off-load/information) into GATES depending on whether USTRANSCOM TCCs are operating the port.

b. **Arrive at POD.** Forces physically arrive at the POD. This ends the movement phase of deployment.

9. Reception: Conduct Port of Debarkation Operations

The deploying force will arrive in the theater at APODs and SPODs. Reception is the process of expeditiously off-loading, marshalling, and transporting equipment, personnel, and materiel to complete the movement phase to a sea or air POD. Reception operations at the POD include all those functions necessary to receive and clear unit personnel and equipment through the POD.

a. **Prepare for JRSOI, Storage/Assembly Areas.** Supported CCDRs ensure final preparations are complete in expectation for the arrival of forces at the PODs per the JRSOI plan developed earlier during the planning phase. Final preparations may include the establishment of specific areas at the POD to organize types of cargo in preparation for staging and onward movement. These areas may include storage areas for explosives that must remain a safe distance from the populated and active areas of the POD and vehicle parking areas that facilitate their onward movement.

b. **Receive Forces/Process Personnel and Cargo at the POD.** Personnel and cargo are off-loaded at PODs. The support organization analyzes ITV data to determine how and where the arriving personnel and cargo are to be moved to appropriate holding areas. Status reports are provided to higher HQ. The units are advised of the general situation and may be tasked for personnel to work on various work parties (i.e., drivers for off-loading, PSA, security, cargo off-load). Personnel and cargo are received and processed for movement. Unit personnel and cargo may move on unit equipment and/or common-user transportation. Appropriate documentation is prepared for subsequent movement.

c. **Conduct POD Yard Management.** POD yard management is essential to maintain the flow of forces and equipment through the POD. POD yard management includes those activities that account for and maintain visibility of personnel and cargo transiting the POD. The activities also ensure cargo is organized within the POD to facilitate marshalling in preparation for onward movement.

d. **Marshal and Move to Staging Area.** Unit personnel and cargo will usually move to an SA. In some situations, unit personnel and cargo may move directly to the TAA. If movement is to an SA, preparations begin there for onward movement to the TAA. In certain instances, the POD, SA, and TAA may be colocated; however, this is not recommended.

e. **Monitor and Control Deployment Operations.** These are activities that endure throughout the deployment and include movement control elements coordinating, monitoring, and reporting movement IAW movement instructions. The movement control system also establishes procedures with HN, commercial contractors, and multinational forces on the use of available transportation resources.

10. Staging: Prepare, Assemble, and Marshal the Force

a. **Perform JRSOI Task.** Assembly and marshalling involves bringing together personnel, supplies, and equipment in preparation for onward movement. Units arrive at the SA and begin preparations for movement to the TAA. Staging is the assembling, temporary holding, and organization of arriving personnel and materiel into units and forces, followed by preparation for onward movement and tactical operations. Support activities in the SA provide life support until units become self-sustaining. In the SA, C2 organizations are stood up to monitor status, receive reports, prioritize movement, provide local security, monitor throughput of subordinate units, and forward status to higher HQ. The force is prepared for movement to the TAA. Equipment and cargo, including WRM, are received, accounted for, and distributed. Units prepare for onward movement by assembling, processing, and accounting for personnel; performing maintenance and operations checks on equipment; and verifying and/or modifying load plans for movement from the SA to TAA. When the unit has received its movement mission and available intelligence (including submitting collection requests to cover gaps in intelligence information), and is task-organized IAW command guidance, it makes final movement preparations and departs the SA.

b. **Assemble Forces and Organize into Units.** Arriving forces and equipment are reassembled and organized into their respective units in the SA. Units prepare for onward movement by assembling, processing, and accounting for personnel. Personnel are accounted for and processed IAW command guidance, JRSOI directives, and unit standing operating procedure. Units are task-organized to execute the mission based on CCMD guidance and the OE. C2 and command post operations are established and liaison elements are sent to higher, adjacent, external, and subordinate organizations as the mission requires. C2 is established with higher HQ, and units maintain close coordination with higher HQ as they make final preparations. Units ensure that security operations are established IAW the security plan. Units may also receive equipment, WRM, and supplies. Units receive their equipment, equipment augmentation, WRM, and supplies as required. Equipment, cargo, and supplies are received, accounted for, and distributed IAW logistic guidance. Units perform maintenance and operational checks on equipment.

c. **Provide Essential Logistics Services.** Unit coordination is established with support activities within the SA to provide logistic support and services. These include operations essential to the technical management and support of the joint force. Logistics services include food, water and ice, base camp, health services support, and hygiene services in an expeditionary environment.

d. **Perform Operability Checks.** Equipment is checked to ensure that it is combat ready and mission capable.

e. **Schedule and Prepare for Onward Movement.** Process personnel and cargo for movement and prepare documentation. Load plans are developed and checked to ensure that essential equipment and supplies can be transported. External movement requirements are identified, and movement requests are submitted.

f. **Sequence Cargo Loads and Conduct Inspections.** Loads are sequenced to ensure the most efficient use of available transportation assets. Safety and security of the force are also considered when making decisions during sequence planning.

11. Onward Movement: Conduct Onward Movement

a. **Move to Tactical Assembly Area.** Onward movement is the process of moving units and accompanying materiel from reception facilities and marshalling or SAs to TAAs or other theater destinations, moving arriving non-unit personnel to gaining commands, and moving arriving sustainment materiel from reception facilities to distribution sites. Support functions are established and positioned to expedite and control the onward movement of the force to the TAA.

b. **Move to TAA/Destination.** Deploying forces may be required to move to a TAA while others may go direct to their destination and not have a requirement for tactical assembly. For example, an Air Force unit may be deploying to a fixed base and will fall in on existing base assets.

c. **Report Force Closure.** Once in the TAA or at the destination, units will report force closure as directed.

d. **Coordinate Movement Security Requirements.** Units ensure that security operations are established IAW the security plan and monitor the movement.

e. **Conduct Movement Control Operations.** A movement control element coordinates movement requirements with the security force and confirms that movement clearances have been approved. Departure, en route, and arrival status are monitored and reported.

12. Conduct Tactical Assembly Area Operations

a. **The TAA Is a Location Designated by the CCDR** where units will transfer authority to their gaining commands and from which they can be integrated into the force and be tactically employed. Units arrive at the TAA and continuously monitor the status of preparation in key operational and logistic areas as they prepare for the mission. Coordination is also made for TAA security operations. Unit reports to higher HQ ready for operations when JRSOI operations are completed.

b. **Establish C2, Security, and Unit Area.** C2 or command post operations are established and liaison elements are sent to higher, adjacent, external, and subordinate organizations as the mission requires. C2 is established with higher HQ, and units maintain close coordination with higher HQ as they make final preparations.

c. **Report Status.** Units continuously monitor the status of preparation in key operational and logistic areas as they prepare for the mission and report status to higher HQ.

Movements and the status of units and forces should be reported from all nodes where JRSOI operations are being conducted.

d. **Coordinate Support Requirements.** Coordination is established with the TAA support activities to provide logistic support and services.

e. **Conduct Force Assembly and Accountability.** Units perform a final unit assembly accountability of equipment, supplies, and personnel and report status to the gaining and losing command.

13. Complete Force Integration

a. **Integration** is the process of establishing deploying units into coherent operational units under the C2 of the supported CCDR. The JRSOI process ends when the unit commander has reported ready for operations and the unit integrates with its higher HQ. The unit is integrated with logistics and operational components of the gaining command and completes any final command directed training and activities before being committed to operational missions.

b. **Integrate Communications Systems with Gaining Command.** Communications systems are completely integrated between the gaining command, supporting commands, units, JRSOI organizations, and commanders at all levels to facilitate the timely and accurate exchange of critical information. The receiving commander should establish positive C2 over the arriving unit in the TAA.

c. **Integrate Support.** The unit establishes direct support relationships with various support elements to include supply, services, maintenance, and medical.

d. **Conduct Field Training Exercises and Rehearsals.** Units conduct field training exercises and rehearsals as part of final training preparation.

e. **Confirm Mission Readiness.** Commanders report their unit's status IAW the readiness criteria established by the supported CCDR and confirm when ready to execute their assigned missions.

ANNEX B TO APPENDIX B
JOINT FORCE REDEPLOYMENT PROCESS MAPS DESCRIPTION

1. Conduct Force and Support Planning

Redeployment operations will normally begin when the unit is notified that its mission is complete and it will be returning to its home station/demobilization station or when it receives orders to redeploy to another theater in support of another GCC's requirement.

a. **Receive Warning Order and Establish Command Relationships.** Formal notification is received which directs deployment planning and preparation. Units receive notification of impending operations via a WARNORD that describes the situation, allocates forces and resources, provides other initial planning guidance, and initiates subordinate unit mission planning. Command relationships are also determined and the Joint Staff confirms supported CCDR, supporting CCDR, and agency relationships by message for a given operation.

b. **Receive TPFDD Guidance.** The supported CCDR publishes supporting information via a TPFDD LOI or newsgroup messages that provide specific theater/operationally focused information to those in support. This information will provide additional detail including ULN. Force Module numbering conventions, refined TPFDD guidance, and other specific directions to forces deploying or redeploying.

c. **Develop Deployment/Redeployment Concept.** Supported CCDRs develop a deployment concept and identify specific predeployment standards necessary to meet mission requirements. The Services and supporting CCDRs ensure that predeployment standards specified are achieved and forces and supporting personnel arrive in the supported theater fully prepared to perform their mission. Supported CCDRs also develop a redeployment CONOPS to identify how forces and materiel will redeploy to home station, to mobilization station, or to support another JFC's operation. The redeployment CONOPS is especially important when force rotations are envisioned for a long-term operation. In addition, planners should consider what WRM, pre-positioned materiel, and/or TPE or supplies may be available or required for forces deploying or redeploying into the OA.

d. **Plan WRM/Pre-Positioned Materiel/TPE Equipment Disposition.** The redeployment CONOPS is especially important when force rotations are envisioned for a long-term operation. In addition, planners should consider what WRM, pre-positioned materiel, and/or TPE or supplies may be available to or required for forces redeploying from one OA into a new supported commander's OA.

e. **Identify HN and Contract Support Requirements and HN Inspection Requirements.** HN and contract support play a vital role in redeployment operations. Coordination must be made for various functions to include convoy support centers, communications, MHE, POE support, and other key support functions. Commanders at all levels assess HN and contract requirements, to include facilities, security, supply and services, and equipment processing and turn-in. In addition, the requirements for customs, environmental protection, and agricultural inspections are reviewed.

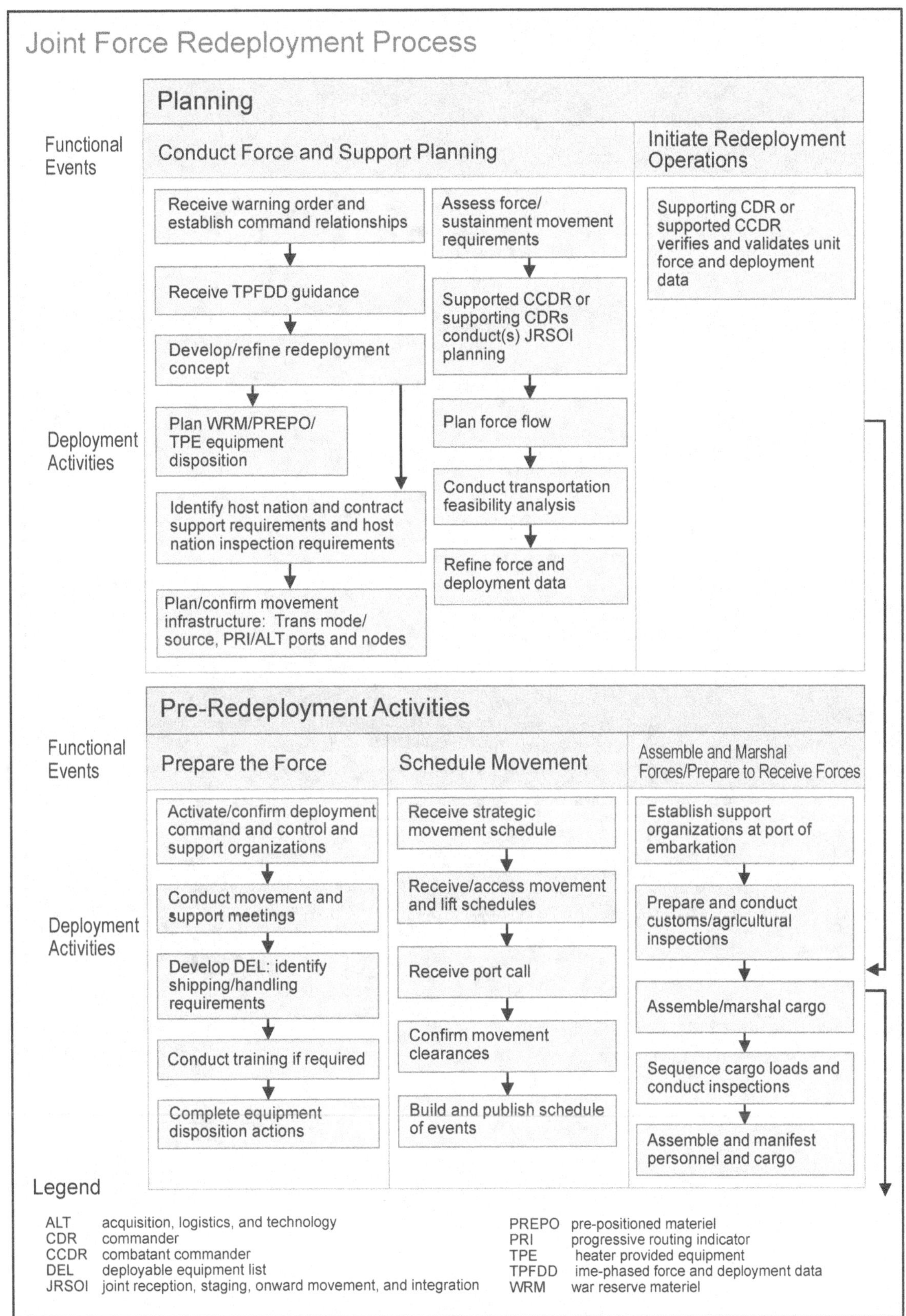

Figure B-B-1. Joint Force Redeployment Process

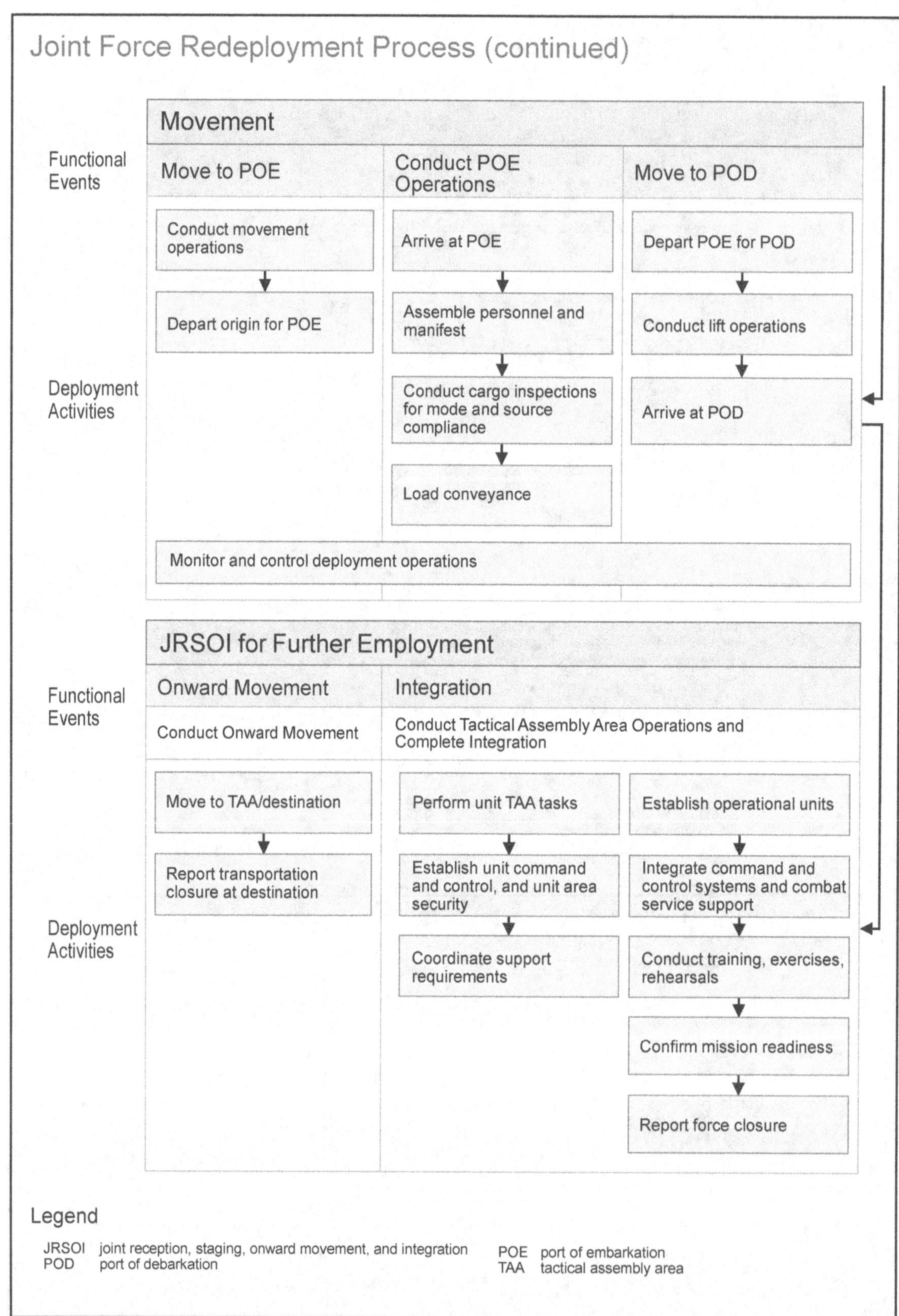

Figure B-B-1. Joint Force Redeployment Process (continued)

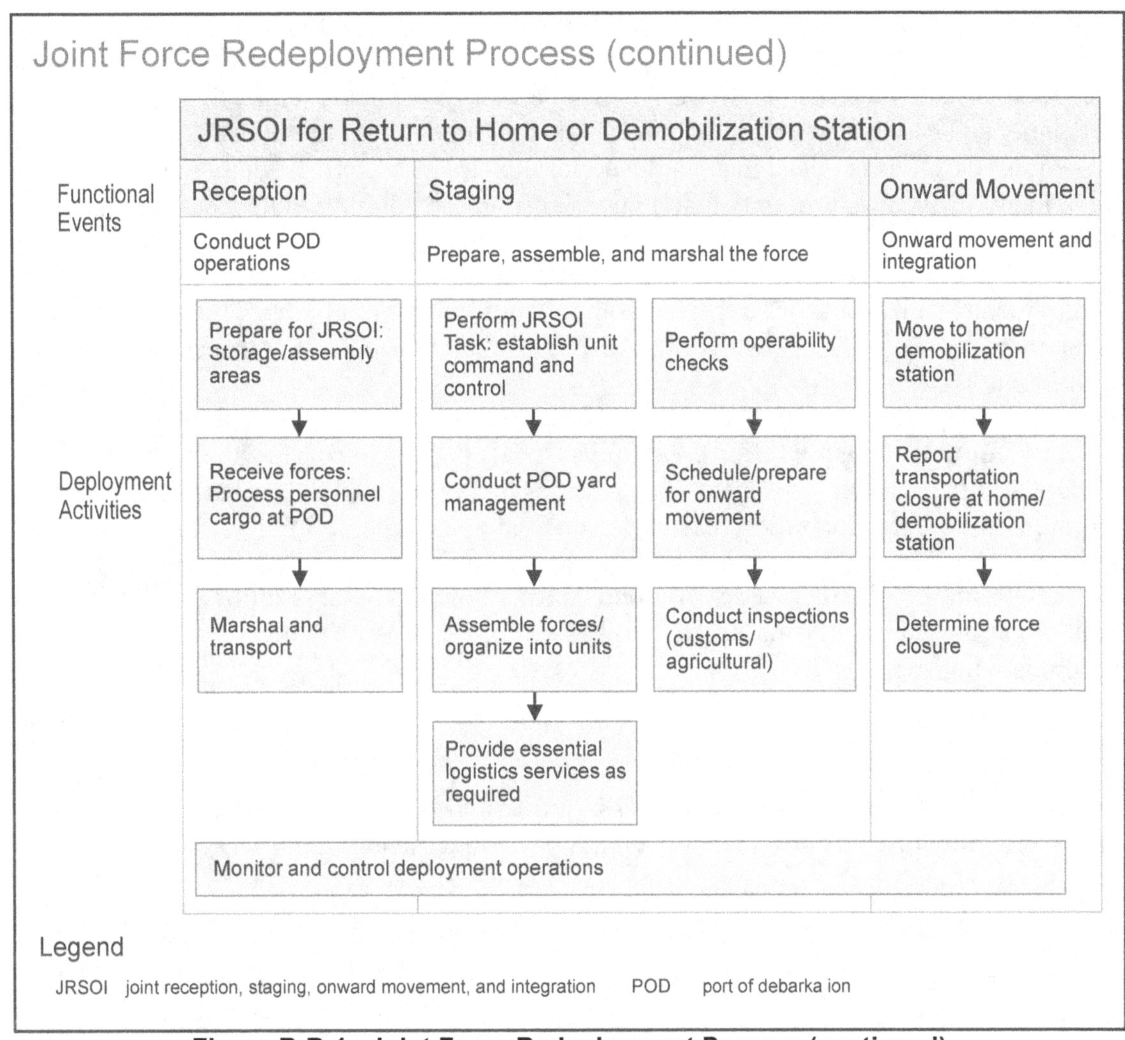

Figure B-B-1. Joint Force Redeployment Process (continued)

f. **Plan/Confirm Movement Infrastructure.** The supported commander plans transportation modes and sources, establishes primary and alternate nodes to include air and sea ports of debarkation, plans for port operations and establishes MSRs whether supporting redeployment to a new OA or back to home/demobilization station. Additionally, supporting commanders and lift providers plan to determine any special cargo handling requirements.

g. **Assess Force and Sustainment Movement Requirements.** This is a critical step during planning for a deployment or redeployment to a new OA. These estimates should include the lift estimates on a macro scale (for example, basic mode/source determination, lift apportionment evaluation, fort-to-port and POD-to-destination), as well as classic logistics planning for projected sustainment and operational supplies (ammunition, fuel, etc.).

h. **Supported CCDR or Supporting CCDRs Conduct JRSOI Planning.** It is imperative early in the deployment process that the supported CCDR begins the planning to receive forces. This applies when forces redeploy from one AOR to another. In this case a

GCC who may have been acting in a supporting role in one AOR may now be the supported GCC for an operation within their AOR. Early planning will ensure there is the appropriate reception forces, material, and equipment available to quickly and effectively process personnel and cargo through the APOD/SPOD and move them to the SA. In addition, the supported CCDR may designate a lead Service to plan and execute the intratheater movement of forces, sustainment, and materiel from the APOD/SPODs to destination.

i. **Plan Force Flow.** JFPs and force providers source and task organize allocated force requirements, filling JFC or supported component force requirements. JFCs or supported components prioritize force flow within the TPFDD based on operational needs and strategic lift limitations.

j. **Conduct Transportation Feasibility Analysis.** Based on the supported CCDR's RDD the lift provider will determine if the supported CCDR's planned force flow requirements are transportation feasible given available strategic lift assets.

k. **Refine Force and Redeployment Data.** Force providers tailor the redeploying units' PAX and cargo information in the TPFDD and will ensure that units identify planned accompanying supplies.

2. Initiate Redeployment Operations

Supporting CCDR or supported CCDR verifies and validates unit force and deployment data. Redeploying units provide PAX and/or equipment lists for TPFDD refinement.

3. Prepare the Force

Multiple actions, events, and activities must be accomplished to get the force ready to redeploy. Planned movement requirements (represented by the TPFDD) are communicated to tasked units and supporting agencies, who take action to prepare and organize the actual personnel, supplies, and equipment for movement. This process also includes getting support in theater prepared to conduct redeployment operations. Preparations are also made to process WRM and excess materiel. Specific activities may include the following. Some may occur simultaneously.

a. **Activate/Confirm Deployment C2 and Support Organizations.** These C2 organizations play a major role in activating and synchronizing support activities for deploying units. These support activities may vary but may include medical and personnel support facilities, supply and maintenance activities, as well as critical deployment nodes such as railheads, airfields, and seaports. These activities may be task organized to support requirements for movement control elements both at the POE installation and POD (e.g., A/DACG, MCCs, POGs, CRG).

b. **Conduct Movement and Support Meetings.** Units confirm readiness, movement available dates, PAX, and cargo details to higher commands. Commands at all levels review planning and execution status and assign tasks to resolve support issues. CCMD components and supporting commanders provide confirmation to the supported commander, who validates to USTRANSCOM that the data in the TPFDD is error-free and accurately reflects the current status, attributes, and availability of units and requirements.

c. **Conduct Training as Required.** Redeploying forces may require new individual or unit training prior to redeployment to a new OA. These may include self-aid; chemical, biological, radiological, or nuclear defense tactics, techniques, and procedures; weapons qualification; vehicle/equipment certification; or other OA specific training that may be required.

d. **Complete Equipment Disposition Actions.** Redeploying units must assess equipment status and coordinate the turn-in or disposal of WRM and excess equipment and materiel. Units must clean, process, and turn in WRM and excess materiel IAW Service disposition instructions.

4. Schedule Movement

a. **Receive Strategic Movement Schedule.** As received from validated TPFDD requirements, strategic lift assets are scheduled and registered in JOPES. These movement schedules are utilized by commands in support of movement planning, coordination, and execution.

b. **Receive/Assess Movement and Lift Schedules.** Commands assess their ability to meet strategic lift schedules. Allocation of ULN(s) to carriers is accomplished in JOPES. ULN lift shortfalls and available lift are identified to the TCCs.

c. **Receive Port Call.** As strategic sealift schedules are being developed, units and/or installations receive SDDC port call messages directing movement to SPOEs in designated windows. For amphibious operations, SDDC port calls do not apply.

d. **Confirm Movement Clearances.** Movement control elements confirm movement diplomatic and ground movement clearances with HN, state, and governmental agencies.

e. **Build and Publish Schedule of Events.** Movement instructions are published in support of JOPES carrier schedules and priority of force movement.

5. Assemble and Marshal Forces/Prepare to Receive Forces

Assembly and marshalling involves bringing together personnel, supplies, and equipment in preparation for movement. Support organizations are established at the POE and positioned to expedite and control the movement from TAA to SAs and throughput of the force through the redeployment pipeline.

a. **Prepare and Conduct Customs/Agricultural Inspections.** In preparation for agricultural inspections, units wash down equipment either in the SA or at the POE. Documentation is prepared and attached to cargo and equipment.

b. **Assemble and Marshal Cargo.** Cargo assembly is conducted within the marshalling areas at the POE. At a minimum, planners must ensure that RFID tags have been applied by this stage of the process.

c. **Sequence Cargo Loads and Conduct Inspections.** Loads are staged and sequenced in support of movement to POEs based upon priority of force movement schedules. Units account for, identify, and process excess equipment and clean, decontaminate, pack, and load unit equipment IAW customs and/or agriculture guidance, and develop initial unit movement data.

d. **Assemble and Manifest Personnel and Cargo.** Final manifesting of redeploying forces (PAX and equipment) is accomplished prior to movement to POE. Documentation is prepared and attached to cargo and equipment.

6. Move to Port of Embarkation

a. **Conduct Movement Operations.** Validated movement requirements developed during deployment planning and scheduled during predeployment activities now must physically move (by some mode of transportation) from origin to the designated APOEs/SPOEs. Equipment of deploying forces may be transported to the POE by commercial rail, truck, or inland waterway. Using the planning factors developed in the earlier stages of the deployment process, the base/installation transportation office requests the necessary DOD and commercial transportation assets (i.e., railcars, trucks, and containers) to meet movement requirements.

b. **Depart Origin for POE.** There may be a requirement for units and equipment to move from the SA to a TAA in preparation for final movement to the POE. Local requirements will dictate whether this is necessary and will be coordinated through the movement control organizations monitoring the redeployment.

c. **Monitor and Control Deployment Operations.** These activities focus on monitoring deployment operations and achieving and maintaining movement control. Deployment coordination centers like the USTRANSCOM DDOC and the supported CCDR's JDDOC or JMC work to balance and regulate the force flow from origin to destination. Along the way, elements coordinate, monitor, and report movement IAW movement instructions, ITV is achieved and maintained, deployment progress and status reports are produced, and changes to the force flow are managed. Force closure will also be reported through these channels. IGC is the designated DOD system for ITV during the strategic movement phase of deployment. IGC collects ITV information from distribution source systems, Services systems, and commercial systems, and then distributes ITV information to customer, Service, and joint systems. A primary control mechanism is the TPFDD, since it specifies the priority of movement and the dates by which cargo and PAX must arrive at the POEs for loading on strategic lift assets. Movement control elements coordinate, monitor, and report movement IAW movement instructions.

7. Conduct Port of Embarkation Operations

Essential actions are accomplished at the POE to complete and finalize all unit movement responsibilities. The result is the load and launch of the strategic conveyance. Critical information is provided to C2 and forward support elements to facilitate efficient onward movement of the force to the POE.

a. **Arrive at POE.** Forces and equipment arrive at the designated POEs. Arrival reporting is accomplished as required.

b. **Assemble Personnel and Manifest.** Documentation is completed for redeploying personnel. Once manifested (based on the DTR Part III, Mobility, Appendix T), a troop commander will be assigned and will be advised of their responsibilities at the APOE and will be provided the troop commander's checklist to complete prior to the unit boarding the aircraft.

c. **Conduct Cargo Inspections for Mode and Source Compliance.** Inspections are conducted within the departure POE alert holding area and/or call forward areas IAW the DTR and joint procedures and policies. This includes safety, customs, and agricultural inspections and equipment wash down.

d. **Load Conveyance.** Cargo and personnel are loaded on lift. Reports are provided with status of units, cargo, personnel, lift, terminals, and loading operations.

8. Move to Port of Debarkation

a. **Depart POE for POD.** Forces physically depart the POE for their designated PODs IAW movement instructions.

b. **Conduct Lift Operations.** Lift operations entail forces moving via one of three modes: airlift, sealift or self-deploying. Assignment of lift for each deploying ULN is accomplished during the TPFDD validation process, and can be queried through JOPES Web SM tool. The deploying force commander is responsible for ensuring accurate manifest data. The lift provider is responsible for entering actual manifested passenger and cargo information in JOPES Web SM tool via GATES. In the case of exercises, the commander who was assigned lead agent responsibilities for a specific exercise as tasked in joint training plans is responsible for using the appropriate feeder systems to ensure data is entered. USTRANSCOM or the lift provider will be responsible for entering actual manifest (carrier onload/off-load/information) into GATES depending on whether USTRANSCOM TCCs are operating the port.

c. **Arrive at POD.** Forces physically arrive at the POD. This ends the movement phase of deployment.

9. Joint Reception, Staging, Onward Movement, and Integration

The responsibility for JRSOI from a POD during redeployment operations is determined by the post-redeployment mission of the redeploying force. Redeployment for further employment will involve JRSOI in the new OA. Redeployment to the home and/or demobilization station or point of origin for return to peacetime positioning or demobilization will involve POD JRSOI coordinated and executed by the Services and USTRANSCOM for common-user PODs and by the respective Service or unit for forces redeploying by organic assets to non-common-user PODs.

10. Conduct Port of Debarkation Operations

POD operations include all actions taken to download and process unit personnel and equipment at an APOD or SPOD and may include customs and agricultural inspections.

a. **Prepare for JRSOI, Storage/Assembly Areas.** Supported CCDRs will ensure final preparations are complete in expectation for the arrival of forces at the PODs per the JRSOI plan developed earlier during the planning phase. Final preparations may include the establishment of specific areas at the POD to organize types of cargo in preparation for staging and ultimately their onward movement. These areas may include storage areas for explosives that must remain a safe distance from the populated and active areas of the POD and vehicle parking areas that facilitate their easy onward movement.

b. **Receive Personnel and Cargo.** PAX, unit equipment, and cargo are downloaded, moved to temporary holding areas, and consolidated for movement to final destination. Units may assist with download and movement of equipment. Customs and agricultural inspections may be conducted if they were not conducted at the POE, were considered inadequate, or to meet other requirements.

c. **Conduct POD Yard Management.** POD yard management is essential to maintain the flow of forces and equipment through the POD. POD yard management includes those activities that account for and maintain visibility of personnel and cargo transiting the POD. The activities also ensure cargo is organized within the POD to facilitate marshalling in preparation for onward movement.

d. **Marshal and Move to Staging Area.** Unit personnel and cargo will usually move to an SA. In some situations, unit personnel and cargo may move directly to the TAA. If movement is to an SA, preparations begin there for onward movement to the TAA. In certain instances, the POD, SA, and TAA may be colocated; however, this is not recommended.

e. **Monitor and Control Redeployment Operations.** These activities are enduring throughout the deployment and include movement control elements that coordinate, track, and report movement to the JFC. The movement control system also establishes procedures with HN, commercial contractors, and multinational forces on the use of available transportation resources.

11. Prepare, Assemble, and Marshal the Force

Units arrive at the SA and begin preparations for movement to the TAA. Staging is the assembling, temporary holding, and organization of arriving personnel and materiel into units and forces, followed by preparation for onward movement and tactical operations.

Support activities in the SA provide life support until units become self-sustaining. In the SA, C2 organizations are stood up to monitor status, receive reports, prioritize movement, provide local security, monitor throughput of subordinate units, and forward status to higher HQ. The force is prepared for movement to the TAA. Equipment and cargo, including WRM, are received, accounted for, and distributed. Units prepare for onward movement by assembling, processing, and accounting for personnel; performing maintenance and operations checks on equipment; and verifying and/or modifying load plans for movement from the SA to TAA. When the unit has received its movement mission, adequate intelligence, and is task-organized IAW command guidance, it makes final movement preparations and departs the SA.

a. **Establish C2.** C2 and command post operations are established and liaison elements are sent to higher, adjacent, external, and subordinate organizations as the mission requires. C2 is established with higher HQ and units maintain close coordination with higher HQ as they make final preparations. Units ensure that security operations are established IAW the security plan.

b. **Assemble Forces/Organize into Units.** Arriving forces and equipment are reassembled and organized into their respective units in the SA. Units prepare for onward movement by assembling, processing, and accounting for personnel. Personnel are accounted for and processed IAW command guidance, JRSOI directives, and unit standing operating procedures. Units are task-organized to execute the mission based on CCMD guidance and the OE established security and unit area. Units ensure that security operations are established IAW the security plan. Units receive their equipment, equipment augmentation, WRM, and supplies as required.

c. **Provide Essential Logistics Services.** Unit coordination is established with support activities within the SA to provide logistic support and services. These include operations essential to the technical management and support of the joint force. Logistics services include food, water and ice, base camp, health service support, and hygiene services in an expeditionary environment.

d. **Perform Operability Checks.** Equipment is checked to ensure that it is combat ready and mission capable. Equipment is reconfigured for onward movement. Additionally, units may install equipment previously removed for airlift; maintain accountability of aircraft pallets, nets, and containers in the marshalling area and break down pallets and containers as soon as practical and return them to the A/DACG; and perform required maintenance checks, including refueling.

e. **Schedule and Prepare for Onward Movement.** Process personnel and cargo for movement and prepare documentation. Load plans are developed and checked to ensure that essential equipment and supplies can be transported. External movement requirements are identified and movement requests are submitted.

f. **Sequence Cargo Loads and Conduct Inspections.** Loads are sequenced according to their chalk, load list, or the schedule of events. Sequencing is accomplished to ensure the most efficient use of available transportation assets. Safety and security of the force are also considered when making decisions during sequence planning.

12. Onward Movement

Onward movement is the process of moving units and accompanying materiel from reception facilities and marshalling areas or SAs to TAAs or other theater destinations, moving arriving non-unit personnel to gaining commands, and moving arriving sustainment materiel from reception facilities to distribution sites. Support functions are established and positioned to expedite and control the onward movement of the force to the TAA.

a. **Move to TAA/Destination.** Deploying forces may be required to move to a TAA while others may go directly to their destination and not have a requirement for tactical assembly. For example, an Air Force unit may be deploying to a fixed base and will fall in on existing base assets.

b. **Report Transportation Closure at Destination.** Once in the TAA or at the destination, units will report transportation closure as directed.

13. Integration

a. The TAA is a location designated by the CCDR where units will transfer authority to their gaining commands and from which they can be integrated into the force and be tactically employed. Units arrive at the TAA and continuously monitor the status of preparation in key operational and logistic areas as they prepare for the mission. Coordination is also made for TAA security operations. Unit reports to higher HQ ready for operations when JRSOI operations are completed.

b. **Establish C2, Security, and Unit Area.** C2 or command post operations are established and liaison elements are sent to higher, adjacent, external, and subordinate organizations as the mission requires. C2 is established with higher HQ, and units maintain close coordination with higher HQ as they make final preparations.

c. **Coordinate Support Requirements.** Coordination is established with the TAA support activities to provide logistic support and services.

d. **Establish Operational Units.** Units perform a final unit assembly accountability of equipment, supplies, and personnel and report status to the gaining and losing commands.

e. **Integrate Communications Systems and C2 Support.** Integrate communications systems with gaining command. Communications systems are completely integrated between the gaining command, supporting commands, units, JRSOI organizations, and commanders at all levels to facilitate the timely and accurate exchange of critical information. The receiving commander should establish positive C2 over the arriving unit in the TAA. The unit establishes direct support relationships with various support elements in the support structure to include supply, services, maintenance, and medical.

f. **Conduct Training Exercises and Rehearsals.** Units conduct field training exercises and rehearsals as part of final training preparation.

g. **Confirm Mission Readiness.** Commanders report their units' status IAW the readiness criteria established by the supported CCDR and confirm when ready to execute their assigned missions.

h. **Report Force Closure.** Units report force closure, confirming they are now fully integrated into the supported commander's operational forces.

14. Conduct Port of Debarkation Operations

Arrival at the POD marks the transition from the intertheater to intratheater movement leg. Transfer of advance arrival information from USTRANSCOM to the gaining command is essential for reception and onward movement.

a. **Prepare for JRSOI, Storage/Assembly Areas.** Supported CCDRs ensure final preparations are complete in expectation for the arrival of forces at the PODs per the JRSOI plan developed earlier during the planning phase. Final preparations may include the establishment of specific areas at the POD to organize types of cargo in preparation for staging and ultimately their onward movement. These areas may include storage areas for explosives that must remain a safe distance from the populated and active areas of the POD and vehicle parking areas that facilitate their onward movement.

b. **Receive Personnel and Cargo.** PAX, unit equipment, and cargo are downloaded, moved to temporary holding areas, and consolidated for movement to final destination. Units may assist with download and movement of equipment. Customs and agricultural inspections may be conducted if they were not conducted at the POE, were considered inadequate, or to meet other requirements.

c. **Marshal and Move to Staging Area.** Unit personnel and cargo may move to an SA at the POD while arrangements are made for their onward movement. If movement is to an SA, preparations begin there for onward movement to their home or demobilization station.

15. Prepare, Assemble, and Marshal the Force

a. **Receive Personnel and Cargo.** PAX, unit equipment, and cargo are downloaded, moved to temporary holding areas, and consolidated for movement to final destination. Units may assist with download and movement of equipment. Customs and agricultural inspections may be conducted if they were not conducted at the POE, were considered inadequate, or to meet other requirements.

b. **Perform JRSOI Task: Establish C2.** C2 and command post operations are established and liaison elements are sent to higher, adjacent, external, and subordinate organizations as the mission requires. C2 is established with higher HQ and units maintain close coordination with higher HQ as they make final preparations. Units ensure that security operations are established IAW the security plan.

c. **Conduct POD Yard Management.** POD yard management is essential to maintain the flow of forces and equipment through the POD. POD yard management includes those activities that account for and maintain visibility of personnel and cargo transiting the POD. The activities also ensure cargo is organized within the POD to facilitate marshalling in preparation for onward movement.

d. **Assemble Forces/Organize into Units.** Units prepare for onward movement by assembling, processing, and accounting for personnel. Personnel are accounted for and processed IAW command guidance, JRSOI directives, and unit standing operating procedure.

e. **Provide Essential Logistics Services.** Although redeploying to home or demobilization station, units may still require some logistics services while awaiting onward movement. Unit coordination is established with support activities within the SA to provide the required logistic support and services. These may be provided by a Service or a joint organization. These logistics services may include subsistence, fuel, vehicle maintenance, water, ice, billeting, or hygiene services.

f. **Perform Operability Checks.** Equipment is checked to ensure that it is combat ready and mission capable.

g. **Schedule and Prepare for Onward Movement.** Process personnel and cargo for movement and prepare documentation. Load plans are developed and checked to ensure that essential equipment and supplies can be transported. External movement requirements are identified and movement requests are submitted.

h. **Conduct Inspections (Customs/Agricultural).** Redeploying forces must comply with USG or a foreign government's requirement to enter the country. Redeploying forces' baggage, equipment, and cargo will be required to clear through US or foreign governments' (if home station is a base in a foreign country) customs or agricultural inspection.

16. Onward Movement and Integration

a. **Move to Home/Demobilization Station.** Units board transportation to home or demobilization station. SDDC controls onward movement of forces/materiel from the PODs according to the redeployment TPFDD and AIS/shipping documentation. The port commander/transportation terminal unit commander and the designated major command receiving the forces develop a reception plan for arriving forces.

b. **Report Transportation Closure at Home/Demobilization Station.** Units report through their Service channels that they have arrived at their home or demobilization station. Destination reception includes all actions necessary to fully recover the unit to include its assigned personnel and equipment. Locations are designated by receiving commands.

c. **Determine Force Closure.** Redeploying units return to home station and report status. In redeployment operations, force closure occurs when the designated commander or Service determines that the redeploying force has returned to home station or other follow-on destination. When units or individuals redeploy, reintegration processing must be done prior to returning active duty members to their permanent duty stations or demobilizing RC members. Reintegration includes medical and security debriefs, clothing and equipment turn-in, and update of personnel and finance records.

APPENDIX C
SAMPLE TIME-PHASED FORCE AND DEPLOYMENT DATA LETTER OF INSTRUCTION

See CJCSM 3122.02, Joint Operation Planning and Execution System (JOPES), Volume III, Crisis Action Time-Phased Force and Deployment Data Development and Deployment Execution, *for additional guidance on construction of a supplemental TPFDD LOI.*

1. Title

US<*Combatant Commander Name*> Supplemental TPFDD Letter of Instruction

2. References

(a) CJCSM 3122 Series, Joint Operation Planning and Execution Systems (JOPES).

(b) JP 3-35, *Deployment and Redeployment Operations.*

(c) JP 5-0, *Joint Operation Planning.*

(d) Global Force Management Implementation Guidance.

The supported CCDR may modify or add references as appropriate.

3. Purpose

To provide standing supplemental TPFDD instructions specific to US <*Combatant Commander's Name*>, <*operations, or specific purpose*> to its Service components, subordinate commands, supporting CCDRs and their components IAW reference (c). Guidance in this LOI is effective immediately and supersedes previous editions. Should a conflict arise between guidance contained in this instruction, subsequent operation-specific guidelines and reference (c) contact <*CCDR Name*> <*responsible code*> for resolution. In operations or exercises where this command is a supporting CCDR, the guidance provided by the supported CCDR takes precedence over corresponding guidance in this publication.

4. Table of Contents

The supported CCDR shall provide an appropriate table of contents.

5. General Information

a. The following Web sites support <*CCDR Name*> operations.

b. The following Web sites support <*CCDR Name*> exercises.

c. The following Web sites support <*CCDR Name*> planning.

d. The following Web sites support <*CCDR Name*> <*additional activity as appropriate*>.

The supported CCDR shall provide appropriate Web sites for reference and add or delete subparagraphs as appropriate.

6. Additional Supplemental Time-Phased Force and Deployment Data Letters of Instruction

Supplemental TPFDD LOIs which have bearing on this document are as follows: *The supported CCDR shall provide a list of additional supplemental TPFDD LOIs either from the supported CCDR's own command or other commands and appropriate Web sites for where they may be obtained.*

7. Points of Contact

a. The following personnel or offices provide *<CCDR Name>* operational support.

b. The following personnel or offices provide *<CCDR Name>* exercise support.

c. The following personnel or offices provide *<CCDR Name>* planning support.

d. The following personnel or offices provide *<CCDR Name>* *<additional activity as appropriate>* support.

The supported CCDR shall provide appropriate points of contact and add or delete subparagraphs as appropriate.

8. Plans, Operation Orders, and Time-Phased Force and Deployment Data

The OPLAN series assigned to *<CCDR Name>* is *<OPLAN Series>*. PIDs for current *<CCDR Name>* plans, OPORDs, and TPFDDs will be published on the *<CCDR Name>* *<J Code>* Web site. *The supported CCDR shall provide or tailor this section as appropriate.*

9. Newsgroups

<CCDR Name> news server is *<address for news server>*. Newsgroups serve as the formal medium for conveying TPFDD related requests, authorizations, verifications, validations, changes, or any general coordination. Any coordination via telephone will be followed up with a newsgroup. General service message traffic having bearing on TPFDD activities will be retransmitted in the appropriate newsgroup as well. The following newsgroups shall be used for coordination on *<CCDR Name>* TPFDDs as follows: *The supported CCDR shall provide or tailor this section as appropriate with a table of associated TPFDDs and newsgroups.*

10. <Combatant Commander Name> Unit Line Number and Force Module Assignments and Structure

<CCDR Name> component commands, subordinate commands, and supporting commands will adhere to the following directed ULN and force module structure when *<CCDR Name>* is the supported commander. *The supported CCDR will specify ULN and*

force module assignments in tabular format. Specific guidance on construct of force modules for validations may be published separately for each exercise or operation.

11. <Combatant Commander Name> Time-Phased Force and Deployment Data Guidance

a. **General Guidance.** All planning, execution, and exercise TPFDD coordination and procedures will be accomplished IAW reference (c) unless modified below or amended by additional supplemental instructions. The guidance in this LOI is directive.

The supported CCDR will specify additional general guidance as appropriate.

b. **Deliberate Planning.** Deliberate planning procedures will conform to references (a) and (c) unless modified below or amended by additional supplemental instructions.

(1) Use of JOPES is directed for TPFDD activities of record.

(2) Use of JCRM is directed to capture the contingency sourcing demand signal and assign FTNs to contingency sourcing requirements.

The supported CCDR will specify additional deliberate planning guidance as appropriate.

c. **Crisis Action Planning.** CAP procedures will conform to reference (a) unless modified below or amended by additional supplemental instructions.

(1) Use of JOPES is directed for executing TPFDDs.

(2) Use of JCRM is directed to capture the initial and emergent force requirements and assign FTNs to the requirements. FTNs will be entered in the FTN field of the appropriate JOPES FRN/ULN to ensure traceability of the requirement.

(3) Upon allocation of the force requirement as documented via the GFMAP annex, the appropriate providing organization will be entered in the associated JOPES FRN/ULN to document the tasked force provider.

(4) For deployment, supporting CCDRs and force providers will request validation of ULNs via a newsgroup validation request message. For redeployment, Service components and subordinate commands will request validation of ULNs via a newsgroup validation request message. Validation requests for more than five ULNs will be consolidated in a force module and the request message will provide the force module reference. Validation requests will cite the legal authority to deploy referencing the order or vocal order authority. In the case of verbal orders, the name, rank, and Defense Switched Network (DSN) number for the individual providing the authorization will be provided. Validation requests must be submitted no later than <*time*>, requests posted outside normal timelines or working hours may be processed on the next business day unless phone notification is provided. A sample is provided in attachment (1).

(5) A 24-hour point of contact (POC) and contact phone number for load plan level of detail will be identified in the ULN POC field.

The supported CCDR will specify additional CAP guidance as appropriate.

d. **Rotation of Forces and Emergent Requirement Planning.** Planning for force rotations and emergent force requirements will conform to references (a), (c), and (f).

(1) Use of JOPES is directed for executing TPFDDs; additional information technologies may be used to enhance the planning process.

(2) Use of JCRM is directed to capture the rotational and emergent force requirements and assign FTNs to the requirements. FTNs will be entered in the FTN field of the appropriate JOPES FRN/ULN to ensure traceability of the requirement.

(3) Upon allocation of the force requirement as documented via the GFMAP annex, the appropriate providing organization will be entered in the associated JOPES FRN/ULN to document the tasked force provider.

(4) For deployment, supporting CCDRs and force providers will request validation of ULNs via a newsgroup validation request message. For redeployment, Service components and subordinate commands will request validation of ULNs via a newsgroup validation request message. Validation requests will cite the legal authority to deploy referencing the order or vocal order authority. In the case of verbal orders, the name, rank, and DSN number for the individual providing the authorization will be provided. Validation requests must be submitted no later than <*time*>, requests posted outside normal timelines or working hours may be processed on the next business day unless phone notification is provided. A sample is provided in attachment (1).

(5) A 24-hour POC and contact phone number for load plan level of detail will be identified in the ULN POC field.

The supported CCDR will specify additional force rotation and emergent force requirement planning guidance as appropriate.

e. **Orders.** The following paragraph shall be used as a standard paragraph in all <*CCDR Name*> orders for TPFDDs in execution. Modification is <*authorized/not authorized*> as appropriate.

THE USE OF JOPES IS DIRECTED. UTILIZE PID <*NUMBER*> FOR DEPLOYMENT AND PID <*NUMBER*> FOR REDEPLOYMENT. REQUIREMENTS MUST FOLLOW PUBLISHED SUPPLEMENT TPFDD LETTER OF INSTRUCTION GUIDANCE AND BE VERIFIED AND VALIDATED IN JOPES ALLOWING USTRANSCOM TO PERFORM TIME-PHASED FORCE CLOSURE ANALYSIS WHEN COMPARED TO OTHER DEFENSE TRANSPORTATION SYSTEM REQUIREMENTS. USE NEWSGROUP <*NEWSGROUP NAME*> <*NEWS SERVER*> FOR COORDINATION AND VERIFICATION OF ALL JOPES TRANSACTIONS. FOR EMERGENCY

VALIDATIONS DURING NON-WORKING HOURS CONTACT THE *<CCDR NAME>* JOPES DUTY OFFICER AT *<PHONE NUMBER>*.

In addition, a separate paragraph may contain guidance for ITV.

IN-TRANSIT VISIBILITY (ITV). TO ENSURE ITV OF DEPLOYING AND REDEPLOYING PERSONNEL, CARGO AND EQUIPMENT, DOD COMPONENTS, AGENCIES AND MILITARY DEPARTMENTS WILL CAPTURE, PROCESS AND TRANSMIT SHIPMENT INFORMATION FOR CARGO EQUIPMENT IN ELECTRONIC FORMAT TO MAXIMIZE ELECTRONIC CAPTURE OF MOVEMENT DATA VIA AUTOMATED INFORMATION SYSTEMS FEEDING THE INTEGRATED DATA ENVIRONMENT/GLOBAL TRANSPORTATION NETWORK CONVERGENCE (IGC) IF UNITS DO NOT HAVE THE MEANS TO SUPPORT AUTOMATED MANIFEST FEEDS TO IGC, UNITS MUST REQUEST SUPPORT THROUGH HIGHER HEADQUARTERS, MILITARY DEPARTMENT CHANNELS OR USTRANSCOM. SHIPPERS/UNITS MUST COMPLY WITH THE PROVISIONS OF DOD REGULATION 4500.9 SERIES, DEFENSE TRANSPORTATION REGULATION (DTR). THE ARRIVAL AND DEPARTURE OF UNIT PERSONNEL AND EQUIPMENT AT ALL NOTES FROM ORIGIN TO DESTINATION WILL BE VISIBLE IN IGC WITHIN 1 HOUR OF THE MOVEMENT EVENT.

The supported CCDR may modify the above paragraphs as appropriate.

f. **Protection of Movement Information.** All personnel will comply with guidelines in reference (c) to ensure the proper safeguarding of plan and TPFDD information.

g. **TPFDD Validation Windows.** Validation windows specified in reference (c) will be observed with exceptions as noted below.

The supported CCDR will specify additional guidance on validation windows as appropriate.

h. **Commercial Ticket Program.** Personnel support exercises will be moved via strategic airlift from POE to POD if the distance between the origin and destination is greater than 300 miles. If the distance is less than 300 miles, land transportation will be used. Units with 100 PAX or more may be moved by strategic lift or commercial charter aircraft. Units under 100 PAX will be considered for movement under the common ticket program. Units with less than 30 PAX will be moved by the common ticket program. Units with between 30 and 100 PAX will be considered to move under the Group Operational Passenger System. Individual units not meeting strategic lift minimums will be considered for aggregated lift if available.

The supported CCDR will specify additional guidance or modify this guidance on the commercial ticket program as appropriate.

i. **Port Handling/In-Land Transportation (PHIT) Funds.** Cargo moved via land mode in support of CJCS exercises are authorized joint funding called PHIT funds. Units may use PHIT funds obtained through the exercise transportation account code for channel movements. PHIT funds can only be used to move people and cargo between unit installations and channel commercial ports. Component commands, organizations, and agencies will need to contact the appropriate component command operations directorate in order to receive PHIT funds.

The supported CCDR will specify additional guidance or modify this guidance on the PHIT as appropriate.

j. **Hazardous Materials.** Records containing HAZMAT must be explicitly identified in the validation request and coded with the proper cargo category code in the level II ULN detail. An aircraft diplomatic clearance worksheet for hazardous cargo is provided in attachment 2. This document is unclassified when filled in, and must be submitted with the cargo load plan. The foreign clearance guide available via SIPRNET at http://www.fcg.pentagon.smil.mil provides details regarding country clearance, entrance and exit criteria. Some country descriptions provide sensitive or hazardous cargo considerations. Additionally USTRANSCOM provides HAZMAT guidance via their unclassified homepage at http://public.transcom.mil via navigation of the following links: Publications, DOC, DTR, Part II, Chapter 204 or via https://business.transcom.mil/customerportal/docs/splash html, DTR 4500.9, Part II, Chapter 204. The sites also provide numerous links to other useful transportation Web sites. Additional questions regarding HAZMAT can be directed either to the SDDC Operations Center, for surface movement (ocean, rail, and truck) or to the 618th Air and Space Operations Center (AOC), Tanker Airlift Control Center (TACC), Aerial Port Control Center for airlift movement execution.

The supported CCDR will specify additional guidance or modify this guidance on HAZMAT as appropriate.

k. **Load and Stow Plans.** Component commands, subordinate commands, supporting commands and agencies will submit load plan information as soon as possible after USTRANSCOM acceptance of the validation request for lift allocation and within 48 hours of request from a lift provider. Load plans will be submitted to HQ AMC/618 AOC TACC for all airlift requirements and stow planning coordinated with HQ MSC and HQ SDDC for all sealift requirements. Direct liaison authorized is granted to coordinate load and stow plans. HAZMAT requirements must be explicitly identified on all load and stow plans.

The supported CCDR will specify additional guidance or modify this guidance on load and stow plans as appropriate.

l. **USTRANSCOM Planning Factors**

(1) For determining sealift movement days:

- RLD to ALD business rule: 1 day for every 450 miles
- ALD to EAD business rule: 25 days off the east coast and 15 days off the west coast
- EAD to LAD business rule: 7 days

(2) For air movement loads:

- C-5: 61 STONs (oversized and outsized) and 51 PAX
- C-17: 45 STONs (oversized and outsized) or 90 PAX
- C-130: 12.0 STONs (bulk) or 80 PAX
- Commercial: 130 PAX

(3) For land movement days:

- 500 miles per day per driver
- Arrangements can be made for dual drivers to double the daily distance at a cost increase to the installation or service

(4) For land movement loads:

- Trucks: average loading capacity is 48 feet and 24 STONs
- Truckload defined as:
    - 60% length usage
    - Over-dimensional height and width items
    - Overweight items
    - Non-over-dimensional or overweight truck count based upon percentage of 24 STON weight limit
    - Cubic capacity based on over-dimension limits of 576 inches (length) × 102 inches (width) × 162 inches (height)

(5) Permits:

- Carriers obtain permits through permit agent or state DOT
- SDDC can expedite the state DOT permit process for shipment declared "Essential to National Defense"

VALIDATION REQUEST MESSAGE FORMAT

From: *<Supporting component, command or agency> <Office Code>*

To: *<Supported CCDR>*

Info: *<Appropriate Commands>*

<Classification>

Subj: *<Supporting component, command or agency> <operation or exercise name>* Validation Request Message *<number> <C-date>*, *<PID>*

Ref: (a) *<Legal authority to deploy (message, verbal orders)>*

(b) *<Others as appropriate>*

1. Per reference (a), the below ULNs in PID *<PID>* are forwarded for validation, or the following force module *<force module designation>* with a ULN count of *<number>* is forwarded for validation.

2. The ULNs in paragraph 1 are free of fatal errors. Changes are not authorized by providing organizations without prior coordination with the office via this newsgroup.

3. Remarks. *<Additional remarks as appropriate>*

Drafted/Released: *<Name/Rank/DSN>* / *<Name/Rank/DSN>*
Classified by: *<Authority if classified otherwise not used>*
Reason: *<Reason code if above is used>*
Declassify on: *<Date if above is used>*

Aircraft Diplomatic Clearance Worksheet for Hazardous Cargo

Purpose and Instructions: Coordinate aircraft diplomatic requests for missions with hazardous cargo between planners, booking agencies controllers, and international clearance specialists. All blocks must be completed to ensure proper and timely coordination. This is not a stand-alone form; it must be attached to the aircraft diplomatic clearance worksheet when submitted.

EXAMPLE

Proper Shipping Name	PCS	Gross WT (LBS)	N.E.W (LBS or KGS)	Class/Div	UN Shipping Number
Rockets	2	1930	106.994 LBS	1.2E	UN1206
Small Arms Ammo	5	175	0.374 KGS	1.4S	UN0012

Note: For ammunition, flares, etc., put the number of boxes for PCS, not units.

HAZMAT for ULN/Mission Number:

Proper Shipping Name	PCS	Gross WT (LBS)	N.E.W (LBS or KGS)	Class/Div	UN Shipping Number

Use additional sheets as required

FROM: MSDDC OPERATIONS CENTER SCOTT AIR FORCE BASE IL//AMSSD-OPC//
TO: CDR ASLAC GOOSE CREEK SC//DOL//
CDR FT STEWART GA//DOL//
CDR FT DIX NJ//DOL//
CDR USMC LOGCOM ALBANY GA//DOL//
CDR CAMP ATTERBURY IN//DOL//
CDR FLRC LEXINGTON KY//DOL//
CDR FT CAMPBELL KY//DOL//
CDR FT CARSON CO//DOL//
CDR USMC TWENTYNINE PALMS CA//DOL//
CDR FT BLISS//DOL//
INFO CDR ARCENT FT MCPHERSON GA
CDR FORSCOM FT MCPHERSON GA
CDR CENTCOM MACDILL AFB FL
CDR COMSC WASHINGTON DC
CDR 597TH TRANS GRP FT EUSTIS VA
CDR 842ND TRANS BN BEAUMONT TX
CDR 595TH TRANS GRP ASH SHUAYBAH KUWAIT

SUBJECT: PORT CALL FOR CHARLESTON 46-10 CHANGE 5

A. FM 3-35, ARMY DEPLOYMENT AND REDEPLOYMENT, APRIL 2010.
B. FORSCOM/ARNG REGULATION 55-1 UNIT MOVEMENT PLANNING DATED JUNE 2006.
C. DOD REG 4500.9-R, PART II, CARGO MOVEMENT, JUNE 2008.
D. CODE OF FEDERAL REGULATIONS (CFR), TITLE 49, HAZARDOUS MATERIALS TRANSPORTATION
E. INTERNATIONAL MARITIME DANGEROUS GOODS CODE (IMDGC)

1. THIS CONSTITUTES THE CALL FORWARD OF ALL EQUIPMENT SCHEDULED FOR SURFACE DEPLOYMENT THROUGH THE SEAPORT OF EMBARKATION (SPOE) NORTH CHARLESTON, SC (1PK). THE LIBERTY PROMISE (VOYAGE DOC IS A4142) WILL LOAD BEGINNING ON/ABOUT 02 DEC 2010. STRICT ADHERENCE TO UNIT SEAPORT OF EMBARKATION (SPOE) ARRIVAL DATE IS REQUIRED. DEVIATIONS TO THIS SCHEDULE ARE NOT AUTHORIZED UNLESS APPROVED BY THIS HQS. HOME STATIONS FOR THESE UNITS ARE INDICATED BELOW. THE ASSIGNED TAC IS A1RA FOR OND US ARMY UNITS AND A1RB

FOR OEF UNITS. TCAIMSS II DATA MUST BE PUSHED UPON RECEIPT OF PORT CALL OTHERWISE CARGO WILL BE FRUSTRATED AT PORT. ALSO, COMMODITY CODE 690-694 WILL NOT BE USED.

2. UNITS MUST COORDINATE SHIPMENT REQUIREMENTS WITH THEIR TRANSPORTATION OFFICE TO ENSURE ARRANGEMENTS HAVE BEEN MADE TO MOVE DEPLOYING CARGO TO THE PORT. TRANSPORTATION OFFICERS REQUIRING COMMERCIAL LINE HAUL SUPPORT SHOULD CONTACT SDDC OPERATIONS CENTER, GLOBAL DISTRIBUTION DOMESTIC, CUSTOMER SERVICE. THE TRANSPORTATION OFFICE HAVING RESPONSIBILITY FOR REQUESTING COMMERCIAL TRAFFIC SHOULD COORDINATE WITH THEIR FORCE PROTECTION OFFICE TO ENSURE ALL COMMERCIAL CARRIERS PICKING UP OR DELIVERING FREIGHT ARE NOT DELAYED AT THE GATE. SDDC AND THE TRANSPORTATION OFFICERS NEED TO EFFECTIVELY MANAGE OUR COMMERCIAL ASSETS FOR THE ENTIRE PLAN AND ENSURE ALL MOVEMENTS HAVE ADEQUATE COMMERCIAL ASSETS TO SUCCESSFULLY COMPLETE THE MISSIONS. A DEPLOYMENT TELECONFERENCE WITH SDDC, FORTS, PORTS, AND COMMERCIAL RAIL CARRIERS IS HELD MONDAY THROUGH FRIDAY AT 0930 EST TO ADDRESS ALL MOVEMENT ISSUES. HIGHLY RECOMMEND ALL ITO'S/TO'S ADDRESSED IN PORT CALL DIAL IN DAILY IF SHIPMENT TO THE PORT IS VIA RAIL.

3. ULNS FOR DEPLOYMENT OUT OF CHARLESTON:

HOME ARRIVAL DATES

ULN	UIC	STATION	NET	NLT	SPOD
URAPS87	DJ7500	CHARLESTON SC	29 NOV 2010	30 NOV 2010	PJ8 (OEF)
T9CRS04	W6HQ98	CHARLESTON SC	29 NOV 2010	30 NOV 2010	PJ8 (OEF)
T9LRP19	W6HQ98	CHARLESTON SC	29 NOV 2010	30 NOV 2010	PJ8 (OEF)
TALJ 01	WA5LW9	FT STEWART GA	29 NOV 2010	30 NOV 2010	PN4 (OEF)
TC3D 01	W7TPAA	FT DIX NJ	29 NOV 2010	30 NOV 2010	PN4 (OEF)
WX7D G9	M67004	CHARLESTON SC	29 NOV 2010	30 NOV 2010	PJ8 (OEF)
T1LAM16	W3ZKAA	SIERRA ARMY DEPOT CA	29 NOV 2010	30 NOV 2010	PJ8 (OEF)

ADDITIONAL ULNS FOR DEPLOYMENT OUT OF CHARLESTON:

T1JRD02	W46E62	CHARLESTON SC	29 NOV 2010	30 NOV 2010	PJ8 (OEF)
T1TRC20	WMPAAA	LEXINGTON KY	29 NOV 2010	30 NOV 2010	PN4 (OEF)
TKL8101	WDQWV4	FT CAMPBELL KY	29 NOV 2010	30 NOV 2010	PN4 (OEF)
TALH 03	WDQWW	FT CAMPBELL KY	29 NOV 2010	30 NOV 2010	PN4 (OEF)
TCLM2	WDQWW4	FT CAMPBELL KY	29 NOV 2010	30 NOV 2010	PN4 (OEF)
T1TRC19	WML6AA	LEXINGTON KY	29 NOV 2010	30 NOV 2010	QA1 (OEF)
T1MSK08	W0DAL7	CHARLESTON SC	29 NOV 2010	30 NOV 2010	QA1 (OEF)
T1MSK07	W0DAL7	CHARLESTON SC	29 NOV 2010	30 NOV 2010	QA1 (OEF)
T1TRC22	W6HNB3	LEXINGTON KY	29 NOV 2010	30 NOV 2010	PJ8 (OEF)

T1TRC21	W90Z99	LEXINGTON KY	29 NOV 2010	30 NOV 2010	PJ8 (OEF)
T9FA 01	WBRCAA	FT CARSON CO	29 NOV 2010	30 NOV 2010	PJ8 (OEF)
W3H0AC1	M21410	TWENTYNINE PALMS CA	29 NOV 2010	30 NOV 2010	PJ8 (OEF)
TMLAZ01	WSQJAA	FT DIX NJ	29 NOV 2010	30 NOV 2010	PN4 (OEF)
TKUW 01	WSYHAA	CAMP ATTERBURY IN	29 NOV 2010	30 NOV 2010	PN4 (OND)
TDU2 01	WV03AA	FT BLISS TX	29 NOV 2010	30 NOV 2010	PK6 (OEF)
TDU1 01	WQVMAA	FT BLISS TX	29 NOV 2010	30 NOV 2010	PK6 (OEF)
URAPS88	DJ7500	CHARLESTON SC	29 NOV 2010	30 NOV 2010	PJ8 (OEF)
URAPS89	DJ7500	CHARLESTON SC	29 NOV 2010	30 NOV 2010	PJ8 (OEF)

ULN DELETED FROM DEPLOYMENT OUT OF CHARLESTON:

TZU2 01	WZWEAA	CAMP ATTERBURY IN	29 NOV 2010	30 NOV 2010	PN4 (OND

SENSITIVE ITEMS WILL BE SCHEDULED INTO PORT ON 30 NOV 2010 ONLY.

4. ALL EQUIPMENT ARRIVING AT THE PORT OF CHARLESTON SHOULD BE CONSIGNED TO:

CDR, SDDC 841ST TRANSPORTATION BATTALION
1050 REMOUNT ROAD
B. 3310
NORTH CHARLESTON, SC 29406

ALL UNITS MUST CALL 24 HOURS IN ADVANCE FOR AN APPOINTMENT. CONTACT FREIGHT TRAFFIC CONTROL OFFICE, PHONE NUMBER 843-743-0446 x197

5. CARGO MUST ARRIVE AT THE SEAPORT OF EMBARKATION (SPOE) PREPARED IAW REFS A THROUGH E. THIS MESSAGE HIGHLIGHTS PREPARATION AND REPORTING ISSUES THAT MAY REQUIRE SPECIAL ATTENTION TO ENSURE SAFE CARGO TRANSIT AND PROPER ACCOUNTABILITY.

6. CARGO ACCOUNTABILITY:

A. CARGO REQUIRING SEALIFT MUST BE DOCUMENTED USING MILITARY SHIPPING LABELS (MSLs). MSLs WILL BE PRINTED BY THE UNIT'S TRANSPORTATION OFFICE AND MUST BE AFFIXED TO CORRESPONDING EQUIPMENT PRIOR TO DEPARTURE FROM HOME STATION.

B. DEPLOYING UNITS MUST RECEIVE ONE SET OF MSLs FOR EACH PIECE OF CARGO REFLECTED ON THEIR UNIT DEPLOYMENT LIST (UDL). MSLs MUST REFLECT THE UNIT IDENTIFICATION CODE (UIC), SHIPMENT UNIT NAME, MODEL NUMBER, AND DIMENSIONAL DATA AS PROVIDED ON THE UDL. LABELS FOR MILITARY VEHICLES MUST BE APPLIED UNIFORMLY. LABELS

MUST BE PLACED ON THE DRIVER'S SIDE (LEFT SIDE) OF THE FRONT BUMPER AND ON THE DRIVER'S (LEFT) SIDE DOOR. EQUIPMENT MUST BE MARKED ON THE FRONT AND REAR BUMPERS WITH THE UIC AND SHIPMENT UNIT NUMBER AS PROVIDED ON THE UDL. CORRESPONDING LOCATIONS MUST BE USED FOR EQUIPMENT WITHOUT BUMPERS OR DOORS. FOR MILVANS, ISUs, AND OTHER BREAKBULK CARGO, TWO LABELS NEED TO BE PLACED ON EACH ITEM, AS PREVIOUSLY DESCRIBED. ANY OTHER SIMILARLY CONSTRUCTED NUMBERS FROM PREVIOUS DEPLOYMENTS MUST BE REMOVED TO AVOID CONFUSION. THIS PROCEDURE APPLIES TO BOTH DEPLOYMENT AND REDEPLOYMENT.

C. RFID TAGS: ALL MAJOR ORGANIZATIONAL EQUIPMENT AND CONTAINERS MUST HAVE ACTIVE DATA-RICH RFID TAGS WRITTEN AT THE POINT OF ORIGIN IN ACCORDANCE WITH CENTCOM REGULATION 700-4. CONENT LEVEL DETAIL WILL BE PROVIDED IN ACCORDANCE WITH THE CURRENT DOD RFID TAG DATA STANDARDS. THE CAPABILITY TO SEE TIMELY AND ACCURATE INFORMATION IS ESSENTIAL CONCERNING DEPLOYING/REDEPLOYING UNIT CARGO AND EQUIPMENT AS WELL AS NON-UNIT AND SUSTAINMENT CARGO MOVEMENTS. THIS REQUIRES LEVEL 6 DETAIL VISIBILITY OF SECONDARY CARGO PACKED INSIDE CONTAINERS, INSIDE BOXES STUFFED IN CONTAINERS, SECONDARY CARGO PACKED INSIDE CARGO VEHICLES AND TRAILERS, AND MAJOR ORGANIZATIONAL EQUIPMENT BEING SHIPPED INTO THE CENTCOM AOR. REQUESTS FOR RELIEF FROM THIS REQUIREMENT SHOULD BE DIRECTED TO CFLCC. AT ORIGIN OF SHIPMENT LEVEL 5 & 6 SECONDARY CARGO DETAILED DATA MUST BE REFLECTED ON THE UNITS DEL FOR THIS DATA TO BE TRANSFERRED TO THE RF TAGS. FORSCOM UNITS REQUIRING RFID TAGS OR ADDITIONAL RFID TAGS SHOULD CONTACT THE LOCAL ITO WHO SHOULD IN TURN CONTACT THE FORSCOM G-4. SDDC OPS POC FOR RFID TAGS IS MR. DAN MONAHAN DSN 770-6489 OR EMAIL DANIEL.MONAHAN@US.ARMY.MIL.

D. VEHICLE LOADS THAT COULD POSSIBLY BE SHIPPED SEPARATELY (SECONDARY LOADS) MUST ALSO BE STENCILED WITH THE UIC AND A SHIPMENT UNIT NUMBER.

E. AN ACCURATE UDL IS ESSENTIAL FOR TRANSPORTATION PLANNING. ANY ITEM NOT ACCURATELY REPORTED WILL BE CONSIDERED FRUSTRATED CARGO AT THE PORT. FRUSTRATED CARGO WILL ONLY BE SHIPPED ON A "SPACE AVAILABLE" BASIS. MAJOR UNIT COMMANDS NEED TO PROVIDE LNOS TO THE PORT POC TO FACILITATE MOVEMENT OF FRUSTRATED CARGO. UNITS NEED TO REPORT VEHICLES AND TRAILERS IN "REDUCED FOR SEALIFT/OPERATIONAL" CONFIGURATION WHEN POSSIBLE ON THEIR UDLs. FOR VEHICLES, TRAILERS AND CONTAINERS CARRYING SECONDARY CARGO, ACTUAL WEIGHTS MUST BE ANNOTATED ON THE UDL PRIOR TO MSLs BEING PRODUCED.

7. HAZARDOUS/SENSITIVE/CLASSIFIED CARGO: UNIT PERSONNEL RESPONSIBLE FOR PACKING, MARKING, LABELING, PLACARDING, AND CERTIFYING HAZARDOUS MATERIAL ITEMS WILL ENSURE ACTIONS ARE COMPLETED IAW REF D OR E. ITEMS SHIPPED IAW DEPARTMENT OF TRANSPORTATION EXEMPTION (DOT-E), DOT SPECIAL APPROVAL OR COMPETENT AUTHORITY APPROVAL (CAA) MUST BE ATTACHED TO THE SHIPPING MANIFEST. SENSITIVE/CLASSIFIED SHIPMENTS SHALL BE TRANSPORTED IAW REF C.

A. THE SDDC PORT WILL USE THE UDL AS ADVANCE CARGO MOVEMENT DOCUMENTATION. UNITS ARE RESPONSIBLE FOR COORDINATING WITH THE ITO TO PUT THE UDL INTO TC-AIMS II, UNLESS PRIOR ARRANGEMENTS ARE MADE WITH THE TERMINAL. IF THE UNIT DOES NOT HAVE ACCESS TO TC-AIMS II, ATCMDS MUST BE GENERATED MANUALLY IAW REF C. APPLIED SEAL NUMBERS WILL BE ANNOTATED ON THE DD FORM 1907, SIGNATURE AND TALLY RECORD, WHICH WILL ACCOMPANY THE GBL TO CREATE A "CHANGE OF CUSTODY" IAW REF C FOR ALL SENSITIVE ITEMS BEING SHIPPED. A SEPARATE PACKING LIST, LISTING THE SENSITIVE ITEMS, FOR EACH ITEM OF CARGO CONTAINING SENSITIVE ITEMS NEEDS TO BE PROVIDED TO THE PORT. THIS CAN BE FAXED OR DELIVERED WITH THE CARGO.

B. TRANSPORTATION OF SENSITIVE AND CLASSIFIED EQUIPMENT MUST BE COMPLETED IAW THE SECURITY STANDARDS OUTLINED IN REF C.

C. CREW SERVED WEAPONS MUST BE REMOVED FROM VEHICLES AND PLACED IN A LOCKED CONTAINER APPROVED FOR SENSITIVE ITEM SHIPMENTS IAW AR 190-11 WITH A SECURITY SEAL.

D. HAZARDOUS CARGO:

(1) HAZARDOUS CARGO MUST BE SEGREGATED AND LABELED IAW REFS D OR E. FOR EXAMPLE, FLAMMABLES MUST BE SEGREGATED FROM OXIDIZERS AND OXYGEN AND ACETYLENE CYLINDERS MUST BE REMOVED FROM THE VEHICLES AND STRAPPED TO SEPARATE WOODEN PALLETIZED CRATES TO FIRMLY AND SECURELY HOLD THE CYLINDERS IN A VERTICAL POSITION. THE CYLINDER CAPS SHOULD BE PROTECTED FROM IMPACT AND CYLINDERS SHOULD BE SHIELDED FROM DIRECT HEAT.

(2) IAW REF C, THE MULTIMODAL DANGEROUS GOODS FORM (DD FORM 2890) DATED MARCH 05, IS REQUIRED FOR HAZMAT SHIPMENTS TRANSPORTED ON COMMERCIAL VESSELS IN US AND INTERNATIONAL WATERS. ORGANIC VEHICLES, TRAILERS, CONTAINERS, AND ANY OTHER UNIT EQUIPMENT CONTAINING HAZMAT ARRIVING AT THE PORT WILL REQUIRE THE FOLLOWING DOCUMENTATION:

(A) COMPLETED DD FORM 2890 FOR EACH VEHICLE/CONTAINER/ EQUIPMENT SHIPPED OR CONVOYED CARRYING HAZMAT IAW REF D OR E. THE DD FORM 2890 MUST BE VISIBLE AND COMPLETED IN FOUR (4) COPIES FOR CONTAINERIZED CARGO. ONE COPY WILL BE RETAINED BY THE CERTIFYING UNIT/ INSTALLATION, ONE WILL BE PLACED INSIDE THE CONTAINER OR PACKAGE, ONE COPY WILL BE AFFIXED TO THE OUTSIDE OF CONTAINER OR PACKAGE IN A WATERPROOF ENVELOPE, AND ONE COPY WILL BE PROVIDED TO THE PORT. THREE COPIES OF THE DD FORM 2890 ARE REQUIRED FOR VEHICLES. ONE COPY WILL BE RETAINED BY THE CERTIFYING UNIT/INSTALLATION, ONE COPY IN A WATERPROOF ENVELOPE WILL BE AFFIXED TO THE VEHICLE, AND ONE COPY WILL BE PROVIDED TO THE PORT.

(B) FOR ALL HAZMAT SHIPMENT OF UNITS DEPLOYING FROM THE US, A DEPLOYMENT EQUIPMENT LIST CONTAINING THE PROPER CARGO CATEGORY CODES MUST BE TRANSMITTED TO THE PORT VIA TC-ACCIS/TC-AIMS. THE SHIPPER WILL ATTACH A DD FORM 2890 TO THE TC- ACCIS/TC-AIMS GENERATED GBL TO PROVIDE THE CORRECT HAZMAT CERTIFICATION INFORMATION OR THE UNIT'S LNO WILL PROVIDE A HARD COPY OF ALL SHIPPING PAPERS FOR ALL EQUIPMENT TO THE PORT DOCUMENTATION TEAMS.

(3) UNIT VEHICLES/CONTAINERS/HAZMAT CARGO WILL BE PROPERLY PLACARDED IAW REFS C, D OR E. ALL HAZMAT CARGO REQUIRES PLACARD FOR OCEAN MOVEMENT. PLACARD IS REQUIRED FOR STRICTEST MODE OF TRANSPORT, AND MUST BE APPLIED BY UNIT/SHIPPER PRIOR TO ARRIVAL AT POE. CONTAINERS WILL HAVE A PACKING LIST, WHICH INCLUDES THE HAZMAT INFORMATION AFFIXED TO BOTH THE INSIDE AND OUTSIDE OF THE CONTAINER IN A WATERPROOF ENVELOPE.

(4) CONTAINERS WILL HAVE A PACKING LIST, WHICH INCLUDES THE HAZMAT INFORMATION AFFIXED TO BOTH THE INSIDE AND OUTSIDE OF THE CONTAINER IN A WATERPROOF ENVELOPE.

E. AMMUNITION OR EXPLOSIVES WILL NOT BE PERMITTED IN THE PORT OR ABOARD THE VESSEL WITHOUT AUTHORIZATION FROM THIS COMMAND. THIS PROHIBITION EXTENDS TO CONTAINER SHIPMENTS ALSO.

FOR HAZMAT QUESTIONS, PLEASE CONTACT LISA TAYLOR AT DSN 770-6918 OR HOSETTA ALLEN AT DSN 770-6788.

FOR TRANSPORTATION PROTECTIVE SECURITY QUESTIONS, PLEASE CONTACT LARRY EARICK AT DSN 770-6834 OR JESSYCA HOWARD AT DSN 770-6881.

8. SEAVANS/MILVANS/QUADCONS:

A. CONTAINERS MUST BE MARKED WITH THEIR ACTUAL GROSS WEIGHT BEFORE DEPARTURE FROM HOME STATION. ACCURATE WEIGHT DATA MUST

BE EASILY IDENTIFIABLE TO PORT PERSONNEL TO AVOID INJURY OR EQUIPMENT DAMAGE. DO NOT EXCEED CONTAINER WEIGHT LIMITATIONS. THE ACTUAL GROSS WEIGHT MUST BE ANNOTATED ON THE UNIT'S UDL IN ORDER FOR THE ACTUAL WEIGHT TO BE ENTERED ON THE MILITARY SHIPPING LABEL (MSL). THE PACKING LIST, WHICH INCLUDES THE HAZMAT INFORMATION, MUST BE AFFIXED TO BOTH THE INSIDE AND OUTSIDE OF THE CONTAINERS.

B. DURING DEPLOYMENT, CONTAINERS MUST BE INSPECTED TO ENSURE THAT THEY MEET THE CURRENT CONTAINER SAFETY CERTIFICATION (CSC) INSPECTION REQUIREMENTS AND HAVE A CURRENT CSC DECAL AFFIXED ON THE CONTAINER IN THE APPROPRIATE LOCATION.

9. VEHICLES/TRAILERS/MISCELLANEOUS:

A. EQUIPMENT ARRIVING AT THE PORT MUST BE CLEAN, FREE FROM FLUID LEAKS, AND IN GOOD MECHANICAL CONDITION. VEHICLES MUST BE EQUIPPED WITH SERVICEABLE AND PROPER LIFTING DEVICES OR SHACKLES.

B. VEHICLE KEYS SHOULD BE SECURELY ATTACHED TO STEERING COLUMN TO ALLOW FOR VEHICLE OPERATION.

C. VEHICLES MUST NOT HAVE THEIR FUEL TANKS GREATER THAN ONE QUARTER (1/4) FULL.

D. UNITS SHIPPING WRECKERS NEED TO ENSURE TOW BARS AND TOOLS ARE PLACED IN THE CAB OF THE VEHICLE TO ALLOW EASY ACCESS AT THE SPOD. THIS EQUIPMENT MAY BE REQUIRED TO DISCHARGE INOPERABLE VEHICLES FROM THE VESSEL DUE TO LIMITED RECOVERY ASSETS IN THEATER.

E. CARGO LOADED IN OR ON VEHICLES MUST BE PROPERLY BLOCKED, BRACED AND SECURED FOR SEA SHIPMENT. LOOSE CARGO LOADS ARE NOT PERMITTED. UNITS SHOULD PREVENT METAL-TO-METAL CONTACT IF THERE IS A POSSIBILITY OF ABRASIVE DAMAGE.

F. JERRY CANS MAY BE SHIPPED MUST BE SHIPPED EMPTY, VAPOR FREE, AND DOCUMENTED ON A DD FORM 2890.

G. GENERATORS MAY BE SHIPPED WITH ONE QUARTER (1/4) FULL FUEL TANKS.

H. BULK FUEL CARRIERS (TRAILERS) MUST BE DRAINED IF APPLICABLE. IF DRAINED BUT NOT PURGED, VEHICLE WILL BE HANDLED AS HAZMAT.

I. INSTALLATION ITOs SHOULD NOTIFY RAIL CARRIERS OF WIDE LOADS ON THE RAILCARS NLT 24 HOURS PRIOR TO TRAIN PULLING SO RAIL CARRIER CAN PLAN THE SAFE ROUTING OF THE TRAIN.

10. EQUIPMENT MAINTENANCE MUST BE ACCOMPLISHED AT HOME STATION PRIOR TO DEPARTURE. WHEN EQUIPMENT IS CONVOYED TO THE SPOE, VEHICLE PREPARATION THAT COULD NOT BE ACCOMPLISHED PRIOR TO DEPARTURE FROM HOME STATION WILL BE DONE AT THE PORT WITHIN A DESIGNATED AREA.

11. THE VESSEL IS THE LIBERTY PROMISE. VOYAGE NUMBER IS A4142.

12. POINTS OF CONTACT FOR THIS MOVE ARE DSN: 770: CW2 EICHELE 5599, MS. HIMEL 5900, MS. FREEMAN 5888, SSG LEWIS 6409 OR MR. KABAJ 5898 OR EMAIL AT SDDC.OPS.CENTCOM@US.ARMY.MIL.

APPENDIX D
REFERENCES

The development of JP 3-35 is based upon the following primary references:

1. United States Government Publications

a. Global Force Management Implementation Guidance Fiscal Year (FY) 2010-2011.

b. Title 10, United States Code.

c. Unified Command Plan.

2. Department of Defense Publications

a. DODD 4500.09E, *Transportation and Traffic Management.*

b. DODD 5100.01, *Functions of the Department of Defense and its Major Components.*

c. Department of Defense Instruction 4140.1, *Supply Chain Materiel Management Policy.*

d. DTR 4500.9-R, *Defense Transportation Regulation Part I, Passenger Movement.*

e. DTR 4500.9-R, *Defense Transportation Regulation Part II, Cargo Movement.*

f. DTR 4500.9-R, *Defense Transportation Regulation Part III, Mobility.*

g. DTR 4500.9-R, *Defense Transportation Regulation Part V, Customs.*

3. Chairman of the Joint Chiefs of Staff Publications

a. CJCSI 3110.01H, *Joint Strategic Capabilities Plan.*

b. CJCSI 3141.01E, *Management and Review of Joint Strategic Capabilities Plan (JSCP)-Tasked Plans.*

c. CJCSI 3151.01B, *Global Command and Control System Common Operational Picture Reporting Requirements.*

d. CJCSI 3500.01G, *Joint Training Policy and Guidance for the Armed Forces of the United States.*

e. CJCSI 5120.02C, *Joint Doctrine Development System.*

f. CJCSM 3122.01A, *Joint Operation Planning and Execution System (JOPES) Volume I: (Planning Policies and Procedures).*

g. CJCSM 3122.02D, *Joint Operation Planning and Execution System Volume III, Crisis Action Time-Phased Force and Deployment Data Development and Deployment Execution.*

h. CJCSM 3130.03, *Adaptive Planning and Execution (APEX) Planning Formats and Guidance.*

i. CJCS Guide 3130, *Adaptive Planning and Execution (APEX) Overview and Planning Framework.*

j. CJCSM 3500.03C, *Joint Training Manual for the Armed Forces of the United States.*

k. CJCSM 3500.04F, *Universal Joint Task List Manual.*

l. CJCSM 5120.01, *Joint Doctrine Development Process.*

m. JP 1, *Doctrine for the Armed Forces of the United States.*

n. JP 1-0, *Joint Personnel Support.*

o. JP 2-0, *Joint Intelligence.*

p. JP 2-01, *Joint and National Intelligence Support to Military Operations.*

q. JP 3-0, *Joint Operations.*

r. JP 3-05, *Special Operations.*

s. JP 3-07.2, *Antiterrorism.*

t. JP 3-08, *Interorganizational Coordination During Joint Operations.*

u. JP 3-10, *Joint Security Operations in Theater.*

v. JP 3-11, *Operations in Chemical, Biological, Radiological, and Nuclear (CBRN) Environments.*

w. JP 3-13, *Information Operations.*

x. JP 3-13.2, *Military Information Support Operations.*

y. JP 3-13.3, *Operations Security.*

z. JP 3-13.4, *Military Deception.*

aa. JP 3-16, *Multinational Operations.*

bb. JP 3-17, *Air Mobility Operations.*

cc. JP 3-33, *Joint Task Force Headquarters*.

dd. JP 3-57, *Civil-Military Operations*.

ee. JP 3-61, *Public Affairs*.

ff. JP 4-0, *Joint Logistics*.

gg. JP 4-01, *The Defense Transportation System*.

hh. JP 4-01.2, *Sealift Support to Joint Operations*.

ii. JP 4-01.5, *Joint Terminal Operations*.

jj. JP 4-01.6, *Joint Logistics Over-the-Shore*.

kk. JP 4-02, *Health Service Support*.

ll. JP 4-05, *Joint Mobilization Planning*.

mm. JP 4-09, *Distribution Operations*.

nn. JP 5-0, *Joint Operation Planning*.

oo. JP 6-0, *Joint Communications System*.

4. United States Army Publications

a. FM 3-35, *Army Deployment and Redeployment*.

b. FM 55-1, *Transportation Operations*.

5. United States Marine Corps Publications

a. Marine Corps Warfighting Publication 3-32, *Maritime Prepositioning Force Operations*.

b. Marine Corps Doctrine Publication 4, *Logistics*.

6. United States Navy Publications

a. Navy Warfare Publication 5-01, *Navy Planning*.

b. NTTP 4-01.1, *Navy Advanced Base Logistics Operations*.

c. NTTP 4-01.5, *Strategic Mobility and Unit Movement Operations*.

7. United States Air Force Publications

a. Air Force Doctrine Document (AFDD) 3-17, *Air Mobility Operations*.

b. AFDD 4-0, *Combat Support*.

c. Air Force Pamphlet 10-1403, *Air Mobility Planning Factors*.

APPENDIX E
ADMINISTRATIVE INSTRUCTIONS

1. User Comments

Users in the field are highly encouraged to submit comments on this publication to: Joint Staff J-7, Deputy Director, Joint and Coalition Warfighting, ATTN: Joint Doctrine Support Division, 116 Lake View Parkway, Suffolk, VA 23435-2697. These comments should address content (accuracy, usefulness, consistency, and organization), writing, and appearance.

2. Authorship

The lead agent for this publication is the Director, Joint Force Development (J-7), Joint Staff. The Joint Staff doctrine sponsor for this publication is the Director for Logistics (J-4).

3. Supersession

This publication supersedes JP 3-35, 7 May 2007, *Joint Deployment and Redeployment Operations.*

4. Change Recommendations

a. Recommendations for urgent changes to this publication should be submitted:

TO: JOINT STAFF WASHINGTON DC//J4-JDD/J7-JEDD//
JOINT STAFF WASHINGTON DC//J-3//

b. Routine changes should be submitted electronically to the Deputy Director, Joint and Coalition Warfighting, Joint Doctrine Support Division and info the lead agent and the Director for Joint Force Development, J-7/JEDD.

c. When a Joint Staff directorate submits a proposal to the CJCS that would change source document information reflected in this publication, that directorate will include a proposed change to this publication as an enclosure to its proposal. The Services and other organizations are requested to notify the Joint Staff J-7 when changes to source documents reflected in this publication are initiated.

5. Distribution of Publications

Local reproduction is authorized, and access to unclassified publications is unrestricted. However, access to, and reproduction authorization for, classified JPs must be IAW DOD Manual 5200.01, Volume 1, *DOD Information Security Program: Overview, Classification, and Declassification,* and DOD Manual 5200.01, Volume 3, *DOD Information Security Program: Protection of Classified Information.*

6. Distribution of Electronic Publications

a. Joint Staff J-7 will not print copies of JPs for distribution. Electronic versions are available on JDEIS at http://jdeis.js.mil (NIPRNET), and http://jdeis.js.smil.mil (SIPRNET), and on the JEL at http:www.dtic.mil/doctrine (NIPRNET).

b. Only approved JPs and joint test publications are releasable outside the CCMDs, Services, and Joint Staff. Release of any classified JP to foreign governments or foreign nationals must be requested through the local embassy (Defense Attaché Office) to DIA, Defense Foreign Liaison/IE-3, 200 MacDill Blvd., Joint Base Anacostia-Bolling, Washington, DC 20340-5100.

c. JEL CD-ROM. Upon request of a joint doctrine development community member, the Joint Staff J-7 will produce and deliver one CD-ROM with current JPs. This JEL CD ROM will be updated not less than semi-annually and when received can be locally reproduced for use within the CCMDs and Services.

GLOSSARY
PART I—ABBREVIATIONS AND ACRONYMS

AA&E	arms, ammunition, and explosives
ACSA	acquisition and cross-servicing agreement
A/DACG	arrival/departure airfield control group
AFDD	Air Force doctrine document
AFWA	Air Force Weather Agency
AIS	automated information system
AIT	automated identification technology
ALD	available-to-load date
AMC	Air Mobility Command
AOC	air and space operations center (USAF)
AOR	area of responsibility
APEX	Adaptive Planning and Execution
APOD	aerial port of debarkation
APOE	aerial port of embarkation
ASCC	Army Service component command
AV	asset visibility
BRACE	Base Resource and Capability Estimator
C2	command and control
CAP	crisis action planning
CBP	Customs and Border Protection (DHS)
CBRN	chemical, biological, radiological, and nuclear
CCDR	combatant commander
CCIR	commander's critical information requirement
CCMD	combatant command
CDRUSSOCOM	Commander, United States Special Operations Command
CDRUSTRANSCOM	Commander, United States Transportation Command
CJCS	Chairman of the Joint Chiefs of Staff
CJCSI	Chairman of the Joint Chiefs of Staff instruction
CJCSM	Chairman of the Joint Chiefs of Staff manual
COA	course of action
COMPASS	Computerized Movement Planning and Status System
CONOPS	concept of operations
CONPLAN	concept plan
CONUS	continental United States
COP	common operational picture
CRAF	Civil Reserve Air Fleet
CRG	contingency response group
CSA	combat support agency
CULT	common-user land transportation

DA	Department of the Army
DCAPES	Deliberate and Crisis Action Planning and Execution Segments
DDOC	Deployment and Distribution Operations Center (USTRANSCOM)
DEL	deployable equipment list
DEPORD	deployment order
DHS	Department of Homeland Security
DIA	Defense Intelligence Agency
DISA	Defense Information Systems Agency
DLA	Defense Logistics Agency
DOD	Department of Defense
DODD	Department of Defense directive
DOS	Department of State
DOT	Department of Transportation
DPO	distribution process owner
DSN	Defense Switched Network
DTR	defense transportation regulation
DTS	Defense Transportation System
EAD	earliest arrival date
ELIST	enhanced logistics intratheater support tool
FEMA	Federal Emergency Management Agency
FM	field manual (Army)
FRN	force requirement number
FTN	force tracking number
FY	fiscal year
GATES	Global Air Transportation Execution System
GCC	geographic combatant commander
GCCS-J	Global Command and Control System-Joint
GCSS	Global Combat Support System
GCSS-J	Global Combat Support System-Joint
GDSS	Global Decision Support System
GEF	Guidance for Employment of the Force
GFM	global force management
GFMAP	Global Force Management Allocation Plan
HAZMAT	hazardous materials
HN	host nation
HNS	host-nation support
HQ	headquarters
IAW	in accordance with
ICODES	integrated computerized deployment system

IED	improvised explosive device
IGC	Integrated Data Environment/Global Transportation Network Convergence
ISB	intermediate staging base
ISR	intelligence, surveillance, and reconnaissance
ITO	installation transportation officer
ITV	in-transit visibility
JCRM	Joint Capabilities Requirements Manager
JDDOC	joint deployment and distribution operations center
JFAST	Joint Flow and Analysis System for Transportation
JFC	joint force commander
JFP	joint force provider
JFRG II	joint force requirements generator II
JLOTS	joint logistics over-the-shore
JMC	joint movement center
JOA	joint operations area
JOPES	Joint Operation Planning and Execution System
JOPP	joint operation planning process
JP	joint publication
JPEC	joint planning and execution community
JRSOI	joint reception, staging, onward movement, and integration
JTB	Joint Transportation Board
JTF	joint task force
JTF-PO	joint task force-port opening
LAD	latest arrival date
LNO	liaison officer
LOC	line of communications
LOI	letter of instruction
LOTS	logistics over-the-shore
MAGTF	Marine air-ground task force
MCC	movement control center
MCIP	military customs inspection program
MDDOC	Marine air-ground task force deployment and distribution operations center
MDSS II	Marine air-ground task force Deployment Support System II
METT-T	mission, enemy, terrain and weather, troops and support available—time available
MHE	materials handling equipment
MOG	maximum (aircraft) on ground
MSC	Military Sealift Command
MSR	main supply route

NALSS	naval advanced logistic support site
NATO	North Atlantic Treaty Organization
NEO	noncombatant evacuation operation
NFLS	naval forward logistic site
NTTP	Navy tactics, techniques, and procedures
NURP	non-unit-related personnel
OA	operational area
OCONUS	outside the continental United States
OCP	operational capability package
OE	operational environment
OPCON	operational control
OPLAN	operation plan
OPORD	operation order
OPSEC	operations security
PAX	passengers
PHIT	port handling/in-land transportation
PID	plan identification number
POC	point of contact
POD	port of debarkation
POE	port of embarkation
POG	port operations group
POL	petroleum, oils, and lubricants
PORTSIM	port simulation model
PSA	port support activity
RC	Reserve Component
RDD	required delivery date
RFF	request for forces
RFID	radio frequency identification
RLD	ready-to-load date
RQT	rapid query tool
SA	staging area
SDDC	Surface Deployment and Distribution Command
SecDef	Secretary of Defense
SIPRNET	SECRET Internet Protocol Router Network
SMS	single mobility system
SO	special operations
SOF	special operations forces
SOP	standard operating procedure
SORTS	Status of Resources and Training System
SPM	single port manager
SPOD	seaport of debarkation
SPOE	seaport of embarkation

STON	short ton
TAA	tactical assembly area
TACC	tanker airlift control center
TACON	tactical control
TC-AIMS II	Transportation Coordinator's Automated Information for Movement System II
TCC	transportation component command
TD	theater distribution
TEA	Transportation Engineering Agency
TMT	time-phased force and deployment data management tool
TPE	theater provided equipment
TPFDD	time-phased force and deployment data
TPFDL	time-phased force and deployment list
TRAC2ES	United States Transportation Command Regulating and Command and Control Evacuation System
TTAN	transportation tracking account number
UCP	Unified Command Plan
UDL	unit deployment list
ULN	unit line number
USAF	United States Air Force
USCG	United States Coast Guard
USG	United States Government
USSOCOM	United States Special Operations Command
USSTRATCOM	United States Strategic Command
USTRANSCOM	United States Transportation Command
VISA	Voluntary Intermodal Sealift Agreement
WARNORD	warning order
Web SM	Web scheduling and movement
WRM	war reserve materiel

PART II—TERMS AND DEFINITIONS

asset visibility. Provides users with information on the location, movement, status, and asset visibility. Provides users with information on the location, movement, status, and identity of units, personnel, equipment, and supplies, which facilitates the capability to act upon that information to improve overall performance of the Department of Defense's logistics practices. Also called **AV.** (Approved for incorporation into JP 1-02.)

automation network. None. (Approved for removal from JP 1-02.)

cargo increment number. A seven-character alphanumeric field that uniquely describes a non-unit-cargo entry (line) in the Joint Operation Planning and Execution System time-phased force and deployment data. (Approved for incorporation into JP 1-02 with JP 3-35 as the source JP.)

common-user sealift. The sealift services provided by the Military Sealift Command on a common basis for all Department of Defense agencies and, as authorized, for other departments and agencies of the United States Government. (Approved for incorporation into JP 1-02.)

deployment. The rotation of forces into and out of an operational area. (Approved for incorporation into JP 1-02.)

force closure. The point in time when a supported joint force commander determines that sufficient personnel and equipment resources are in the assigned operational area to carry out assigned tasks. (JP 1-02. SOURCE: JP 3-35)

force requirement number. An alphanumeric code used to uniquely identify force entries in a given operation plan time-phased force and deployment data. Also called **FRN.** (Approved for inclusion in JP 1-02.)

force tracking. The process of gathering and maintaining information on the location, status, and predicted movement of each element of a unit including the unit's command element, personnel, and unit-related supplies and equipment while in transit to the specified operational area. (JP 1-02. SOURCE: JP 3-35)

force visibility. The current and accurate status of forces; their current mission; future missions; location; mission priority; and readiness status. (Approved for incorporation into JP 1-02.)

global force management. A process that provides near-term sourcing solutions while providing the integrating mechanism between force apportionment, allocation, and assignment. Also call **GFM.** (Approved for inclusion in JP 1-02.)

host-nation support agreement. None. (Approved for removal from JP 1-02.)

information resources. None. (Approved for removal JP 1-02.)

infrastructure. None. (Approved for removal from JP 1-02.)

intermediate staging base. A tailorable, temporary location used for staging forces, sustainment and/or extraction into and out of an operational area. Also called **ISB.** (JP 1-02. SOURCE 3-35)

joint flow and analysis system for transportation. System that determines the transportation feasibility of a course of action or operation plan; provides daily lift assets needed to move forces and resupply; advises logistic planners of channel and port inefficiencies; and interprets shortfalls from various flow possibilities. Also called **JFAST.** (JP 1-02. SOURCE: JP 3-35)

joint reception complex. None. (Approved for removal from JP 1-02.)

joint reception, staging, onward movement, and integration. A phase of joint force projection occurring in the operational area during which arriving personnel, equipment, and materiel transition into forces capable of meeting operational requirements. Also called **JRSOI.** (Approved for incorporation into JP 1-02.)

joint total asset visibility. None. (Approved for removal from JP 1-02.)

key employee. None. (Approved for removal from JP 1-02.)

marshalling area. A location in the vicinity of a reception terminal or pre-positioned equipment storage site where arriving unit personnel, equipment, materiel, and accompanying supplies are reassembled, returned to the control of the unit commander, and prepared for onward movement. (Approved for incorporation into JP 1-02.)

materials handling equipment. None. (Approved for removal from JP 1-02.)

N-day. None. (Approved for removal from JP 1-02.)

naval advanced logistic support site. An overseas location used as the primary transshipment point in the theater of operations for logistic support. Also called **NALSS.** (Approved for incorporation into JP 1-02).

naval forward logistic site. An overseas location, with port and airfield facilities nearby, which provides logistic support to naval forces within the theater of operations during major contingency and wartime periods. Also called **NFLS.** (Approved for incorporation into JP 1-02.)

off-load preparation party. None. (Approved for removal from JP 1-02.)

port operations group. A task-organized unit, located at the seaport of embarkation and/or debarkation that assists and provides support in the loading and/or unloading and staging of personnel, supplies, and equipment from shipping. Also called **POG.** (Approved for incorporation into JP 1-02.)

port support activity. A tailorable support organization composed of mobilization station assets that ensures the equipment of the deploying units is ready to load. Also called **PSA.** (Approved for incorporation into JP 1-02.)

power projection. None. (Approved for removal from JP 1-02.)

R-Day. None. (Approved for removal from JP 1-02.)

reception. 1. All ground arrangements connected with the delivery and disposition of air or sea drops. 2. Arrangements to welcome and provide secure quarters or transportation for defectors, escapees, evaders, or incoming agents. 3. The process of receiving, off-loading, marshalling, accounting for, and transporting of personnel, equipment, and materiel from the strategic and/or intratheater deployment phase to a sea, air, or surface transportation point of debarkation to the marshalling area. (Approved for incorporation into JP 1-02.)

recovery and reconstitution. 1. Those actions taken by one nation prior to, during, and following an attack by an enemy nation to minimize the effects of the attack, rehabilitate the national economy, provide for the welfare of the populace, and maximize the combat potential of remaining forces and supporting activities. 2. Those actions taken by a military force during or after operational employment to restore its combat capability to full operational readiness. (JP 1-02. SOURCE: JP 3-35)

redeployment. The transfer or rotation of forces and materiel to support another joint force commander's operational requirements, or to return personnel, equipment, and materiel to the home and/or demobilization stations for reintegration and/or out-processing. (Approved for incorporation into JP 1-02.)

staging. Assembling, holding, and organizing arriving personnel, equipment, and sustaining materiel in preparation for onward movement. (Approved for incorporation into JP 1-02.)

staging area. 1. Amphibious or airborne - A general locality between the mounting area and the objective of an amphibious or airborne expedition, through which the expedition or parts thereof pass after mounting, for refueling, regrouping of ships, and/or exercise, inspection, and redistribution of troops. 2. Other movements - A general locality established for the concentration of troop units and transient personnel between movements over the lines of communications. Also called **SA.** (JP 1-02. SOURCE: JP 3-35)

tactical assembly area. An area that is generally out of the reach of light artillery and the location where units make final preparations (pre-combat checks and inspections) and rest, prior to moving to the line of departure. (JP 1-02. SOURCE: JP 3-35)

transit area. None. (Approved for removal from JP 1-02.)

transportation closure. The actual arrival date of a specified movement requirement at port of debarkation. (Approved for incorporation into JP 1-02 with JP 3-35 as the source JP.)

unit line number. A seven-character alphanumeric code that describes a unique increment of a unit deployment, i.e., advance party, main body, equipment by sea and air, reception team, or trail party, in the time-phased force and deployment data. Also called ULN. (Upon approval of this revised publication, this definition will modify the existing definition and be incorporated into JP 1-02.)

unit movement control center. A temporary organization activated by major subordinate commands and subordinate units during deployment to control and manage marshalling and movement. Also called **UMCC.** (JP 1-02. SOURCE: JP 3-35)

unit movement data. A unit equipment and/or supply listing containing corresponding transportability data. Tailored unit movement data has been modified to reflect a specific movement requirement. Also called **UMD.** (Approved for incorporation into JP 1-02 with JP 3-35 as the source JP.)

validation. 1. A process associated with the collection and production of intelligence that confirms that an intelligence collection or production requirement is sufficiently important to justify the dedication of intelligence resources, does not duplicate an existing requirement, and has not been previously satisfied. (JP 2-01) 2. A part of target development that ensures all vetted targets meet the objectives and criteria outlined in the commander's guidance and ensures compliance with the law of armed conflict and rules of engagement. (JP 3-60) 3. In computer modeling and simulation, the process of determining the degree to which a model or simulation is an accurate representation of the real world from the perspective of the intended uses of the model or simulation. (JP 3-35) 4. Execution procedure whereby all the information records in a time-phased force and deployment data are confirmed error free and accurately reflect the current status, attributes, and availability of units and requirements. (JP 3-35) (Approved for incorporation into JP 1-02.)

Intentionally Blank

JOINT DOCTRINE PUBLICATIONS HIERARCHY

JP 1
JOINT DOCTRINE
JP 1-0
PERSONNEL
JP 2-0
INTELLIGENCE
JP 3-0
OPERATIONS
JP 4-0
LOGISTICS
JP 5-0
PLANS
JP 6-0
COMMUNICATIONS SYSTEM

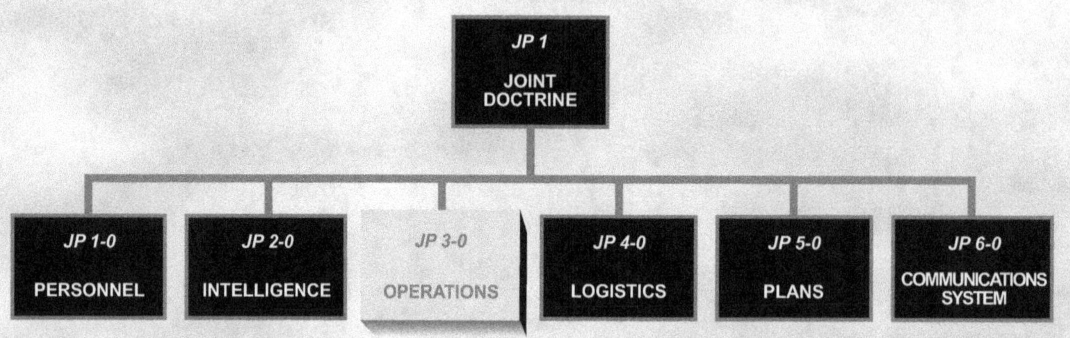

All joint publications are organized into a comprehensive hierarchy as shown in the chart above. **Joint Publication (JP) 3-35** is in the **Operations** series of joint doctrine publications. The diagram below illustrates an overview of the development process:

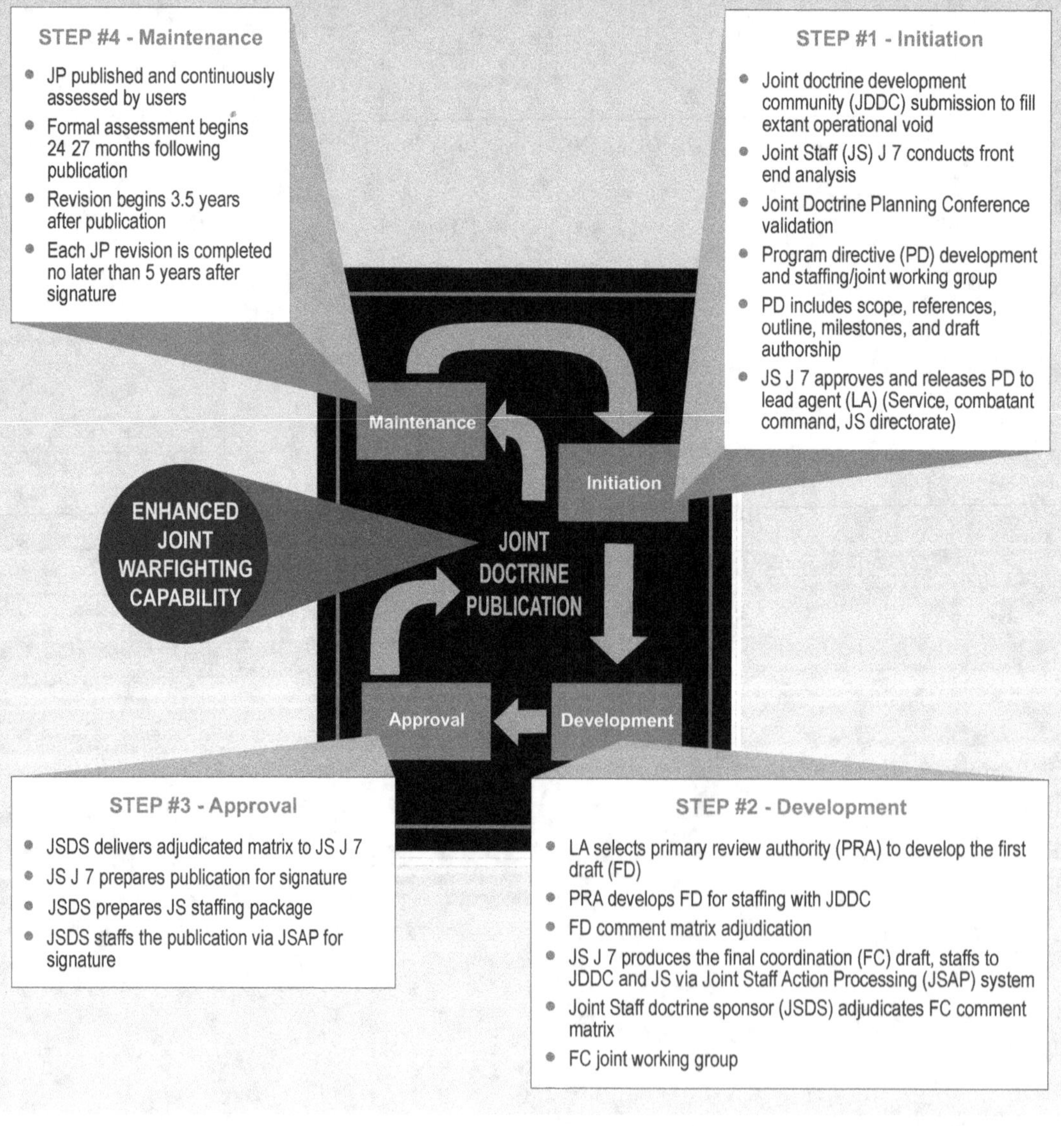

STEP #4 - Maintenance
JP published and continuously assessed by users
Formal assessment begins 24 27 months following publication
Revision begins 3.5 years after publication
Each JP revision is completed no later than 5 years after signature
STEP #1 - Initiation
Joint doctrine development community (JDDC) submission to fill extant operational void
Joint Staff (JS) J 7 conducts front end analysis
Joint Doctrine Planning Conference validation
Program directive (PD) development and staffing/joint working group
PD includes scope, references, outline, milestones, and draft authorship
JS J 7 approves and releases PD to lead agent (LA) (Service, combatant command, JS directorate)
Maintenance
Initiation
ENHANCED JOINT WARFIGHTING CAPABILITY
JOINT DOCTRINE PUBLICATION
Approval
Development
STEP #3 - Approval
JSDS delivers adjudicated matrix to JS J 7
JS J 7 prepares publication for signature
JSDS prepares JS staffing package
JSDS staffs the publication via JSAP for signature
STEP #2 - Development
LA selects primary review authority (PRA) to develop the first draft (FD)
PRA develops FD for staffing with JDDC
FD comment matrix adjudication
JS J 7 produces the final coordination (FC) draft, staffs to JDDC and JS via Joint Staff Action Processing (JSAP) system
Joint Staff doctrine sponsor (JSDS) adjudicates FC comment matrix
FC joint working group

www.ingramcontent.com/pod-product-compliance
Lightning Source LLC
Chambersburg PA
CBHW081324310526
45789CB00018B/2334
* 9 7 8 1 5 0 0 6 5 4 0 2 3 *